TALES OF TRAVEL, LOVE, AND SURVIVAL IN THE FOREIGN SERVICE

HOPE GANDER GOODWIN

PAGE PUBLISHING, INC.
New York, NY

First originally published by Page Publishing, Inc. 2018

ISBN 978-1-64350-295-3 (Paperback)
ISBN 978-1-64350-297-7 (Hardcover)
ISBN 978-1-64350-296-0 (Digital)

Printed in the United States of America

Tales of Travel, Love, and Survival in the Foreign Service is dedicated to my fantastic husband, Joe, and our extended family. We were abundantly blessed with six wonderful children: Joan, Joe II, Gretchen, Jill, Jennifer, and Juliana; four sons-in-laws: Scott, Mike, John and Michael; seven grandchildren: Angela (Dale), Jennifer (Adam), Taylor, Joseph, Trevor, Chloe and Isabella; and our first great-grandson, Nolan.

Raising children abroad was more challenging than my growing up on a Missouri farm, which provided a secure and happy childhood. I am very proud of the strength, compassion, and generosity, which our global nomad offspring possess and practice after developing broad minds from their world travels and experiences of living abroad. I am proud that we are all survivors and that we have actively attempted to make a difference in this fragile but exciting world together.

CONTENTS

Royal enstollment performed June 25, 1994 in Atiavi, Ghana
as Joe was given development chief title of Togbi Godwin I and
Hope was honored with the queen mother title of Mama Atiavi I.

FOREWORD

In 1993, I wrote the following letter to the First Lady Hillary Clinton. Her response follows. I was angry and resentful when I composed it. With permission of the ambassador, I also mailed a copy to the American Foreign Service Association. AFSA in turn forwarded it to every member of Congress, which ultimately made a difference. My expressed grievance against the proposed cuts of foreign service spousal survivor benefits was subsequently removed from the bill. Sometimes a peaceful protest, even by an introvert like me, pays dividends in understanding.

This letter summarizes my personal experiences in the foreign service as of 1993. Many more travel adventures and opportunities to become *survivors* awaited us.

April 26, 1993

First Lady Hillary Rodham Clinton
The White House
1600 Pennsylvania Avenue
Washington, DC

Dear Mrs. Clinton:

I feel compelled to write to you concerning my dismay over current proposed cuts in survivor benefits for foreign service spouses as I believe you will take the time to read my letter, listen with your heart, and learn what enormous sacrifices are required of a foreign service family. At this moment, I feel as though my country is contemplating betraying me, unappreciative of the heavy burdens that I have carried as gracefully as humanly possible. Though I rarely complain about the many sacrifices, dangers, and ultimate repercussions of living abroad that we have endured with faith, love, and good humor, I now wish to relate some of our personal experiences and concerns.

Allow me to introduce myself. My name is Hope Gander Goodwin, and my wonderful husband, Joe, is the USAID director in Accra, Ghana. We are the parents of six terrific offspring—five daughters and one son. We as a family have spent the past twenty-two consecutive years living abroad while my husband worked for seventeen years for the US Agency for International Development plus five years of working for two USAID-funded university contracts. All this time I have served my country with dignity and pride also as I share a tremendous commitment to the development assistance goals with my husband, who treats me as an equal partner and respects my opinion.

Although not yet a widow, I definitely qualify and consider myself to be a survivor. I could write a book about our adventures and misadventures. It would all be true, but readers would think it fiction and wonder how so many things could happen to one person or to one family in a lifetime. Guess we are just blessed! Judge for yourself, please.

HEALTH RISKS: A very real worry for any parent living abroad is the constant health risk. As one might expect from such a large family, we have had our share. You will agree that mothers in Little Rock (or my Monroe City, Missouri, hometown) do not have to cope with such hazards as we face daily abroad. I vividly recall many worrisome episodes that our family have experienced abroad under less-than-desirable conditions such as the following: *cerebral malaria* nearly claimed the life of one daughter while she was on medical evacuation to South Africa for *cancer*; *hepatitis* caused another child to repeat a year of school as a result of long, slow recovery; a severe allergic reaction to medication given to me during an *emergency Cesarean* section in Latin America resulted in my being in *critical condition* for six days; I gave *birth without benefit of pain relief* under very crude conditions in Africa; I underwent *cancer surgery* in a foreign land because our contract would not cover my return home; we nearly lost our three-year-old baby from *dehydration* from a dangerously high fever and unidentified infection, and the same child was seriously ill from *"jungle fever"* while on an Amazon River trip and no doctor could be found in the jungle; scary *asthma attacks* during desert sandstorms; living at high altitude which caused us to spit up blood from dryness, lips and nose to crack constantly, shortness of breath, and constant indigestion; tests for possible to *tuberculosis*; losing fifteen pounds in three days from violent *amebic dysentery*; spending Christmas Eve in an African hospital with another daughter hooked up to *IVs* and just praying that the needle was sterile; holding down a child at a local dentist with *no anesthetic* to pull out her teeth; horrendous boils caused by *mango worms*; husband lost twenty-five pounds from a tapeworm; cases of *ringworms*; eaten alive by *bedbugs* in hotels; numerous *tsetse fly bites* while on a camping trip; severe reactions to *spider bites*; *venomous snakes* inside our house; oldest girl endured to our side of the bargain. I hope the USG will recognize these facts and bear some responsibility for vulnerable survivors like myself.

SECURITY RISKS: Along with our two youngest girls (then seven and three years of age), I was literally trapped between two army tanks for the most agonizing forty-five minutes of our lives in a certain Latin American country until they had killed four snipers in front of our eyes. During one revolution, commandos tried to capture our neighbor who was a presidential candidate and bullets were flying in our backyard. I packed the kids into a bathtub for protection from stray bullets. I have been threatened with an AK-47 automatic weapon by a group of men. I suffer from terrorist nightmares as a result of these and other occasions. I have been spat upon in one country and thrown off a public bus in another just for being an American during less popular times. Our home has been burglarized four times with numerous other attempts foiled. Our ten-year-old discovered a night watchman whose throat had been slit by thieves. Our pockets have been picked on numerous occasions, losing passports, credit cards, jewelry, airline tickets, and money. We survived two evacuations due to political unrest and endured the stress/pain of separation of nearly a year. There have been a large number of people like us who have endured the trauma of being evacuated and forced to leave behind all their possessions and pets and (as in my case) for long indefinite periods. Several families currently serving with us lost all their earthly possessions in Liberia and Somalia, and although they are brave and philosophical, they can never ever replace their children's baby pictures, etc. Our family lived through martial law in Bolivia with six changes of government during one turbulent sixteen-month period. Some other things that we have encountered are too sensitive to mention, but rest assured these have also taken a toll on our minds and bodies.

MOVING STRESS: The moves were always emotional as you can imagine dealing with eight cases of anxieties and insecurities created by the moves. Packing/moving is physically exhausting (we have lived in seventeen different houses in the past twenty-two years) and most stressful when the boxes leave, as one never knows if or when one will see those precious possessions again. We are justified in worrying as we had one shipment of air freight vanish forever; due to water damage, we lost four lift vans of household effects (which included family photos and other irreplaceable items); a forklift pierced one lift van and destroyed treasured paintings; we have had shipments vandalized; one time we had to wait fourteen months for our effects to reach the next post, eleven months another time, and routinely receive our goods in about six months. Meanwhile, kids outgrow their clothes and toys. They do not feel "at home" until they are surrounded by their familiar things.

EDUCATION: Moving to another topic, which is dear to my heart, is education for the children. Our kids have gone through so many adjustments and different educational systems: American, British, Brazilian, international, and even a year of Calvert correspondence course (with me as their untrained teacher). Although they are masters at making adjustments, the quality of their education abroad has definitely lacked substance and really did not prepare them for life in the United States. It has been a difficult reentry for each of the older five and now we face being assigned to Washington next year in the senior year of high school for our youngest daughter. In my opinion, our children have suffered academically, lack career awareness, and have had trouble adapting to American lifestyles. On the other hand, they are all caring, culturally sensitive, and broad-minded individuals. As parents, we often feel guilty about what our career choice has required of our kids, but we hope it will make them stronger people in the long term.

SENSE OF LOSS: Over the years, I have grown accustomed to doing without many of life's material comforts, which doesn't bother me. However, one thing to which I will never adjust is the absolutely irreplaceability of time, experiences, and emotions which can never be shared with our dear families back home. I grew up in a loving family unit in a very safe and stable environment in rural Missouri. Therefore, it pains me deeply that our children have not had the opportunity to know their grandparents (two of which have died since we came abroad) and their other relatives and have never known the security of having roots and permanent friends (who won't move away or who they have to leave behind with each move). Last week I received devastating news of the death of my oldest nephew, and I feel so helpless being so far away and unable to truly share in the grieving process with my brother and family. We simply could not afford the price of the airfare for me to go home. The irony is that for the sake of USG interests, we spent over $4,000 out of our own pocket past ten years in five different countries to help with college cost. Although I am one of the more fortunate spouses to find employment abroad in recent years, I am still far below where I would have been (both in terms of job satisfaction and financial benefits) if I had not been a "trailing spouse."

UNPAID WORK: I wish to mention the unselfish sacrifices made by our ambassador's wife, Bonnie Brown, who is a lawyer by training but who is not allowed to hold a paying job here. Sound familiar? Like you and I, Bonnie is very committed to representing US interests and to many causes of helping the women and children of Ghana and donated a minimum of forty hours per week of labor. We both spend many hours planning, shopping for, preparing, and hosting official functions. Like you, we must attend numerous official functions, smiling graciously, and often feeling guilty about the daughter left at home. The University of Ghana vice chancellor told me that he noticed that I never stopped smiling and clapping during the five-hour ceremony while over one thousand graduates received their diplomas individually and that he felt that I deserved a diploma for representing the United States so well. We spouses devote many hours to community service. I have served on school boards, church boards, and embassy association boards. We actively participate in women's groups devoted strictly to charity work. I have done my share of fundraising, sewing for hospitals, reading to orphans, giving adult literacy classes and nutrition lessons, and visiting the handicapped school. The payment has been the smiles on the faces of the recipients. We spouses (both men and women) feel that our employer is slapping us in the face by passing a bill to cut our survivor benefits. I am particularly concerned about the proposal to cut off children's benefits at age eighteen. That means, if I were to lose my husband, our youngest would not have the opportunity to attend college as I would have no means to send her. Juliana has already paid a high price for having parents who are so busy and committed to saving the world. Is that any way to reward her?

LANGUAGE BARRIERS: We have had to learn Portuguese, Spanish, and French. The kids also learned some Kiswahili and Arabic. Sounds glamorous? It is not! Dealing and communicating in a foreign language can be extremely stressful. Studying about and adapting to different cultures is the interesting part although not easy.

Thank you for your patience in reading my letter. Your apparent accessibility gives me the courage to write.

Sincerely,
Hope Gander Goodwin

THE WHITE HOUSE

WASHINGTON

November 19, 1993

Ms. Hope Gander Goodwin
Agency For International Development
P.O. Box 1630
Accra-Ghana

Dear Ms. Goodwin,

Thank you very much for your thoughtful and compelling letter.
I am honored and touched that you chose to share your personal
experiences with me. The strength and courage you both have shown
in coping with a difficult situation is an inspiration for all of
us.

Your comments about survivor benefits for foreign service
spouses are an important source of information for President
Clinton and me.

Thank you again for taking the time to write to me. My
thoughts and prayers are with you.

Sincerely yours,

Hillary Rodham Clinton

Hillary Rodham Clinton

CHAPTER 1

Farmer's Daughter

Success has always been easy to measure.
It is the distance between one's origin
and one's final achievements.
—Michael Korda

This revised autobiography is derived from true stories originally written for my grandchildren in 1996 while we were working in Cambodia. Family and friends have encouraged me to update this incredible life journey. To recognize any achievement or so-called success in my life it is necessary to write this chapter about my origin and the positive influences on my first two decades of life. Or you could read the book first and return to this chapter to learn how firm a foundation was laid by my parents to make me strong enough to endure.

"We've come a long way, baby," my husband affectionately says to me often. That is literally true. Whenever we lived halfway around the world from our native home, my heart always felt the distance.

While shaking hands with a newly arrived American ambassador in an African post, he startled me with his rather undiplomatic remark: "With a firm grip like yours, you must be the daughter of a dairy farmer." Momentarily, I gasped in embarrassment as the guest in the receiving line behind me laughed.

Defensively, I retorted, "That I am Mr. Ambassador and mighty proud of it."

As it turns out, the chief of mission was also a Midwesterner with a farm background and had meant his comment to be a compliment. It is amazing how large a percentage of the diplomatic corps hail from the area known as God's country.

Nestled among tall oak trees in Marion County, Missouri, a modest farmhouse witnessed my 4:00 a.m. birth on September 2, 1943, the third child and first daughter born to Clifford Robert and Alice Josephine (Jarboe) Gander. They named me Delores Hope, although I was christened Dolores Hope because the priest felt that it was a more proper Catholic spelling. My older brothers, Don and Paul, had difficulty pronouncing the first name, and after two years of calling me Doe Doe, the folks decided it would be more appropriate to use the middle name.

Hope sounds like a positive name and has become popular, but I disliked it as a young girl because my brothers nicknamed me Hopey Dopey. I was unaware that Hope was also the middle name of Grandma Gander until I mentioned in her presence how much I hated my name. Well, that strong pioneer woman who crossed the continent in a covered wagon at age six gave me a tongue-lashing that I will never forget. Grandma thought I had been disrespectful. She praised the uniqueness and virtues of the name and informed me that I "had better live up to its value." If Grandma were alive, I would hope that she felt that I have honored her name. I am pleased that our oldest granddaughter now bears the same middle name.

From family photos, it is apparent that my city-raised mother delighted in making feminine clothes for me after dealing with the bib overalls and grungy work clothes for her husband and two sons.

Mother was a beautiful city lady who fell in love at the tender age of sixteen with a handsome hardworking and honest farm boy her age. They dated for five years waiting to grow up and earn enough money to marry. As a bride, Mother found herself outside of her element on the farm. Although she adapted and became a true partner and wife who would make any man proud, she certainly remained a lady in every sense of the word. Aunt Jackie described Mother as valiant, and I would agree that was my courageous mother.

I have a vivid memory of my mother down on her knees in her huge vegetable garden, crawling along the hot earth, picking peas while wearing a neatly starched dress, nylon stockings, makeup, and sunbonnet. She always combed her hair and put on fresh lipstick the moment she heard Dad coming into the house. To his credit, Dad kept himself freshly shaven daily and changed his sweaty clothes frequently to remain attractive to her. Both gestures were a sign of their mutual respect and love, which endured for seventy-two years before Dad left this world.

Without a doubt, dad literally wore the pants in the family. To comply with his wishes, Mother most always wore dresses even when pants became popular and more practical. Referring to my dad and his occupation, I remember mother repeating her mother's warning that "you can't make a silk purse out of a sow's ear." She never quit weaving her handiwork into that silk purse and managed to refine that sows ear into a prized and special breed. My father was an interesting, fascinating, and most charming storyteller. His lifetime hobby was finding Indian relics, and many articles were written about his massive collection of artifacts, which number in the thousands. Dad could relate when and where he found each one. One of the woolly mammoth elephant teeth he found in our riverbed is displayed at the Mark Twain Visitor's Center Museum near Monroe City, MO. Sadly, in 1994 he had six operations on his right eye, which left him without any vision in that eye. But the unsinkable Cliff Gander continued into his late eighties to find relics and hunt deer and wild turkeys, with his remaining cataract covered eye, an artificial vein pumping blood from his heart, and significant loss of hearing. That man was no quitter.

Dad may not have finished high school but had a clever mind with a built-in calculator. We moved to a 160-acre farm when I was sixteen months old, which Dad paid off in record time by working long hours with careful management. Mother always was right there walking and working beside him.

A valuable secret I learned from mother is how she mastered the art of making Dad think things were his idea. However, Dad had plenty of great ideas of his own, like taking mother on an annual anniversary trip for sixty-seven years straight. He delighted in planning their trips, divulging their destination just before leaving while mother packed in advance for all possibilities. Until we kids were old enough to be left to tend the chores, we were taken along on their October adventures, often to view the changing of the leaves in the

Lake of the Ozarks. It was exciting for us to get out of school for a few days but must not have been very romantic for our parents. Their commitment to renewing and recognizing their love is an admirable example that Joe and I have tried to emulate.

Growing up on a farm was good training in discipline and accepting responsibility. I would not trade places or past experiences with anyone in the world. From the time I was six until I went away to college, I got up at four o'clock to help round up the cows for milking. At first, it was done by hand, but in later years, Dad ran a demanding mechanized grade-A dairy operation, which required the milk to be chilled down to 33°F by seven o'clock in the morning when the bulk milk truck arrived. Milking was done every twelve hours, seven days a week, which required commitment. Dad always said he was married to the cows.

Even though I was a shy, short, skinny kid with lots of freckles, I could not have had a happier childhood. My parents loved each other and set fine examples for their kids. My big brothers teased and tolerated me but were always very nice fellows whom I admired. Life was never boring as there was always so much work to be done. For leisure, I took pleasure in reading, painting, listening to Harry Carey announcing the St. Louis Cardinals baseball games on the radio, sewing, writing poetry, raising parakeets and goldfish. I even had a pet cow that would let me ride her by dangling hay from a string tied to a stick.

Although we lived eight miles from Monroe City, my mother made great sacrifices by seeing that I had all the same opportunities afforded my classmates. She faithfully drove me to piano lessons for three years (alas, I did not possess her musical talent), tap dancing lessons and acrobatics, Brownie Scouts, Girl Scouts, plus seven years of truly active participation in the 4-H club where she volunteered as a leader and taught my cooking and sewing projects. Winning blue ribbons at the county fair always made her proud. Mother was an accomplished quilt maker and made beautiful crocheted, knitted, and embroidery handicrafts. Among other talents, she was a perfectionist housewife with a flair for decorating and refinishing furniture. I inherited her love of travel.

My favorite memories of my youth are of the square dances and being with friends. It was a very happy, carefree time, safe and secure, with little peer pressure or temptations compared to what the next generation encountered.

I was a dreamer by nature and the farm provided the solitude and the serene beautiful backdrop to let my imagination run wild. For instance, while riding on the sweaty backs of the team of work-horses, I would dream of being a female jockey and winning the Kentucky Derby. My husband indulged my childhood dream by escorting me to the derby in 2008. I wore fancy hats along with the rest of the 162,000 spectators.

Long before I could see over the steering wheel, I learned to drive a tractor. As driver, I had the easy part while Dad and the boys hoisted the heavy prickly bales of hay onto the wagon. They kicked the round bales over before picking them up to make certain that a poisonous copperhead snake was not lurking underneath.

To cool off after a hard day's labor in the fields, the boys and I would slide down the riverbank into the muddy North River, which formed the northern boundary of our farm and contained large catfish, snapping turtles, and water moccasins. It was exciting to challenge the unknown. I nearly drowned once when I stepped into a turtle hole and was rescued by our fun city cousin, Tom Ream, who was my exact age and spent many summers with us. He and his mother, Aunt Della, even took a trip to Canada with our family one summer. Tom was also there to fetch help when I rode my new bicycle down the steep pond dam straight into a fence post, being hurdled like a missile over the fence, and knocked unconscious. Tom ran back to the house and informed my poor mother that I was dead. Perhaps that incident is the cause of the chronic and severe headaches, which I suffered for so many years. Thankfully, those headaches no longer plague me.

When I was very young, a tornado struck our farm. I remember the frightened look on my father's face as he watched the hog house picked up by the force of the tornado and turned into mere splinters. Dad ordered my brothers and me to lie against the wall and threw himself over our bodies. It sounded like a freight train charging through our house, and when it stopped, it was the most eerie silence I have ever heard. Over the years that farm has experienced floods and more tornadoes, and the house has been struck by lightning various times. The 1918 farmhouse still stands proudly and affords the most beautiful view of the world from the front porch. There is truly *no place like home.* After having been privileged to visit about 120 countries and all seven continents, I can still say that with sincerity. I am grateful that my sister Alice bought the home and restored it.

Farm food is absolutely the best in the world and my mother was an exceptional cook and a gracious hostess. Her example has been an inspiration to me as we have entertained frequently at all our posts. While traveling the world for the past forty-six years, I have tasted a tremendous variety of exotic foods, including fabulous French cuisine and my favorite spicy Indian foods. However, nothing compares to my memories of the big banquets the wives prepared for the thrashing crews on the farm. Farmers at that time would help one another to harvest their wheat and corn crops. A huge dinner (as the noon meal is called in the Midwest) would be fixed for the hungry workers. The menu usually consisted of crispy fried chicken, mashed potatoes and gravy, corn on the cob, fresh tomatoes, creamed peas, homemade dinner rolls, and fruit and cream pies, washed down with lots of iced tea and fresh lemonade. The men ate first so they could return to the field. Kids ate with the women and then helped with the mountain of dishes. Good memories of fellowship. It was a kinder world where folks loved and helped their neighbors.

By the way, those chickens were homegrown. Getting baby chicks, every spring was exciting. They were such cute little things but required a lot of tender loving care. The chickens all matured at the same time, which meant Mother and I had to kill and dress about thirty chickens daily for a week for the freezer. Mother had the dirty work of killing the chickens and I made her tell each one she was sorry as she wrung its neck. As I plucked their feathers, I always thought that undress was a much more appropriate word than "dressing" the chickens. We reaped the benefits of our hard labor by having delicious fried chicken all winter.

My favorite neighbor was Versa Corder, who always smelled like lilacs and grew beautiful flowers. Versa visited weekly and mother would iron while Versa rocked me to sleep on her soft lap. I liked to visit her home and admired her collection of African violets and all the handicrafts which she made. One day I was attacked by a sow whose little piglets started squealing as I happened to be walking past them on the way to Versa's home. Fortunately, her husband, Carl, was outside and rescued me after I fell down and had the sow's sharp hooves skid down my back.

Sometimes I felt very lonesome and cheated because I did not have a sister. I did not have a great deal of interaction with my brothers who were always busy helping Dad, except I do recall sharing two spankings with them, which we all deserved. Once, we experimented with smoking cigarettes that the boys had "borrowed" from dad's drawer. He was not so upset by our taking the cigarettes without permission as much as he was by our choice of hideouts. Dad caught us in the barn loft full of hay. None of us knew what we were doing. I got sick and never smoked again. We all thought we were real clever until we heard Dad climbing the ladder. He was not smiling. The other time I remember disobeying him was after Dad had built a new deep pond and warned us not to swim there. One hot July day, my cousin Tom, my brother Paul, and I thought there would be no harm done in taking a quick dip. Whoops, we got caught. I can attest that a switch on warm wet skin smarts. I never swam in that pond again.

For helping Mother dust the furniture and vacuum-clean the big house, I received an allowance of $0.25 a week. Don's room was across the hall from mine and I remember him reading *Popular Mechanics* magazines until late at night. It is no wonder that he learned to fix anything and everything.

When we were teenagers, Paul let me teach him how to dance and we listened to his collection of Johnny Mathis, Teresa Brewer, and the Platters records. Paul became an excellent dancer and I was proud to be his partner. We even won a jitterbug contest.

A playhouse that I built in a pear tree was my retreat from the world below. I spent hours playing in that tree alone, dreaming about my future, deciding to become a nun, meditating, and always praying hard for a baby sister.

Much to the total astonishment of my parents who were in their fortieth year of life, my prayers for a baby sister were answered when I was twelve. The folks always kidded me that it was my fault, but I know now they had more to do with Alice Bell's surprise birth on January 9, 1956, than I did. We all adored the beautiful child with blond curls and sparkling green eyes. For the first eighteen months, Alice had the colic and I paid my dues by patiently walking the floor with her. Alice kept everyone young and amused. When she learned to talk, Alice never stopped asking questions. Her inquisitive mind challenged us to come up with satisfactory answers. She grew up to be a highly successful mechanical engineer and an executive with Michelin tire company, where she met her dear husband, Joel Dobson.

Alice and I have had the pleasure of becoming acquainted as adults. I no longer think of her as my little sister but rather as my friend. We were amazed to discover how similar the characteristics of our sweet, humorous husbands were. Sadly, after a nine-year struggle, Joel succumbed to the dreadful Alzheimer's disease in 2010 at the tender young age of sixty-two. Our family will forever miss Joel.

When Alice was a few months old, Don moved to St. Louis after graduation and worked at McDonnell Douglas aircraft. He then joined the air force from which he retired to farming after twenty-six years of faithful service including a year stint in Thailand during the Vietnam War.

Both my brothers married exceptionally wonderful women. I have the greatest admiration for my sisters-in-law, the former Elizabeth Ketsenberg and Anne Yates. These two marvelous ladies deserve canonization in our family's eyes. Being married to a stubborn Gander is not easy. Just ask my husband.

I attended Holy Rosary Catholic School in Monroe City for both elementary and high school. Attending the same school for twelve years provided a sense of stability and security, which I regret that my own children never knew. Being in Holy Rosary meant having an extended family system. Everyone cared about each student.

I attempted to hide and overcome my shyness by participating in extracurricular activities.

High school was great fun. During freshman year, I played some basketball, but my short height was a definite disadvantage. For the next three years, I loved being chosen as a cheerleader and attending every basketball game. I cheered extra loud whenever my brother or my boyfriend scored a basket. I broke my hip while practicing our routine in bobby socks on a slick floor which unfortunately eliminated our squad from regional cheerleading competition.

To my delight, I was lucky enough to be selected to play major parts in several school plays, beginning with first grade when I played the part of Gretel while my classmate Ed Charlson was Hansel. Mother made me a wonderful costume, which has delighted three generations of little girls. I teamed up again with Ed for lead roles in the junior and senior plays. I was elected to be a class officer several times and was honored to be the Sodality leader.

Then there was the joy of the choir where I sang off-key but totally uninhibited. I remember wearing hats to church and singing at all the funerals and at midnight mass on Christmas and Easter. There were spelling bees, peace rallies, and CYO dances. My brother should have been called patient Paul. Once Paul got his driver's license, I was never far from his side. It must've been a real drag to let his younger sister tag along everywhere, while a welcome relief for my chauffeur mother. Paul never complained once that I recall. I always thought he drove the Chevy too fast but did not dare to criticize lest I would lose my chances to go with him to all the games and dances. My escort to the junior prom was Jim Buckman, a beau I had off and on since second grade. Senior prom found me in a yellow chiffon flowing gown with rather itchy petticoats, feeling like the belle of the ball as I proudly entered the paper-magnolia-decorated gym on the arm of the handsome college guy named Joe Goodwin, who grew up in the neighboring village of Indian Creek, better known as Swinkey.

The Holy Rosary class of 1961 consisted of fourteen girls and only three boys who had shared the common bond of growing up together from playing spin the bottle to sharing secrets. I ranked fourth in my class and received the all-around good student award.

When our class sang "You'll Never Walk Alone" at the graduation ceremony, everyone burst into tears, including the pianist. The song was never finished. To this day, I feel that I never walk alone when I return home for visits. There is always someone in a small-town community who can be counted on to hold your hand in time of need. Friendships are genuine and enduring.

Ever since the first grade, I aspired to becoming a missionary nun. The Korean conflict was happening at that time and our class adopted orphans as pen pals. That inspired me to want to be a nursing nun and work in an orphanage in Asia. For eleven years, I never lost sight of that goal. With the assistance of Sr. Mary Alice, I was accepted into the Dominican convent in New York where I expected to go after graduation. Religion was a big part of my life, not because my parents forced it upon me but because I found it comforting. I was never into material things so did not dread the thought of taking a vow of poverty. Thinking back, I believe that my life was balanced. I liked boys and even thought it wise to date as many guys as would ask me out so that I would never wonder what I had missed when I entered the convent. Boyfriends came and went, but I was still absolutely convinced that I had been called to serve God behind the black and white Dominican habit.

My vocation was lost, rather replaced, when I fell in love with Joseph Baxter Goodwin on our first date on October 15, 1960. We both knew immediately that we were destined to share our goals and lives. Joe also planned to live and work abroad. We were and still are a perfect match. We felt comfortable and had so much fun together from the first moment we met playing miniature golf. Twenty days later Joe gave me his class ring and asked me to "go steady."

Even knowing how much I loved Joe, it was very difficult for me to accept that I would no longer become a nun. Joe was patient and most understanding when I tried to break up our relationship because I was ridden with the guilty feeling that I was letting God down. Joe gently and lovingly pointed out that marriage is also sacred and insisted that united we could make more of a difference in this world than individually. He was so right. What fun we have had in the process of trying!

The moment that I was absolutely certain that Joe was the human being with whom I wanted to spend the rest of my life was a very humorous moment from my perspective, but a terrible one for Joe. It was a snowy January night. We were leaving a class party. Impulsively deciding that I wanted to drive Joe's ugly 1955 gray Plymouth, I grabbed the keys from his hand and raced toward the car. Joe was chasing me when he slipped on the ice and fell into an open sewer. I gasped in disbelief and did not know whether to run or return to help him, but I knew the situation would test his marvelous sense of humor. Covered in you know what up to his chest, Joe gallantly pulled himself out of the stinking filth, stood up and recited a riddle that popped into his head: "By the sewer I lived, by the sewer I died. They said it was murder, but it was sewer-cide." I wanted to hug and kiss him for being such a good sport. Instead, Joe smelled so bad that I rode in the back seat on the opposite side hanging my head outside the window despite the freezing temperature. Needless to say, he did not walk me to the door that night. I just hoped that he would call me the next day, so I could apologize. He did, and I did.

I doubt if Joe admitted to his parents just how he happened to land in a sewer. Lucille and Baxter Goodwin were wonderful, hardworking farmers and very serious people, who would probably have disapproved of my immature act if Joe told them the truth. They were not overjoyed when we announced our engagement. It was nothing personal. They simply feared that Joe would not finish college if we were married. They underestimated our commitment.

We were engaged for three years not because I harbored doubts but because we were so young when the love bug fatally bit us. Joe was barely eighteen and I was a mere seventeen. I did not want to be a teenage bride, and so we agreed to marry on Labor Day, September 2, 1963, which was my twentieth birthday.

While we waited for our big wedding day, we both continued our studies and dreamed about our future life abroad. My first year of college was spent at a Catholic girl's school in Ottumwa, Iowa. It was a wonderful experience except for missing Joe every moment. Marilyn Whiston, a classmate from Holy Rosary, was my compatible roommate for the first semester. For the second semester, we were asked to switch with girls from Colombia and Peru so they could practice English. Living with Clara was an advantage for me as it improved my Spanish and knowledge of Latin American customs. Maria Teresa Glave was a sweetheart too.

While I was in Iowa, Joe attended Northeast Missouri State University in Kirksville which was only sixty miles away from me in Iowa. Bless his heart, he drove back home to work for his grandfather each weekend to earn enough gas money to come visit me briefly every Sunday afternoon before my 7:00 p.m. curfew. Joe and I wrote daily love letters. He called me every Wednesday evening. I wasted money by crying through most conversations because I missed him so much.

At the end of the academic year, my college offered me a full scholarship for the sophomore year. Occasionally, I still regret my decision to decline the generous offer. I listened to my heart and not to my head. But Joe and I could not abide our separation, and both had planned to transfer to the University Missouri that fall so we could be closer to one another. Nevertheless, my school sponsored me to spend the summer of 1962 to work and teach catechism in an African American community in Lafayette, Louisiana. The code-name for all the fundraising the school did in order to send me was "Project Hope" in honor of my name, not any resemblance to the real medical Project Hope ship.

Racial tensions had escalated in 1962. Joe and my parents were apprehensive as I boarded a bus for faraway Louisiana. Buses were being boycotted that year and they were concerned for my safety. I stopped to visit my brother Don and wife, Liz, as well as their family, who were stationed in Jacksonville, Arkansas. That was immediately after the famous riots at Central High School in Little Rock which we drove past to see the physical damage. Don put me back on a bus looking as concerned for me as Joe had been. I was excited, idealistic, and optimistic. I finally got to live in a convent; only the nuns were gone for the summer and we lay "teachers" had the run of the serene place. My class of fifteen-year-olds was charming. It was an incredible summer. I was the only white person attending both funeral and a wedding for which my students honored me with an invitation. I do not know how much religious knowledge they gained from me during those months. I do know how much my life was enriched and how much I gained from the personal contact with my students and their lovely families.

I flew back to Missouri because my sister was having kidney surgery. On my first flight, we lost an engine, we made an emergency landing at a fogged-in Memphis airport, and I vomited on a total stranger from the fright. No wonder I hate to fly, even after having logged about two million miles. The memory of that first flight has not faded with time.

Joseph Baxter Goodwin and Delores Hope Gander
were married on September 2, 1963 in Holy
Rosary Church in Monroe City, Missouri.

CHAPTER 2

Earning My PhT Degree

Far away there in the sunshine
are my highest aspirations.
I may not reach them, but I can look
up and see their beauty,
believe in them and try to follow where they lead.
—Louisa May Alcott

No, the chapter title is not a typo. I joke that while Joe pursued his PhD, I definitely earned my PhT degree (*put husband through*). That was not an uncommon practice for women of my generation. Educating men was considered more important as men were expected to be the principal breadwinner. Some of our close friend's wives also worked to put their husbands through college, although few neither endured it for as many years nor produced four babies in the process like we did.

I proved my mother-in-law's fears that I would "never work" to be unfair and unfounded. Before the long seven-and-a-half-year education journey ended, Lucille became a big supporter of mine and constantly chided Joe to quit school and get a job to support his growing family. Sadly, his mother died without realizing that we had succeeded in gaining a PhD in agricultural economics. Lucille was herself a schoolteacher and a great influence on Joe, and would have been secretly proud. She never allowed herself to show emotions or affection. However, her fondness for the grandchildren was obvious. Our kids and their first cousins quickly learned to hide behind her skirt for protection whenever they misbehaved. Joe reminded his mother that she did not believe in "sparing the rod and spoiling the child" when he and his three siblings were young. In fact, Joe had to cut his own branches for her to give him a whipping, difficult as it is for me to believe that he was ever a bad boy.

One of my favorite musicals is *Fiddler on the Roof* a story to which I can certainly relate because we have five daughters and understand the struggles of parents to hold on while letting go. In fact, I weep in all sentimental movies but that one floods my tear ducts every time. There is a terrific line when the main character, Tevye, in referring to his oldest daughter and her poor tailor husband remarks that "they are so happy that they don't even know how miserable they are." You could easily have been talking about Joe and me. While we were struggling to get an education, we were as poor as church mice, only we were so rich in happiness that we did not realize how bad off we were financially until much later in life.

Returning from our week honeymoon, Joe romantically swept me off my feet to carry me over the threshold into the dark, tiny basement apartment where I had lived with another girl during the previous summer. Joe struggled to unlock the door with me cradled in his arms. Lo and behold, there stood my roommate who had not yet moved out—a definite mood killer situation. She finally left us to settle into our humble home. Reality began.

The following day I returned to work at the University of Missouri extension service while Joe began the first semester of his junior year of undergraduate studies at the University Missouri Columbia. For income tax purposes, I declared Joe as my dependent, which increased my monthly take-home pay by a total of $3 to a net salary of $184 a month. Our rent was $60 a month, including utilities. To my disappointment, that tax break increase paid for less than a week's worth of Joe's nasty smoking habit. Joe had promised to quit smoking the moment we got married. He honestly tried. Kicking an addiction on one's honeymoon is not advisable. Before the week was over, I took a rain check on his promise. Seven years passed before I was able to cash in, when he finally stopped smoking for health reasons as well as a desire to please me. I'm eternally grateful for his wise decision despite his subsequent weight gain of thirty pounds.

Our game plan when we married was to finish the bachelor's degree, join the Peace Corps, and then have children. That was our strategy. The best made plans do indeed go astray.

When we were married for just over five months, I realized that I was pregnant. However, six weeks later, before we'd even adjusted to the idea, I suffered a miscarriage. It was a blessing in disguise because two days later Joe and I both came down with a bad case of German measles, which we contacted from his sister, Carol, during a weekend visit home. Even so all this was a shock to my system. To make matters worse, I foolishly felt that this was God's way of punishing me for not becoming a nun. We subsequently joked that God continued to punish me by sending three babies over the next two and a half years.

Our beautiful firstborn, Joan Lorene arrived December 12, 1964, six months before Joe obtained his bachelor's degree. The Peace Corps did not accept couples with children, so we decided to go on to graduate school. Joe was offered and accepted a scholarship in the Department of Agricultural Economics at the University of Missouri. I continued to work at the University while running to the day care center during my breaks and lunch in order to nurse and check on Joan.

While we pursued a master's degree along came our nine-plus-pound bouncing son, Joseph Baxter II (whom we called Jody until he grew up), on March 5, 1966, followed by our sweet daughter Gretchen Linn on June 26, 1967. After Jody was born, I decided to operate a day care center in our tiny efficiency apartment as I could not stand the thought of leaving our own two babies. For the next eighteen months, I cared for six babies under the age of two, all in diapers. It was a big responsibility, but I loved all the little ones. Good thing I was blessed with an abundance of patience and persistence.

The problems came when I conceived Gretchen and vomited for the first five months and lost fifteen pounds. No medications helped. I could only keep Jell-O and cottage cheese down. Every diaper I changed sent me running to the bathroom in spasms. It was miraculous that Gretchen was born healthy with a normal birth weight. Joe and my doctor never left my side during the long and difficult thirty-six-hour labor. I was grateful for the doctor's skill but appalled by his chauvinistic remark when he saw our female child emerge. "Wasn't worth all this trouble to have a girl" was the doctor's thoughtless and unforgivable comment. I could not believe my ears as my eyes beamed at our precious child.

Joe finished his master's degree two months after Gretchen joined the family. We set off for the University of Maryland where Joe had accepted a three-year DEA Fellowship to pursue his PhD in agricultural economics. I remember my father standing sadly by the station wagon full of kids and boxes and say we would never be back. Of course, we would be back, and I tried to reassure him. He responded that he knew we would visit but never return to live. I thought we would prove him wrong but "Father knows best." Except for a brief period during an evacuation from the Sudan, we didn't live in Missouri from 1967 until 2011. Since half of our kids are Missouri residents, we decided to return to our home state.

In August 1967, the journey to Maryland took thirty-six hours as there were few bypasses around big cities and every stoplight bore our name. With no funds to stay in a motel, we paused at rest stops along the way. The baby crib mattress fit perfectly in the back of the big Chevy station wagon and our three babies, ages thirty-two months, seventeen months, and two months slept like little angels most of the way. There were no car seats or seat belt restrictions for that generation of youngsters.

Arriving at the outer loop of the Washington area Beltway in fast-moving traffic to which we were definitely not accustomed, we found ourselves forced to make a quick choice of either Baltimore or Richmond. We wanted neither city. We were looking for College Park, Maryland. A car was turned upside down in the middle of the place where the road split. Fortunately, traffic pushed us into the correct turn. Eventually we arrived safely at our destination, exhausted and feeling like a fish out of water in that size city. Washington is a transit area where people were not as friendly as back home. It required an attitude adjustment.

After finding a three-bedroom apartment to rent, we had to wait one week for it to be ready for occupancy. The hotel was costing us $17 a night, which was beyond our meager budget. So we drove past Baltimore looking for a rest area where we could sleep. Locating none and feeling desperate by nine o'clock, I called a cousin that lived in the area. I did not know John D. Phelps or his charming wife, Betty, very well and had not seen them in years. They graciously invited us to spend the night. As it happened John and Betty were leaving the next day on an anniversary trip and allowed us to housesit in their absence. That was a real godsend.

Our furniture had not arrived from Missouri by the time the apartment was ready for occupancy, but we did not want to wear out our welcome at the Phelps home. Consequently, we moved into our apartment where we lived for three weeks with nothing but the baby mattress on the floor. We all sat, ate, and slept on the bare wood floor even while we celebrated both of our birthdays and our anniversary. Needless to say, I took the kids in the playground often while Joe was off at the University. The best and only seat in the house was the toilet, which is where I nursed the baby.

Washington was a rude awakening in more ways than one. I knew we were in trouble when I read an article in the *Washington Post* reporting that a family of four living in the DC area with a combined income of under $11,000 was considered to be below the poverty line. Here we were a family of five with an annual fellowship income of $4,800. I am a good manager of resources but knew my skills would be tested to the limit. After making our rent and car payments, there was very little left for food and gas and miscellaneous items were out of the question. We did not eat well for the next three and a half years. Good-natured Joe took a stale bologna sandwich and butter and jelly sandwich to the office every day. Back in Missouri, we had been well fed, between the side of beef that my parents had given us and the pork, eggs, and canned vegetables from his parents. But there we were one thousand miles from home and too proud to ever let our folks know how bad off we were financially. We never applied for food stamps or any kind of assistance even though we qualified. There was always that light at the end of the tunnel and were determined to make it on our own.

We decided to surprise our families and drove home for the 1967 Christmas holidays. Naturally, we drove straight through. The worst part of the journey was being in a blinding snowstorm on the Pennsylvania Turnpike. Never did like that stretch of road. Coming back to Maryland, we got so tired that we had to stop to wash our faces with snow to be more alert. We arrived in our apartment complex at four o'clock in the morning. At least we thought it was our apartment. Looking up at the third-floor corner unit, we could see a light burning through the curtains on the windows. Curtains? But we had no funds for curtains or carpets or air-conditioning, television, or any such luxuries. Our reactions were different. I was thinking that Joe, knowing how I disliked living in a fishbowl, had sweetly arranged for those window coverings. Joe blew that sweet thought when he asked me accusingly if I had remembered to pay the rent and suggested that we had been evicted.

Nervously we turned the key in the lock. Opening the door, I suddenly believed in Santa Claus for a brief moment. That Christmas we had been unable to afford any presents for our youngsters. They were too young to realize the difference and besides they received ample toys from their grandparents while home. Not only were there curtains on the windows, an old carpet on the living room floor, but also a Christmas tree and presents for all three children from Santa. I recognize the writing of my neighborhood friend Sarah Klotz. I regret that we lost touch for a number of years as we moved but have reconnected in recent years. Sarah was a good friend as were Julie Knox and Sandy Horvath and their families.

Before any reader begins to feel sorry for our impoverished state, I must say that the situation was not all bad. In fact, if we ever felt pity for ourselves, it has slipped my mind. Washington offers many wonderful opportunities which are free. Joe and I always enjoyed taking the children to the zoo frequently. We spent many Sundays visiting the Smithsonian museums and introduced the children to interesting things. Picnic lunches at the park provided the kids space to run more freely than in the confinement of apartment living. Our children were always smartly dressed in clothes that I proudly sewed myself.

Joe loved playing with the kids. Their favorite game was hide-and-seek. Once he hid all three in a cardboard wardrobe carton in which we kept our winter clothing. He had covered them up and instructed them to be very quiet until Mommy found them. I searched high and low. Not a peep from those toddlers gave away their hiding place. Their silence caused Joe to panic, thinking they might have suffocated, and he ran to reveal their secret spot. To our relief they were just fine and thought they were pretty clever to fool me.

One graduate course followed another, and Joe's credits piled up while I earned supplemental income by babysitting. We could not have survived without it.

Christmas of 1969 found us driving back to Missouri to attend my brother Paul's wedding to wonderful Anne Yates. I was six months pregnant at the time, but we had not told anyone. My mother was so thrilled to see the grandkids that she did not notice my bulging tummy for about fifteen minutes. Or maybe she was used to seeing me look like that. Anyway, we all had a jolly laugh.

On the way back home, I began premature labor somewhere in West Virginia. We did not know what to do so Joe just kept driving faster and faster. When we reached Maryland, we learned I was dilating and was promptly confined to bed for one month with my feet propped up. The doctor assured me that if I could complete at least seven months the baby's lungs would be better developed and have a better chance for survival. The timing was terrible. Joe was in the midst of taking final examinations. The children were too small to care for themselves, so he had to spend more time at home and less time studying. He is not a cook but managed to feed us somehow. The ironing piled higher and higher, but I had no choice but to stay in bed. Labor pains would strike every time I went to the bathroom. I knitted two sweaters while lying flat on my back.

Not only did I make it to the seventh month, but the eighth month, the ninth month, plus two more weeks. One week past my due date, I had a dream about the baby's sex, birth date, and weight. I told Joe about my dream, and he suggested I write it down. Joe had learned not to make fun of my intuition or my dreams. I wrote, "Baby girl with a tiny pink bow in her hair will be born April 4, weighing 7 lbs. 4 oz." Looking at the piece of paper, I thought this prediction would be wrong, not just the silly bow idea. How could it go another week? And the birth weight had to be wrong; none of our babies had been that small. Until that dream, I had been convinced that we were having a second son. The child within me had played football just like our son. This was the presonogram era.

On Saturday, April 4, 1970, Angela Jill made her dramatic appearance, weighing seven pounds and four ounces, exactly like my dream. The only thing she was missing was the bow. However, when Jill gave birth to her second daughter, Taylor, she was wearing a tiny pink bow in her hair the first time I saw her, and I felt my dream came true.

Jill was almost born in an elevator stuck between two floors of Providence Hospital in Washington, DC. When she decided it was time to come, she wasted no time. Arriving at the emergency room Joe let me out and went to find a parking place. There had been a shooting and lots of policemen were roaming around the emergency room. An older fellow, sitting in a wheelchair took one look at me, got out of the wheelchair, and said I looked like I needed it worse than he did. He called for the crowd to let me through. Just then Joe came running in and pushed the wheelchair into the elevator. A young male orderly happened to step inside the elevator with us and pushed the button for the maternity ward.

Suddenly I felt a very familiar pushing pain. I could feel the crown of the baby's head between my legs. Then the most unbelievable thing happened. The elevator stopped and hung between floors. The orderly tried to pry open the door. I mentioned that I knew the baby was coming quickly. The young hospital orderly pushed emergency button and set off the alarm. He panicked, shouting, "Don't do this to me. I have never delivered a baby." Don't do this to *you*?

Joe was squeezing my hand, telling me to "hold on, honey." Knowing how claustrophobic I get on elevators, Joe was worried that I might hyperventilate. But that was the least of my worries. I wanted out. The baby wanted out. It seemed like an hour that we were stuck in the elevator, but Joe assures me it was more like ten minutes. Somehow, someone pried open the door, but there was a large step up to get to the next floor. It would've been a good leap for a normal person, but seemed impossible for me at that stage. Joe lifted, pushed, and rolled me onto the floor. He could have dropped me down the open elevator shaft.

There was no time to prep me for delivery or even give me a hospital gown. A doctor I had never seen before was called out of another delivery room and arrived in time to catch the baby. Joe had gone back downstairs to register me and was certainly surprised, and I suspect very relieved, to find that I had already delivered our darling child when he returned. Angela Jill was born with a dimple in her chin, a twinkle in her eye, and a charming smile for everyone. She made up for lost time by running or skipping everywhere. She rarely walked as a child.

I preferred shopping without kids after perfect strangers asked if we did not know anything about birth control. Tiring of rude comments Joe responded to a lady who said to us, "You must be Catholic."

With a tongue-in-cheek reply, Joe responded, "No, just unlucky Protestants." Offended, she scurried down the aisle. Of course, we were proud to be Catholic and having a big family was our choice. We had wanted a dozen children when we married but settled for half a dozen instead.

Our most serious problem while at Maryland was a lack of health insurance. In 1970, our medical bills amounted $2,100 while Joe's fellowship was only $5,000 a year. He did some consulting at the Inter-American Development Bank but had limited time as he was finishing his course work and studying for his examination. Despite having walking pneumonia and a fever of 103°F when he took his oral exams he passed with flying colors. However, there was still a dissertation to be written and the medical bills to be paid. Both tasks seemed daunting but eventually we succeeded in doing it all.

One day, Joe called me while I was back visiting family in Missouri and asked how I would like to move to Africa. I replied something to the effect that he must be crazy. It seems that there was a job coming available in Ethiopia with the US Agency for International Development and Joe was encouraged by his professor to apply. Joe applied to USAID, but we heard nothing for seven months before being contacted that he was accepted. Expecting to live in Addis Ababa, we bought winter clothes. Then, instead of being sent to Ethiopia, we were assigned to Accra, Ghana, in West Africa which has a tropical climate.

A funny thing happened while we were waiting for our security clearance. An FBI agent showed up at my neighbor's door while I was visiting Sarah. He showed his badge and explained that he was doing a security check of her neighbor. Sarah invited him in but neglected to introduce me. I sat there listening to the entire interview while she gave the agent a glorious report on the wonderful Goodwin family. And no, Joe did not beat his wife or children. And no, the Goodwin's did not drink. I had difficulty keeping a straight face. Another agent even located Joe's former neighbor working in the field on his Missouri Farm. Security checks today are easier with the entire information modern computers offer.

While the security check was underway, we started on our medical clearances. As this was our first posting, our family received eleven injections each against every disease imaginable. Indirectly, I felt all sixty-six shots, including those of my big baby husband who hates injections. While most of the injections were routine, the reaction from the typhoid fever shots sent everyone to bed with a high fever for a day and sore arms for a week.

There was a serious epidemic of Hong Kong flu sweeping America that winter. I was the first to catch it in our family. Never in my life have I had flu to match that violent strain. Many people died. One week before our scheduled departure, our petite eleven-month-old baby Jill caught it and was still sick when we departed. We should have postponed our travel to Ghana but thought it was our duty to go.

Security clearance in hand, on March 14, 1971, we finally bade farewell to our friends and a cousin, Opal Branch, at Dulles Airport. At Dulles, it was necessary to take buses to the planes for boarding. As we stepped into the bus to take us to the plane three-year-old Gretchen asked, "Is this Africa?" Her innocent question made us laugh. She must've thought all our preparations were much ado about nothing. We were beginning a three-day trip and wondered how frequently the kids would ask that usual "how much longer "question.

Our first crossing of the Atlantic Ocean during the Ides of March date was rough. The winds caused constant turbulence which reinforced my fear of flying. After filling three airsickness bags, the stewardess insisted that I take three Dramamine tablets. I should have known better as I have limited tolerance for medication or alcohol and am allergic to many pills. However, I was embarrassed, miserable, and willing to try anything. Obediently I took the pills and immediately passed out. Assuming that I was sleeping peacefully, Joe was relieved for my sake. He was too busy taking care of the kids to worry about my problems. Jill's flu condition was a major concern. Joe realized that she was at the point of dehydration and asked if there was a doctor onboard the plane. One promptly appeared and gave her medication that helped. Jill's green diarrhea from the flu messed up Joe's brand-new suit of the same color. Knowing how fussy he is about his clothes, I salute Joe for being such a good sport about that incident.

When we finally landed in London early the next morning, Joe had great difficulty waking me up. In fact, I have no memory of going through customs, obtaining luggage, or riding in a taxi. When we arrived at our hotel, I regained consciousness when I heard the price quote. The cost for two rooms was the equivalent of $300 a night (not so much today but a lot of money in 1971). So back into the taxi we went to a hotel with more affordable lodging. Then we all collapsed and slept and slept for the next fifteen hours.

When we woke up, baby Jill was much improved, so we took the kids to visit Madame Tussauds wax museum, which was fascinating. Starving and thirsty, we wandered into a pub. Our booth had a plaque that stated that Charles Dickens used to sit there. We then enjoyed our first ride on a double-decker bus. Everything about London was enchanting. The next day we rented a taxi, toured Windsor Castle and the Tower of London, and watched the changing of the guard at Buckingham Palace. Typical tourists except we were dragging along four tykes who were too young to absorb all this culture, except for Joan, who was six and enchanted with the royalty. After that exposure, Joan always pretended to be a queen or princess in all her make-believe games.

CHAPTER 3

Ghana: Our First Post

It's what you learn after you know it all that counts.
—John Wooden

My introduction to Africa was a crude encounter in Nigeria on the way to our first foreign service post in Accra, Ghana. Upon landing in Lagos, passengers were instructed to take all hand baggage and disembark while the plane was being cleaned. We were traveling with four small children and an abundance of carry-on bags. Having just come from winter weather in England, we were not dressed for the tropics. Stepping off the plane with our arms loaded down and inappropriate clothes covering our bodies, we felt like we had entered a steam bath. The weather in Lagos was oppressive. The people at the airport did not form a great welcome committee either.

We piled our bags on the floor and shed our coats and sweaters. Joe went off to buy us a cold drink. A well-dressed Nigerian man approached and started circling around me and the children looking disdainfully at our pile of possessions. Without uttering a single word, the Nigerian man came up and spat point-blank into my face. I was shocked. By the time Joe arrived with bottles of 7-Up, my tears were washing away the unwelcome and unwarranted spit.

"What in the world happened to you?" Joe bewilderedly asked upon seeing my messy face.

"I want to go home. We have made a terrible mistake. I do not want to go to Ghana anymore. Just put me back on the plane to London, please," I begged. And I was serious. If it had been possible, I would've taken our youngsters and returned home without knowing what wonderful adventures I had missed. I've often wondered what triggered that man's unusual behavior.

Fortunately, such an idea was not an option. Two hours later, we landed in Accra as the sun was setting and a cool breeze was blowing. Ghanaians have a well-deserved reputation for being the friendliest people on the African Continent. Even the customs officials had ready smiles and bid us an "akwaaba" welcome. Just when I began to relax a bit, we exited the immigration area and were besieged by porters fighting over who would carry our bags. USAID had sent two vans to pick us up and the drivers helped push our way through the crowd. That is a typical scene in many airport exits around the world, but the first experience can be a bit overwhelming.

Arriving at our house, we found a casserole baking in the oven and a salad in the fridge, thanks to Kathy Ford, the very thoughtful wife of Joe's new boss. I could not have coped very well that particular night without that delicious meal to feed the family. While we were exploring the four-bedroom home and deciding on who would occupy each room, Bill and Billie Stewart arrived to welcome us with their four daughters and we all bonded instantly. Another fun young couple, Pat and Meg Gage, dropped by also. Their hospitality was familiar, exactly like being back in Missouri. Those were the days before the Community Liaison Office (CLO) existed and organized sponsors for new arrivals. Our kind colleagues simply had formed their own welcoming committee and made us very happy.

Looking back, I was so naive and ill-prepared for living abroad. That first night in Ghana, I made Joe leave the light on the entire night as there was a lizard clinging to the ceiling directly above our bed. I was convinced that it would fall on us if we turned out the light and I did not know whether or not it was poisonous. Nobody had mentioned geckos at any of our orientations. I actually stayed awake all night watching its motionless but creepy-looking body. It turns out that harmless gecko lived in our bedroom for the next three years, growing larger and larger from its steady diet of mosquitoes and insects.

When we arrived in Ghana on St. Patrick's Day 1971, the country was in the second year of the Second Republic. In 1957 Ghana became the first of the sub-Saharan colonies that achieved independence (from Great Britain in this case) and Kwame Nkrumah became the prime minister. At independence, Ghana was primarily an agricultural economy, with cocoa being the principal export crop. Ghana at that time was the worlds' biggest producer of cocoa in the world. Gold mining was the other principal industry and export. In fact, before independence, Ghana was known as the Gold Coast. Principal food crops were maize (corn), cassava, and plantain (the latter two products are starchy tubers). Nkrumah attempted to industrialize Ghana rapidly through a program of increasing government control of the economy. The policies failed, and the Ghanaian economy deteriorated. Since Nkrumah had assumed increasing dictatorial powers, the military led a coup in 1966, which overthrew the government. In 1969 there were new elections. The US government through USAID provided assistance to the new government in the form of balance of payments support and technical assistance in agriculture, health, and police training.

Joe was assigned to the Agriculture Office as the economist. The Agricultural Office provided support in extension, seed multiplication, and the agricultural faculty at the university. In addition, it advised on other US supported investments such as the government guarantee supported farm at Ejura, Central Ghana. USAID activities in these fields kept Joe busy. Within a week of landing in Ghana, Joe was sent on a three-week field trip to evaluate the US-supported mechanized maize farm. I would have been totally stuck at home without a car except for the kindness of Billie Stewart who took me to the commissary and the kids to the swimming pool at Lincoln school (the American Community School). We had purchased a new Ford station wagon before leaving the United States, but as it had to be shipped by ocean freight, it took several months to arrive in Ghana. Until then I had to depend upon my new friends for support.

The front yard at our new house had a beautiful fan palm tree and red flame of the forest trees while the big backyard had many banana and mango trees. I was fascinated by all the tropical flowers and plants. Exploring the beautiful garden with our six-foot, six-inch tall gardener, Ernest, I would point out a variety that was new to me and ask, "What's that called?" Ernest would only laugh, and I repeated my question. He looked at me like I was really stupid and would respond either "tree," "flower," or "plant." I gave up and bought a book. One day, Ernest really thought I had lost my mind. We had several banana trees in our backyard, and one tree had a green stalk of bananas that we anxiously awaited to ripen. Finally, after a month or more of waiting for the bananas to ripen he brought me a huge stalk of beautiful bananas. A few minutes later, I saw him chopping down the tree from which those bananas had just been cut. I ran out and asked what he was doing. I said that was the only tree that had any bananas on it and now he was cutting it down. I was met with another burst of laughter. Finally, he got the courage to explain to me that one must cut back the banana tree once it has been harvested in order for a new stalk to spring forth from the middle of the plant. Live and learn.

Our children had only experienced apartment living, so it was great for the kids to have space to play. Our main concern was poisonous snakes. Green mambas were a definite threat as there was a huge weedy vacant lot behind our yard. One day the gardener bent over to pick up the green water hose and the "hose" uncoiled and struck at him. There was a green mamba camouflaged on top of the hose of the same color. It is good that Ernest was tall and agile as he jumped backward in a flash and the deadly snake missed its target. The gardener killed the reptile with his machete. That was a learning experience for the kids to know what to avoid.

Ernest built a marvelous playhouse out of strips of cane and bamboo which kept the kids busy for about six months until a windstorm demolished their fun place. Then our sea freight finally arrived with a swing set, which he assembled. To our amusement, the kids preferred playing in the empty shipping boxes rather than on the hot metal slide or swings or with their toys.

We used both the local economy and the embassy commissary for our food and drink. The Ghanaian economy was still recovering from the economic hardships of the 1960s and many imported items were not available in country. Shopping posed new issues for us. The first weekend in Accra, we went to the local supermarket to shop. Among other items, we put a case of beer in the shopping cart. When we arrived at the checkout, we were asked where were our empty bottles (there was a shortage of beer bottles as they were often used for other purposes). We explained that we were new to the country and had no bottles. That was no excuse; we were told to go to the shop where empty bottles were sold and then return. We did, and the problem was resolved.

Items such as lettuce and celery were not grown in Ghana, nor were they imported. If we wanted these items, we had to go to a neighboring country, Togo, to buy them and other "luxury products." Because these goods were not available locally, the household help did not necessarily know how to prepare them. This led at times to humorous misunderstandings. The wife of the military attaché was having a cocktail party and had arranged for celery to be flown in from Europe. She gave the celery to her cook and told him to prepare it. He said he did not know what to do. She told him to take the leaves off, cut it, and refrigerate it. When it came time to serve the celery, she opened the frig door and found only the leaves, cut as per the instructions the cook understood. She asked the cook where was the stalk from the celery. She was told it was in the garbage outside. She promptly told him to bring in the celery stalks, wash them, and cut it up. The celery was the hit of the party and it was some months later before she relayed the true story.

Another time Joe and I were invited to dinner at a friend's house and were informed we would be having lettuce salad as she had gone to Togo and brought back a head of lettuce. Just as dinner was about to be served, she went in to check on the lettuce salad. She screamed when she discovered her cook had thought it was cabbage and boiled it. Needless to say, we were all disappointed.

Ghanaians used the expression "chop" in a different way from us and that also sometimes caused comical confusion. My friend gave her cook some green peppers and asked him to chop them. When she returned to the kitchen in search of the peppers, they were gone so she inquired where he had put them. Patting his stomach, he replied, "Oh, madam, I have chopped them." So we learned that to *chop* meant to *eat*.

We enjoyed organizing croquet games on Sunday afternoons. To celebrate the arrival of our ice cream freezer we invited friends to come over for croquet and homemade ice cream. They arrived while Joe and I were assembling the ingredients in the kitchen. We quickly threw the freezer together and asked Ernest to crank it for us. After playing a round of croquet, Joe tested the pressure on the handle of the freezer. It spun freely so he suggested Ernest should crank it harder. The dear fellow pumped as fast as he could for about forty-five minutes as sweat dripped from his brow. Something had to be wrong. We opened the top and discovered that in our haste we had forgotten to put in the paddle. Ernest could crank forever, and it would never have become too hard to turn. The ice cream had frozen anyway without the paddle to turn it. We all laughed except Ernest, who again must have been asking himself what kind of crazy advisors had the United States sent to Ghana. After that incident whenever we made ice cream, Ernest would open the top and double-check for the paddle before he started cranking. No dummy, that man.

Joe settled into his job and enjoyed the opportunity to be applying his years of studies. He had an opportunity to travel both in-country and to other African countries during the first three plus years in Ghana. One memorable event was attending an international agricultural conference in Addis Ababa, Ethiopia. The highlight was an audience with Emperor Haile Selassie II at the royal palace where the entrance hall was guarded by the emperor's pet cheetahs. The participants were individually presented to the Emperor and in the following cocktail hour were served Tej, a honey wine, from gold goblets.

I was never idle despite the advantage of having four people helping in the house. We employed a cook/steward, a nanny, a gardener, and a night watchman. This was my first exposure to this dubious luxury, and it took some adjustment on my part. But I soon became involved in outside activities while baby Jill took her nap. The Brownie troop of nineteen very enthusiastic young girls, including our daughter, Joan, needed a leader so guess who volunteered. The American Women's Club provided a nice diversion, and I was on the committee which assembled a unique cookbook. The profits from the cookbook were used for charity. Our chapter on substitution is still useful. Tennis and bridge were also a big part of my social life.

I also was kept busy with frequent entertainment. Another major adjustment for both Joe and I were the demands of going to and giving official cocktail parties and dinners. Ghana had a rather large diplomatic community with whom we interacted, as well as the various government of Ghana agencies. We were expected to attend official functions, and as wives, we were often expected to contribute food to functions at the ambassador's residence.

The foreign service of 1971 was considerably different from that of today. There were no dual postings or tandems, where husband and wife could be assigned to the same post. If two foreign service officers married, one was expected to resign. What this meant in practice was the woman would resign and the man continued his career. Neither were there salaried jobs at post for spouses (the annoying term used was "trailing spouses" in those days and were almost always women). Spouses were expected to engage in volunteer work, care for the children, learn the local language, and be interesting conversationalists at cocktail and dinner parties. A review of the spouse was also included in the rating of the foreign service officer and could affect the career of the officer, either positively or negatively. I was amazed when I read Joe's first personnel evaluation report. It was glowing except for the boss's comment that Joe "kept a messy desk but his wife's entertaining skills made up for that defect in the young officer." No kidding. Fortunately, the rating of spouses was dropped in the mid-1970s.

I played hostess to two sewing groups which made clothes for various charities. The groups met in our home two mornings a week. The ladies of the Sew n' Sews group left their machines at my house rather than carry them back and forth. One December night, a thief came to collect them. Around midnight I had been taking care of Jill who was sick. As I was returning to our bedroom, I heard a strange sound akin to the breaking of a steel bar. Without waking Joe, I went to the closet withdrew two golf clubs and positioned one in each hand. My rationale was that the intruder might grab one golf club and I was prepared to then defend myself with the second one.

Most significantly, I was eight and a half months pregnant with Jennifer. Creeping down the stairway in my bare feet, I was unable to hold onto the railing because I was balancing the golf clubs and the weight of my belly. Hearing a noise in the living room, my heart raced, and I wondered if I should go back and get my sleeping husband. Drawn like a magnet, I continued down the last three steps. There stood a thief with six sewing machines all lined up ready to take them through the window, whose louvers he had removed. Well, I let out a bloodcurdling scream and scared the robber half to death. He cut himself as he leapt out of the open window and darted across the vacant lot. Joe jolted out of bed and raced down the stairs. He could hardly believe what I had done. Neither could I when I considered the precious child in my womb. Ernest was now convinced that I was completely mad, and I was starting to agree with him.

No harm done to the baby, it seemed. Joe thought the fright might bring on labor prematurely. Personally, I was ready. The baby was due on Christmas Eve just like our first child had been, but Joan had arrived December 12, twelve days early, so I was hoping for an early arrival of our fifth baby. The American Embassy nurse advised me to go to military base in Spain for delivery. Deciding that it would be too difficult for the family for me to be away for three months, I pleaded for permission to stay in Ghana for the birth. "Unthinkable," replied the rather gruff former army nurse. She reminded me of another dependent who had died in Accra a few years earlier for lack of blood for a transfusion needed after delivery. I quietly located possible O+ blood donors.

My obstetrician at the four-bed North Ridge Clinic was a Ghanaian who had been trained in England. I felt confident and comfortable with him. However, when it appeared that I might not be able to have a natural birth since the baby was staying in the sideways position, I decided to depart the day after Thanksgiving. The doctor turned the baby several times to no avail. The prospect of having surgery was not appealing. This was before the threat of HIV/AIDS existed. Joe was nervous about the increased risk of infection in a tropical climate.

When I went to Pan Am to purchase my ticket the agent took one look at me, realized I was beyond seven months, and refused to sell me passage. The nurse was furious with me. She made me sign a statement saying that since I had defied her advice to leave Ghana for the delivery, the US Embassy would take absolutely no responsibility for me. That was a troubling thought. When I seriously asked if they would send my corpse home, she did not answer. I went home and prayed that it would not become an issue for Joe to resolve.

We had a wonderful Christmas celebration. Among other gifts, I remember the beautiful Indian wooden rocking chair which Joe bought from our friends, John and Iona Anania, for me to rock the new baby. I had always wanted a rocking chair with a lovely cotton quilt hanging over the back.

Believe it or not, Joe had suggested we host a big turkey dinner on Christmas Day. I reminded him that our child was due the day before, so he countered with a proposal for New Year's Day since my babies were usually a couple of weeks early. What made me agree? I will never know! I was already preoccupied with a large farewell dinner party we were hosting on December 30 for our friends the Gages who were transferring to Liberia. I managed to get through that exhausting party. The due date passed, and we waited rather nervously and impatiently. About nine o'clock on New Year's Eve we were making the turkey stuffing when labor began. Father Mike Yochum was visiting from Northern Ghana so we had a built-in babysitter. Dr. Kwaku predicted that labor would be prolonged and wouldn't let Joe stay with me. Joe reluctantly left but was unable to sleep due to fireworks going off all night. Ghana celebrates the arrival of the New Year in style.

My labor put Joe in a bind about the dinner party that we (the royal "we," which usually meant me) were hosting the next day. The turkey was thawed, and I had prepared pies in advance. So not wanting to disappoint the twenty-two invited guests, he decided not to cancel. Actually, I was glad that Joe had the responsibility of the dinner party to distract him as well as gain an understanding of what is involved. He made five trips between home and the clinic that day to check on me and seek advice. It was comical to watch Joe's normal nonchalant "nothing to it" attitude about entertaining change to complete panic. After getting the guests seated at the table, Joe realized that the turkey was not fully cooked. The cook had not understood about waiting for the thermometer in the bird to pop up and had taken it from the oven too soon. By the time the turkey was ready, and they finally ate; the mashed potatoes were cold and lumpy. As soon as the desert was served, Joe rushed back to the clinic just in the nick of time.

Waddling off to delivery without the luxury of a wheelchair, I was directed to a room with a sign which read "Labour." Since I had been in labor for twenty-four hours already this was disturbing to me. I protested that I was ready for delivery room. But my terminology had confused the doctor. Yes, he understood that birth was imminent and that I was ready for "labour." Realizing that England must use different terms for this stage, I entered the sparse but clean room. The wide green delivery table resembled a Ping-Pong table and was devoid of stirrups, pillow, sheets or anything similar to what I had known in America. There was an oxygen tank lying in the corner but no anesthesiologist available to administer any comfort or relief.

Joe and I had learned the Lamaze breathing technique but had not expected to have a totally natural childbirth or actually apply what we had practiced. This was our fifth baby but Joe's first time to assist me with delivery. His presence kept me calm and confident and delivery was reasonably quick.

We were so proud of our adorable baby, Jennifer Alice Adjoa. To my dismay, the doctor did not clean her passages, check her vital signs, or clean her up before wrapping a piece of rough green canvas around her. No soft blanket welcomed Jennifer. She was handed to her radiant father. I remember how Joe beamed with pride and kept repeating, "Just look at what we did, sweetheart."

Jennifer was a happy baby, especially when tied with cloth onto the back of Margaret, our charming nanny. However, we worried because the baby was so quiet and slow to speak. It was only after we left Ghana when she was sixteen months old that we realized the problem. Five languages had been spoken in our household. Within two weeks after being in the United States, Jennifer began speaking English quite well when that was the only language she was hearing.

Our assignment to Ghana allowed us to finally begin to see some of the world. We had spent a couple of days in England on the way to Ghana. We used our time in Ghana to visit the neighboring adjacent countries. As they were all former French colonies and our French nonexistent, we usually traveled with someone who knew the language.

One memorable trip for me was joining Joe in Abidjan where he was attending a workshop. I agreed to go for a couple days and was to fly back to Accra a day earlier than Joe as I was uncomfortable leaving the kids very long. Well, my return was a disaster. First, I didn't speak French yet and was a little nervous about going to the airport alone. Joe assured me that I would be fine and went off to his official function. The first taxi that I took broke down and we haggled over what was a fair price. Then I hailed another taxi and it also broke down on the way to the airport. When I finally made it, there I discovered that my flight was delayed by eight hours with no explanation for the reason. About midnight, we were told the flight was canceled, and we were taken to a sleazy rent-by-the-hour motel. Meanwhile Joe was comfortably resting in a lovely hotel completely unaware of my predicament. Remember, this was 1973 before cell phones and there was no telephone for me to contact him. The room was so tiny that I had to put the suitcase on the bed and there was no lock on my door. I was the only woman passenger and worried all night about my safety. I reached home twenty-four hours later than scheduled and the kids were concerned about me. Joe got home about fifteen minutes later, and I was ready to scream when he greeted me with "See I told you that you could manage on your own." When I related the details of my journey home, Joe laughed which was not a smart reaction. I can now laugh too.

In March 1972, Joe and two friends, Bill Stewart and Bruce McMullen, undertook a 1,500-mile trip from Accra to Niamey, Niger, via Togo and Dahomey (now called Benin). The return trip took them through Ouagadougou, Upper Volta (now called Burkina Faso). The trip was undertaken in our Ford station wagon and was predominantly on dirt and gravel roads, which in turn resulted in the destruction of two of the tires on the car. Joe enjoyed the trip as it provided the first opportunity to see lions, giraffes, hippos, and several species of antelope in the wild. Joe and I made a couple of trips to the Ivory Coast, which was at that time the place to visit in West Africa. Abidjan, the capital had modern hotels, an ice-skating rink, and a bowling alley as well as great restaurants. The Ivory Coast became independent in 1960, three years after Ghana. In contrast to the strategy of "industrialization first," the founding president of the Ivory Coast, Houphet-Boigny, emphasized the development of the agricultural sector first. Following his strategy, Ivory Coast became a world leader in coffee, cocoa, and oil palm production. The rural wealth in turn fueled growth and diversification of the economy, which attracted tourism and investment.

Every year we were overseas we earned a rest-and-recuperation vacation, which meant a trip to the USA or any destination with a similar cost. In 1972 we traveled to Spain and Morocco on the way home to visit our families. In 1973, we decided to use our travel option to fly to Kenya and go on safari. Several other people in our community had recommended a wildlife safari in East Africa. As often happens with the Goodwin's, our flight to Nairobi was eventful. It started when we arrived at the airport to check-in at the Pan Am counter (actually, Pan Am was a major carrier in that era). When we went to check in, the Pan Am staff informed us that the entire family was being upgraded to first class. Since it was a long flight to Nairobi and the food and seating was much better, we were very appreciative. Unfortunately, as we were in line to board the plane, the Pan Am staffer explained that there had been a mistake and that they only had one upgrade for our family, not all six. Given that the tickets had been an unexpected bonus, we were not upset. However, when the upgrades were reallocated to other people in front of us, we were somewhat annoyed. The next issue was, who gets the first-class seat? I suggested that Joe take it, but he insisted that I should take first-class seat as I always had air-sickness problems and could not look after the kids. Unfortunately, it was a waste as I was sick and could not enjoy the benefits offered in first class.

Having resolved the first-class seat issue, we assumed the flight would now be uneventful. Not true! The Pan Am flight from New York that day had a "young millionaires" group among the passengers. As was common in those days when international air travel was a less common occurrence, when a plane arrived at a new location, passengers would get off and go into the terminal in transit status, to shop and obtain bragging rights that they had been in the country. That day was no exception as a number of the passengers deplaned with transit passes. While the transit passengers were in the airport shopping, the new Accra passengers boarded the plane. It was then that they discovered that there were not enough seats for the passengers now on the plane and the passengers in the transit area. What to do? Pan Am made the decision that they would keep the transit passengers in Accra, and they could continue their flight on the incoming Pan Am flight the next day. That decision was not well received by many of the transit passengers. When the transit passengers boarded the plane to get their carry-ons, many refused to leave. Fistfights occurred in the plane aisle and police had to be called to restore order. Then the baggage of the transit passengers had to be taken off the plane, which resulted in a delay of several hours. Finally, we did depart for Nairobi, leaving a number of angry transit passengers behind, especially the US millionaires who were not accustomed to such treatment.

When we arrived in Nairobi, we were met by Marvin Miracle and his wife. Joe and Marvin had met at an international conference in Accra. At that time, Marvin was on a sabbatical from the University of Wisconsin and living in Nairobi. Upon hearing that we were planning a safari to Kenya, Marvin had graciously suggested we stay with his family while we were in Nairobi. We accepted his kind offer to stay a couple of days in Nairobi. We arranged for a vehicle and driver to take us to Northern Kenya to the Meru and Samburu Parks before returning to Nairobi and then drove southeast to Tsavo Park and Amboseli Reserve. We had a fabulous time. One of my favorite photos is of our excited children watching elephants from our lodge balcony.

In Northern Kenya, we saw species unique to that area such as the Grevy's zebra, the beisa oryx, and the gerenuk. In Tsavo and Amboseli, we saw countless elephants, a number of rhinos and lions, and the numerous antelope and buffalo. Tsavo had over twenty-thousand elephants. Unfortunately, the next ten to fifteen years saw widespread poaching and dramatic decline in the number of animals such that the Kenya experience has declined, relative to when we visited and thought it was paradise.

We departed Ghana in May 1974 after a thirty-eight-month tour of duty. Our experience was very pleasant, except for the January 1972 military coup that overthrew the civilian government and created great uncertainty. With the coup, Ghana entered into a period of military rule until 1979.

My seventeen-year-old sister, Alice, came to visit in December 1973, which was great fun to share our experiences with her and to create new memories. We took her north as far as Ouagadougou. Alice returned home and wrote an interesting piece about her trip for her high school newspaper. It was neat to read the things that had captured her attention that we had already begun to take for granted.

Joe enjoyed his work in Ghana. In addition to his work in the USAID mission, he volunteered to lecture in the Department of Agricultural Economics at the University of Ghana. In assisting in the design of a rice production and marketing project, he collected research data which he intended to use for his dissertation. With incredible bad luck, all the data disappeared with our lost shipment of airfreight. Three years of work were gone forever. That forced us to take nine months of leave without pay from USAID and not return to Ghana for a second tour as planned. Instead, we stayed in Maryland doing a PhD dissertation on a new subject and I typed his thesis with our toddler Jennifer playing by my side and the older kids attending St. Lawrence School. My typing skills returned. Each error was time-consuming as it meant correcting six carbon copies. We spent all our savings, but we accomplished our goal. Joe dedicated his book to his wife, who made the PhD possible and to his children who made it necessary. Amen!

While we were writing the thesis, Joe received a job offer to join Purdue University as an agricultural economist in a multidisciplinary agricultural research team working in Sete Lagoas, Brazil. Joe was attracted to the job as it would provide him an opportunity to get field experience in his discipline. In his work with USAID, he had been involved in designing and managing projects but never implementing them. He felt that the experience in implementation would help him to be a better economist and manager. USAID offered several assignments but in the end, we made the decision to resign and accept the position in Brazil. We took a 20 percent decrease in salary but felt in the long-term the technical experience would be worth it. The job also offered the opportunity to live in Brazil, a country that had always fascinated both of us.

CHAPTER 4

Beautiful Brazil

The Big Move

In March 1975, we packed out of the rented house in Oxen Hill, Maryland. Our kids left their school before the end of the semester. We called to bid our families farewell in Missouri and excitedly headed for new adventures in Sete Lagoas, Brazil. We stopped overnight in Miami and were joined by my cousin Tom Ream, who had settled in Key West. Our visit with Tom was short but sweet and we treasure that memory as he lost his battle with throat cancer at a young age.

Background

Brazil is the largest country in Latin America in both size and population. The language is Portuguese, having been established as a Portuguese colony in the sixteenth century. Brazil shares many characteristics of the United States. It is a federal republic. It is a nation of immigrants. Besides the Portuguese, there are large numbers of people with German, Italian, Japanese, African, and Middle Eastern ancestry. Like the United States, there are few remaining indigenous inhabitants. Slavery played an important role in the development of the economy. Brazil did not abolish slavery until the 1880s.

Also like the USA, Brazil has large mineral deposits and its agricultural sector is extremely diversified, with large areas of sugarcane, citrus, coffee, cocoa, maize, soybeans, and livestock. During the period 1950–1978, Brazil was a recipient of large amounts of economic assistance under the foreign aid program. An especially important role of the foreign assistance program was strengthening agricultural universities in Brazil. In the 1970s the agricultural economic assistance expanded to the Brazilian national agricultural research system. Purdue University was selected to work with the Brazilian National Research Corporation (EMBRAPA) to strengthen its corn and sorghum research capability. The assistance included equipment, MS and PhD training of its staff in the United States, and provision of technical assistance at the National Corn and Sorghum Center at Sete Lagoas in the state of Minas Gerais in Central Brazil. Purdue provided a team that included engineering, plant breeding, agronomy, plant physiology, entomology, pathology, and economics. The team was to help expand the research program, provide hands-on training, and fill in for Brazilian staff sent to the United States for degree training at the MS and PhD level. Joe's job was to be the agricultural economist member of the team.

Language Training

Purdue was anxious to fill the position, and rather than providing us with adequate language training, gave us forty hours of Portuguese training, and told us we would learn the language in the field. That was criminal in my view. The National Corn and Sorghum Center was located in a rural town of one hundred thousand people and few spoke or understood English. Likewise, few of the research station staff spoke English. Consequently, when we initially arrived in Sete Lagoas I was only able to communicate with the three American wives of the Purdue staff.

Purdue had included funding in our contract for language training in-country, so we needed to start as soon as possible. The other Purdue families already in Sete Lagoas recommended a sweet older lady, Dona Josephina, so we contracted for lessons to be given in our home three times a week. Dona Josephina's husband had been a minister and she had learned English on her own. She was very patient with us and we looked forward to the lessons. We studied diligently. We found help in simple ways. Joe read Donald Duck comic books. I watched the Brazilian soap operas to try to pick up words or slang. Eventually I became so fluent in Portuguese that I dreamed and wrote poetry in that beautiful language. I can still understand Portuguese forty-five years later but have lost the speaking ability.

While our lack of understanding of Portuguese was extremely frustrating, it did have humorous moments. When we visited a Brazilian neighbor who spoke English, the six-year-old daughter of the family started speaking to Joe in Portuguese. The mother explained to the little girl that he could not speak or understand Portuguese. The little girl looked at Joe in disbelief and said, "How can he not speak or understand Portuguese? I am only six years old, and I can speak and understand Portuguese." The world as seen by a six-year-old threw down a challenge. The urgency of learning Portuguese correctly was brought home to Joe when he thought he had ordered a beer and they brought him ice cream. The words in Portuguese sound very similar but there is a big difference.

We knew we had arrived when we began to have dreams in Portuguese. I was edified when a man selling roses asked me what state I was from. I replied Missouri. He asked if that was near Sao Paulo. I said Missouri is located in the central USA. He acted surprised to learn that I was an American because he thought my accent was Brazilian. That was the best compliment I ever had.

Friendly Welcome

Despite our lack of communicability in Portuguese, we found the Brazilians to be extremely friendly and appreciative of our effort to learn their language. They loved our children and allowed them the run of the Lago Palace Hotel during our first month in country. A waiter, Jose Maria, could speak a bit of English and took us under his wings. A bellhop named Claudio helped to keep an eye on the kids in the lobby and by the pool and even invited all our family to meet his parents and share a lovely meal in their home. The receptionist allowed Jill and Gretchen to sit on her lap while she answered the telephone. On our second weekend in Sete Lagoas, the owner of the hotel, Señor Oligario, invited us to his farm home and provided transport. He didn't have a land line so could not notify his wife that we were coming. No problem. Stella produced a beautiful meal and we had a wonderful afternoon with a lot of hand gestures, nodding and smiling, and a nap in the hammocks on their patio. Later we lived across the street from the Oligarios and our families became close.

Meanwhile Joe was welcomed at the EMBRAPA Center with open arms and was quickly involved in all things professional and personal. He even became the center's goalie for the Saturday soccer games. Our family was included in all the wonderful *Churrachos* (Brazilian barbeques) at the center too. We formed lifelong friendships.

Shipping

As in Ghana, we arrived with no car, and no expectation of a shipment of our household effects for several months. Actually, it took fourteen months for our possessions sent via sea freight to arrive in Brazil from Ghana. By that time, the kids had outgrown their clothes, and out of necessity, we had replaced most of the household items. To add insult to injury, we were hit with a $2,500 bill for being overweight on the shipment. That was caused by an inequity in allowances which existed. Government contractors were not granted the same benefits as "direct hire" government employees. We had been allowed to ship 7,200 pounds to Ghana while in direct hire status. As a university contractor, we were only given a 2,500-pound allowance. Since we didn't get to return to Ghana to pack out, friends had to manage the task for us. Hence, we were over the weight allotted under the new contract with Purdue. It took another twenty years before benefits were made more equitable.

Housing

Contrary to our Ghana experience, we did not have a furnished house awaiting us. We were installed in a hotel that would be our home for a month until we found a house. We didn't have the benefit of an executive officer to handle the rent, so I had to go to the bank and make the monthly rent payments. Then we waited a couple months for reimbursements. It was the same situation with paying utilities. We lived in two different houses during our time in Sete Lagoas because we moved after we experienced several home invasions in the first house.

Education

Schooling for the children was obviously a priority and we needed to rapidly reach a decision about where we would send the children. The nearest American school was fifty miles away in Belo Horizonte, and the children needed transport. The move to Brazil was the most difficult of our career. We were in a foreign country where we couldn't speak the language; we had no transport, no home, and no school for the children. It took six months to resolve all those issues.

Among the Purdue families in Sete Lagoas, one family had their children in the local school (the mother was Brazilian which helped considerably) and the other two families with school age children did home study. The first option we explored was to place the children in a local school. Given that there was no English-speaking ability in the local school this meant throwing the kids cold turkey into a Portuguese learning environment. We decided to try it, but the results were less than satisfactory. The teachers in the Sete Lagoas school did not know how to handle the situation. Our children knew no Portuguese and the teachers knew no English. Lack of language ability compounded our initial schooling problems, as neither Joe nor I could help the children with their homework since we were effectively illiterate in Portuguese at that point.

After two days of class, our children were demoted two grade levels, which was demoralizing to them. After two weeks, we decided to try the home schooling approach.

I am not a trained teacher but was thrown into the role of teacher/tutor/mother for four of our kids taking the Calvert correspondence course while caring for our two-year-old Jennifer at the same time. It was a nightmare for me. I studied longer than the kids as it took a lot of preparation on my part and they would race through the course. To emphasize that for a few hours I was not their mother but rather their teacher, I had them go out the back door, knock on the front door, and say, "Good morning, Mrs. Goodwin." At first, they thought it was a dumb idea but eventually they got the point that I was making and genuinely buckled down to work. After six agonizing months of doing that, I felt near a nervous breakdown. At that point, we decided that they would have to make the long journey to Belo Horizonte to attend the American school.

We hired a taxi driver to take the children to school and wait for them every day. The driver's name was Coello and they all bonded with him. Their days were long, and we worried constantly about them being on the treacherous roads. All too often the kids would come home with descriptions of the road accidents they had seen. We had a fit when we learned that Coello would turn off the car and coast down the steep hills because he thought he was saving gas. The sad thing is that on their very last day of school when we were leaving Brazil for good, Coello and the kids were all crying as they said goodbye. Coello's tears blinded him and he pulled out in front of a car, causing considerable damage to both vehicles. We felt so sorry for him as we had to leave him with a taxi to repair and the loss of guaranteed income.

Although we considered the American school in Belo Horizonte to be a better solution than home schooling, it also presented new problems. During that period, it was popular to have open classrooms. That meant that students advanced at their own pace. Well, that system works for those more disciplined but not for others. So we felt that our children had a mixed bag of results. Some were more motivated than others. Somehow, they all survived and thrived.

Transport

It was four months before we had a car. In order to promote their auto industry, Brazil did not allow the import of cars at that time. We had to purchase a made-in-Brazil vehicle. Having a larger family meant we could either purchase a Chevrolet or Volkswagen station wagon. Given that we had exhausted our savings after being on leave without pay for ten months while writing the PhD dissertation, we decided that rather than buy a new car we would find a used one.

In fact, we owned two used cars during our tour, first a Volkswagon station wagon and then later a Chevy sedan. Neither vehicle was large enough for our family, but we managed to travel around the beautiful and diverse country with all the kids squeezed in the back seat anyway.

In-Country Travel

In 1976, we made a long road trip to southern Brazil and Paraguay and Iguazu Falls with all five kids in a sedan. I was pregnant with Juliana and experiencing nausea, so we stopped frequently along the roadside. EMBRAPA had a conference in Piracicaba in the state of Sao Paulo which had prompted our trip. After the meetings, we headed for Iguazu Falls which is absolutely gorgeous. These are a series of 275 falls expanding almost two miles wide and dropping 269 feet. We stayed at the famous Hotel das Cataratas near the falls and the kids had a great time with the macaws and wildlife on their beautiful grounds.

From Iguazu we drove to Asuncion, Paraguay, and were excited to find a shop that sold blue jeans for all the kids. Another vivid memory I have of Paraguay was seeing the farmers on ox carts with huge wooden wheels.

On the return trip through southern Brazil, we visited Curitiba in Parana and Florianopolis on the Island of Santa Catarina, all beautiful places.

Rio de Janeiro was four hundred miles from Sete Lagoas, but it held a fascination for us, so we took an overnight train with all the family and our faithful nanny Dalva to help with the baby. Instead, I had to take care of her because she experienced motion sickness on the rocky train. While we were checking into a Rio hotel and distracted, the kids wandered off. The manager asked if we had lost one and we realized that seven-year-old Jill was missing. Her brother had shoved her into an open elevator door and it took off before he could get inside. When the door opened on another floor, Jill got off. How could this all happen so quickly? Thank goodness nothing bad happened to her and a maid brought her back to the lobby.

We enjoyed visits to Sugar Loaf Mountain and Corcovado that trip as well as another one when we flew back to Rio with Joe's Uncle Hank, Aunt Gladys, and cousin Mary Curran. We all huffed and puffed up 425 steps to Corcovado and saw the beautiful 125-foot-tall statue of Christ the Redeemer overlooking Rio.

Joe and I took a third trip to Rio along with fellow Purdue team members Bob and Ilka Shaffert. We stayed at a hotel in Ipanema. I was excited to get to the famous beach. But I stood too close to the bed while putting on my bathing suit and hit my foot on the board around the bottom of the bed and broke my middle toe. It throbbed all weekend. The foot swelled so big that I could not put on my shoe. I had to fly back to Belo Horizonte and then get a bus to Sete Lagoas and then a taxi to home without Joe's assistance because he and Bob had flown elsewhere for business.

When I finally reached our house, I was met by the kids telling me that our son had been hit by a car and was in the hospital. I forgot about my broken toe and ran the two blocks to the hospital where Joe II lay without having had any treatment all day. The hospital would not touch him without a parents' permission. Our friends the Rykerts had tried to assist but the hospital refused their signature. Joe had a torn ligament in his leg and the driver had not even stopped to check on him. By the time I was able to finally take him home all bandaged up, my leg was also swelling. This was not a pleasant experience for either of us.

Losing a Parent While Abroad

We had lived in Brazil less than one year when on February 28, 1976, Joe's wonderful mother, Lucille Victoria Goodwin, died suddenly at the young age of sixty-seven from a blood clot. Joe was away working in Brasilia when I received a telegram stating that she had a seizure and had been in the hospital for a week. I had no way to get in touch with Joe, so I took a bus to the airport in Belo Horizonte to meet Joe's plane as he was due home that day. Unbeknownst to me, Joe had changed to an earlier flight, so we didn't connect at the airport. When he got home the kids told him what had happened, but I had taken the cable with me, so he was unsure of the details. When I finally got home several hours later, we discussed our course of action. We repacked his suitcase and went back to Belo to try to get a ticket for him to go home to see his mother. Unfortunately, it was during Carnival and there was no availability of seats on the flight to Rio. The ticket agent even laughed at us when we said his mother might be dying and we needed to get him home. She said everyone claims to have a dying mother when they want to get to Rio during Carnival. Frustrated, we had to return to Sete Lagoas without a ticket.

Joe was able to leave the next day and called his sister when he got to New York. Mary Jean told him that she didn't think their mom was going to make it. In fact, Lucille had already died while he was flying home, but she didn't want to tell Joe that over the phone. It is very difficult to lose a parent but especially tough when you don't get the chance to tell them that you love them one last time. That is a high price too often paid by foreign service personnel.

Purdue would not pay for me to go back for the funeral, but I wanted to be there with the family, so I bought my ticket to the USA. I made arrangements for a friend to stay with our children and tearfully bid them farewell. Another bus ride to Belo Horizonte and then I was defeated by the Brazilian system. One needed an exit visa in order to leave, and I did not have the required document, which I would have to obtain from the police station back in Sete Lagoas. Long story short, I was unable to attend my mother-in-law's funeral as a result and have always regretted not having the chance to pay my respects and to support Joe and his dad and siblings at that sad time.

Health Problems

Joe and I decided that we would like to have one last child. We didn't care whether it was a girl or a boy. We just felt that we had enough love to share with another child. When I didn't conceive after six months, I finally went to a Brazilian doctor. Much to my surprise, he discovered that I had a large tumor on the outside of my uterus. On Christmas Eve 1975, I had surgery in Belo Horizonte because again

Purdue would not pay for me to go back to the United States, and we had no extra funds. Joe had taken a 25 percent cut in salary in order to take the job and we had been struggling financially after having been through the ten months of leave without pay. The tumor tested positive for cancer and my uterus was left scarred but intact. But we then worried about whether we should try for our sixth child because we didn't know if the cancer would return. Who would raise our large family if anything happened to me? I was only thirty-two at that time and it was a gut-wrenching question. The doctor advised us to wait another six months to allow my womb to heal. So we did.

Lo and behold, we were able to conceive a beautiful blue-eyed baby daughter, Juliana Lucille, who was born by emergency C-section on March 3, 1977. My womb had so much scar tissue left from the surgery to remove the tumor that I could not dilate in the right area and it was near busting point. Unfortunately, I had pneumonia when she was born so wasn't allowed to be awake nor was Joe permitted to be with me.

I had a severe allergic reaction to whatever anesthetic was administered for the surgery and swelled up tremendously. I was in such bad shape that they would not bring our precious baby for me to hold until she was thirty hours old. Joe kept reassuring me that she was healthy, but I was so frightened that they were trying to shield me from the truth. Finally, he convinced them that I would get better if I could see Juliana. She was perfect and good medicine for me. I started to improve after being able to hold our precious child.

There was no nursing care for the mothers, so someone had to stay in the room. Joe thought it should be him, so he slept in the other bed. Normally Joe is a very sound sleeper, but one night he jolted awake, sensing danger. My IV had run out of medicine and I was getting air pumped into my veins. I was aware this was happening but could not speak. Joe lay with his back to me asleep. I actually prayed for God to wake him up and he did. Joe ran for help. It was a close call.

To this day, I know that wanting Juliana saved my life. I would never have gone to see an ob-gyn in another country speaking another language if it had not been for the desire to have another baby. I wouldn't have known the problem existed in time.

Different Customs

Every country has its own customs and sometimes we learned the hard way. For instance, I had no idea that wives fixed the plates for their husbands. Our first open house Christmas party was a disaster because I tried to do it American style. I had bought thirteen dozen eggs and made huge amounts of eggnog, not realizing that was not a Brazilian tradition. I baked mountains of cookies. I made my famous snow-on-the-mountain date cake. I fixed all kinds of dips, cheese, and crackers. I made fruit punch. At last everything was set out with stacks of Christmas plates and I thought the table looked beautiful. Our guests began to arrive. We kept urging them to help themselves to the food and beverages. Nobody moved. Nobody touched a morsel. I was confused and could not understand why they were refusing our hospitality. Finally, one brave Brazilian lady who had lived briefly in the USA picked up a plate and served her husband. Others followed. We were still left with punch bowls of untouched eggnog and lots of sweets.

Fast-forward six months to the USA bicentennial of 1976. I proposed that we host an American-style party at our house to mark the big occasion. Joe, remembering the disastrous Christmas party, tried his best to dissuade me. We even had a big argument about it which was unusual. But I was stubborn. I insisted on serving hot dogs and hamburgers, baked beans, and chips and beer. Joe swore that I was crazy. But I held my ground and invited all his colleagues from EMBRAPA, plus friends and neighbors. The guest list numbered seventy-five people and I prepared lots of American food while Joe continued to protest. I put him in charge of arranging games such as three-legged races, sack races, and water balloons. Again, Joe didn't think that would go over well in Brazil. Was he ever wrong! If you invite them, they will come. The Brazilians not only came but many of them brought uninvited guests or called friends to join us, and in the end, I served around 125 meals. And the games were a huge success, especially because we gave prizes to the winning teams. Some people that had seemed so stern were out on the field beside our house competing with gusto. It was a blast and I am glad that I followed my instincts. It more than made up for the Christmas party fiasco.

Now one trait that disgusted me was that Brazilian men were too often chauvinistic. Time after time, the men would advance to the front of line in the grocery store or wherever I was shopping. One time when I was eight months pregnant with Juliana, a man shoved in front of me just as I finished putting my purchases on the counter and banged me in my bulging stomach with his bottles of beer. Not even a simple apology whispered from his lips. I vowed revenge and tried unsuccessfully to stop them from doing that in the future. I even scolded the cashier for permitting it to happen all the time, but she only shrugged. I am not proud to report that on my last trip to the store that I carried a hatpin with me. I was so frustrated that I had reached the point of no return. If any man had bucked the line that day, he would have had a sharp jab in the groin from me and I probably would have been arrested for assault. I am not proud but admit I kept the pin ready between my fingers. God saved me by not putting any men within my reach. Not one guy tried to get in front of me that day. I feel better for having confessed my sin of anger and malintent.

Sad Farewell

Despite this last paragraph and all the bad things that happened to me while we lived there, I loved Brazil and had many Brazilian friends. Recently I acquired two wonderful new Brazilian/American friends in Julia Goughnour and Sueli Burkhart.

In December 1977, the Goodwin gang of eight emotionally bid farewell to our dear friends and colleagues in Sete Lagoas, Brazil. We had loved working for Purdue for three years, living in Brazil, on loan to EMBRAPA, the National Corn and Sorghum Research Center. It was one of the most difficult departures we ever made from an overseas post, only surpassed in 1994 when leaving Ghana, the second time around.

We were scheduled to fly out of Belo Horizonte and were to leave our hotel at five o'clock in the morning with a seventy-seven-kilometer drive to the airport. We invited the whole EMBRAPA staff to our hotel for drinks by the pool from five to seven o'clock on the evening before our flight. We figured that would give us a chance to say farewell and thank everyone, have dinner, and then pack. It seemed like a good idea. Instead, the event turned into a major wake. People drank, and they stayed. So we ordered food—lots of food. They drank, and they stayed longer, then Luis Marcelo Sans (Juliana's godfather) brought out his guitar and started serenading us with incredibly sad songs. The tears started to flow down everyone's cheeks, faster than the liquor pulsed through their bloodstreams. Watching grown Brazilian man weeping unashamedly, and begging, begging us not to leave, was a touching and disarming experience. As mentioned, I had always disliked the machismo that many men had exhibited in Brazil. However, this group of men was sincere in their open display of affection.

The length and intensity of this impromptu party was getting to me. Joe looked so sad. He had never wanted to leave Brazil as he loved his work so much. To this day, he maintains that it was the highlight of his career. Joe and our son were disappointed that I did not share their enthusiasm for the idea of emigrating. I had very different feelings about Brazil from my husband, and this had created some unspoken friction. The problem is that neither of us adequately expressed or communicated our feelings about the subject at the time.

Without a doubt, I truly loved the people and had formed many close friendships; people with whom I still correspond annually. But I had undergone tremendous stress from many very unpleasant experiences in Brazil. Suffice it to say that I was ready to move on and start a new life, but I regretted and resented the fact that Joe was not more sympathetic to my feelings. Indeed, I felt Joe was being selfish to even suggest that we stay permanently. He knew, or should have known, how close I had come to having a nervous breakdown during that first most difficult year in Sete Lagoas while I was home schooling four of our children, with a two-year-old vying for my attention. I have never felt more isolated in my life because I could not communicate with our neighbors at that point.

Joe and I have long since come to understand and appreciate one another's feelings about that period of our lives. We love, respect, and accept our partner's feelings for what they represented. It is a closed chapter.

Meanwhile, back at the Lago Palace Hotel on the night of our departure, at 4:00 a.m. I excused myself from the crowd who still had not left, in order to go to our room and start packing. Lo and behold, they decided that I needed help and followed me. I knew it was a mistake but could not be rude. I would neatly pack something and suddenly someone would start crying, begging us not to leave, and remove the object I had just packed. The commotion woke Juliana, who was just nine months old, and she started screaming when she saw the people in our bedroom. Brazilians love children and they were enamored by our blue-eyed doll that had been born in their country. A couple of women decided that Juliana was Brazilian, and therefore we could not take her out of the country. Not funny! The two of them grabbed Juliana out of bed and started fighting over who would hold her. She responded with wails for her mother. I was exasperated.

At this point, you may wonder why I waited until the last moment to pack. I am normally an organized person and pack far in advance. However, that last day had not gone the way I had planned. Our maid, Dalva, was very dear to me. She was more like a friend or a sister. We shared everything. I had even helped in the delivery of her baby just one month earlier while her husband, Nilton, begged a doctor to come help us. The doctor ignored Nilton's pleas, saying that it was not time because it was a first child. Dalva had a heart condition and high blood pressure. When her eyes rolled back into her head so I could not see the pupils, I feared we had lost her and the baby. Thank God, they both lived. Joe and I became the boy's godparents. I wanted him to have something for his future. We gave them money to be deposited into a savings account. That last afternoon Dalva brought the baby to the hotel and asked me to keep him while she went to the bank to open the account. She was gone so long, and the baby got hungry. She was breast-feeding him, and I had nothing to give the child. The hours passed and Dalva did not return. I walked the floor and sang to my handsome little godson. Then I started to get this funny feeling and the crazy idea that perhaps she had abandoned him in hopes that we would adopt him. I know it sounds far-fetched, but I had no other explanation for her prolonged absence. Finally, her husband came and told me Dalva had passed out while waiting in the bank line. Her blood pressure was elevated because she was upset about our leaving. She had no identification on her. Finally, she recovered and sent Nilton to collect the baby. With all the drama, I had no time to pack during the day.

What a nightmare! The clock was now ticking away, and I was making no progress. We had accumulated gifts and more stuff than our suitcases would hold. Each child would have to help carry the load. Joan, then age thirteen, was upset with me for making her leave behind her old teddy bear and a huge pink quartz crystal, which she had found. After all, she was carrying her pillow, purse, camera, and two other bags. I had to say no to the rock and stuffed animal. She/we simply could not carry another thing.

We finally managed to extract ourselves from the clutches of our friends and load the vans. They did not go home until we pulled away at 5:15 a.m. We had an unbelievable amount of luggage with seventeen suitcases, a typewriter, and a sewing machine, plus numerous carry-ons. I cringe when I recall how we used to have to travel with six kids and all that baggage. When in 1993, Joe and I went on a Greek Island cruise alone, we took with us only one shared piece of luggage. Perfect.

We arrived at the Belo Horizonte airport at dawn. I smile as I recall the remarks of the two airline security people when our family had to put all our possessions on the conveyor belt. I pretended not to understand their native Portuguese tongue. "Are these crazy people Italians?" one asked.

The other responded, "No they are Americans. Italians know better."

Joe and I had a good chuckle about that when we were out of earshot.

Goodwin children Joe, Gretchen, Jill, Jennifer and Joan in
front of the Congonhas do Campo church in Brazil in 1976.

CHAPTER 5

Machu Picchu Misadventure

This journey deals with the period of transit in December 1977 between Brazil and West Lafayette, Indiana, where Joe was on the faculty of Purdue University.

The sensible thing to do when traveling with an abundance of children and much luggage would be to take the straightest route home. Right? Right! But not when you are Joe and Hope Goodwin, who want to see the world. We thought that we would probably never live in that part of the globe again, so we decided we should tour Bolivia and Peru on our way back. If we had realized that Bolivia would be our next assignment, we could have saved considerable money and skipped the stop.

One of Joe's childhood classmates was studying Spanish in Cochabamba, Bolivia, at that time. Of course, we wanted to see Bede Smith while he was so close to us, even though it required an overnight stay in Santa Cruz, Bolivia. More taxis and hassles with luggage and kids, but I'm glad we made the extra effort. We had a delightful time with Bede and the children thought his jokes were terrific. While in Santa Cruz, we purchased a large leather wood lined trunk in which we deposited most of the excess baggage. We used that big old trunk for years before it was overtaken with mildew and had to be discarded. I never missed that luggage as it always reminded me of the bad things that happened on that vacation.

I just hinted that the trip was going downhill. In fact, we went uphill from there—up to the mountains to La Paz. My memory is foggy of that trip, so I suppose nothing bad happened to us, except that nine-month-old Juliana slept and slept from the altitude and would not eat or drink. I do remember that we bought six wool ponchos, only to learn that we were all allergic to them. I also remember that Joan had purchased a big llama carpet or wall hanging as a surprise present for her father for Christmas.

When we arrived in Lima, Peru, customs did not look fondly upon our entourage. They insisted on opening all sixteen bags, putting a big yellow sticker on each one which had been inspected. Joan was watching this process and getting upset because her surprise gift for her dad was about to be spoiled. Without anyone noticing, Joan picked up one of the stickers and placed it on her suitcase. I understand why she did it but nervously realize that if Joan had been caught, we could have been arrested.

Our goal in touring Peru was to visit the famous deserted Inca city, Machu Picchu, located high in the Andes Mountain. We also sought to visit the ruins at Cuzco, the imperial capital of the Inca Empire. We flew from Lima to Cuzco, where we accessed the train to Machu Picchu. It was a switch back train at the beginning, which climbed the steep mountainside by means of switching, back and forth, back and forth. We disembarked from the train, then were taken by bus to the top of the mountain, again going back and forth around incredibly sharp curves. It made my stomach churn as I looked down at the barren cliffs of stone. Reaching the top, the bus driver emphasized that the train would depart on time either with or without all the passengers. We were told to be back to our bus at a certain time. Later I realized that my husband was so excited about reaching Machu Picchu that he had not listened well to the driver's warning.

Machu Picchu first came to modern day attention in 1911 when Hiram Bingham stumbled upon the ruins. One theory is that the Incas built this noble city to protect their women from the Spanish conquistadors as well as provide safety for the Inca warrior rulers. The majority of the human remains exhumed there are women. It also was a place of worship for the people who saw gods in the sun and the mountain. As a study in archaeology, Machu Picchu is a wondrous sight built of white granite. Machu Picchu's long hidden glory has emerged from beneath its jungle shroud and displays the craftsmanship of master masons. The unmortared stones fit together snugly and in perfect harmony. There is a plaza with two temples, one containing a huge stone altar, the other three large windows that gave us a magnificent view from eight thousand feet above sea level. The city has beautiful stone terraces and numerous houses.

I remember the gleam in Grandma Gander's eyes as she told me about Machu Picchu when I was a young child. Grandma was an armchair traveler. She read *National Geographic* faithfully and kept every issue. I regretted that she had died that previous year. She would have delighted in knowing that her namesake had actually visited Machu Picchu. I also wish I had been able to purchase her collection of *Geographic* magazines when she died, but I was pregnant with Juliana and unable to travel back for her funeral. We took a guided tour of Machu Picchu. At least we started out together as a family on the tour. Explanations were long because everything was translated into several languages and baby Juliana got bored and fussy. I had to take her aside so as not to disturb the other tourists, so I missed most of the tour and vowed to return one day, sans kids.

After Joe and the rest of the youngsters finished the guided tour to Machu Picchu, we reunited for lunch. Joe and Jody, as our son was called at that time to avoid confusion, announced they would like to climb a mountain peak nearby. Naturally, the older girls wanted to go along. I was not thrilled about the idea. It looked steep and dangerous for people without proper climbing gear or any experience. Of course, they promised to be careful. How could I deny such happy faces the pleasure of exploration together? Okay, I agreed, but reminded them to be back in plenty of time for the bus which would descend the hill to take us back to the train station. They nodded, and off they went to explore the peak.

Four-year-old Jenny and baby Juliana stayed with me. I waited rather anxiously for the rest of my family at the lodge at the site. Sometimes it seems like I have spent half my life waiting for Joe Goodwin. As the time approached to board the buses, I strained my eyes in search of a familiar figure on the mountainside. I did not recognize any of them. In turn, the buses filled with passengers and proceeded slowly down the treacherous, narrow, winding mountainside. No Joe or Goodwin gang appeared in sight. Both concern and annoyance surged inside of me. Finally, only one bus remained. A few people straggled in from various directions. The bus driver honked his horn to give the last and final call. I begged him to wait five more minutes for the rest of my family. Another woman made the same plea. He said he would be pushing it to make the train on time but reluctantly agreed to wait three minutes more. Visions of my family being stuck on the cold mountain danced through my head. Just as the driver yelled "*Vamos,*" which means "Let's go," I saw Jill running toward the bus. She was panting breathlessly as she reached me but said the others were close behind. A red-faced Joe, our kids, and the other people for whom we were waiting arrived in the nick of time.

The driver cursed them all, slammed the door, and took off like a bat out of hell. This delay nearly cost us our lives. As we went around the second turn, much too fast, the bus began to slide on the loose gravel. We came to a sudden stop and found ourselves hanging precariously with the front wheels of the bus over the edge of the cliff. The bus tilted at such an angle that from my seat in the back of the bus I could see the train station three thousand feet below. If we went over the cliff, there was not a single tree or bush to catch us. It was solid rock straight down. People began screaming in terror and demanding that the driver open the door. Instead, the driver yelled for all to remain calm and stay in their seats. He said if anyone moved, the bus could go over the brink. He shoved the gears into reverse. The tires spun dirt and gravel. We were in a worse position and tilting further.

The driver started praying out loud. That was a queue for me to hit the panic button. I don't scream or carry on when I am afraid. I tend to internalize it. My hands clutched Joe's arm. I wanted to tell him that I loved him, but the words could not escape my lips. I was speechless. I looked into his concerned eyes. His face was no longer red, but it quickly turned pale. He whispered, "I love you, darling," and patted my hands.

Smoke was now coming out of the hood. Perhaps it was from the tires as the driver continued to try to thrust the bus backward. The wheels spun round and round. The engine moaned and groaned. Suddenly, inexplicably, the tires caught solid ground and we lurched back onto the road, nearly slamming into the canyon wall. Passengers cheered. The driver got out of his seat and took a bow. Then we proceeded very, very slowly down the mountain, being extra careful on each curve. Everyone generously tipped the driver and bid him *adios* and *gracias*.

We managed to get on the train seconds before it started to roll down the track. When we got the family settled down, I asked Joe to go and buy me a drink. I didn't want Coca-Cola. I wanted alcohol. I am not a drinking woman and I have a very low tolerance for alcohol. However, after that experience, for the first time in my life, I felt like I needed a drink. Joe returned with a bottle of champagne and paper cups. Champagne always gives me a headache, and drinking out of paper cups is not my idea of elegance. Nonetheless, I was grateful for the bubbly stuff, which produced extra bubbles in that altitude. The train went jogging along while I chugged down glasses of champagne. I soon felt the buzz.

All of a sudden, the train screeched to a halt in the middle of the dense jungle. An enormous tree was lying across the track. Some passengers began speculating on how the tree got there. There was a group of guerrillas named the Shining Path in Peru. They had been wreaking havoc and terrorizing the country and had even bombed tourist places to call attention to their cause. I expected to be ambushed at any moment and hid my jewelry in the baby's diaper bag. Joe brushed off such a possibility with his usual sense of humor and talked me into getting off the train. If I hadn't been plied with champagne, I probably would've elected to stay put. The crew was already working on cutting the tree apart, a task that took almost two hours. The whole time we chatted with other passengers, I was keeping a keen eye on the jungle, fully expecting the Shining Path to burst forth and rob and kill us all with machine guns.

One fright a day is enough, I had thought. I didn't deserve a second concern the same afternoon. Joe was right not to worry. My fears did not materialize, and the delay was no more than a minor inconvenience. Actually, it was rather a pleasant diversion, for we met some nice people. I have always tried to look for the good in every situation. That is my nature. Our trip to Machu Picchu had been just one more unforgettable experience. I somehow knew that someday I would return and enjoy the intrigue of history more than I had the first time. We did in 2005.

CHAPTER 6

Purdue University

After spending three years working in Brazil under a Purdue University contract, Joe was extended as an assistant professor to work back on campus with graduate students. It was a great experience for him.

Meanwhile, the kids and I did our best to adapt to our new environment. We arrived in West Lafayette, Indiana, on Jenny's fifth birthday, January 1, 1978, after spending the Christmas holiday with our families in Missouri. We had rented a large old house on campus. It had big gaps in the windows and there was snow inside our bedroom. I stuffed newspapers in the cracks but that didn't help much. The outside temperature remained below zero for a month straight.

The winter of 1978–1979 was one of the bitterest winters on record. The house only had registers with heat coming up from the floor. The temperature inside never got above 55°F and the kids would get dressed standing on top of the registers. Purdue University was actually closed for the first time in fifty years due to the amount of snow and freezing temperatures.

We enrolled the kids in St. Lawrence Catholic School, where they had to wear uniforms. It wasn't an easy or particularly happy time for any of the children. It is never easy to change schools in the middle of the school year when friendships had been formed. The Catholic school was also much more disciplined and rigorous than the open classroom system that they had been under in Brazil.

During our period of living there, we did enjoy visits from my parents, Aunt Edith and Uncle Vic, my brother Paul and Anne and kids, our cousins the Lambs, the Mahons, and former colleagues and friends from Brazil. We got to make a few trips back to Monroe City.

Fourteen months later, we were packing out again. This time we were headed for La Paz, Bolivia, to work on a coca substitution project for the University of Florida. I felt so sorry for the kids to change schools again before the end of the school year. They were always paying a price for the life they had not chosen. As a mother, my heart was always heavy and grateful to our kids.

CHAPTER 7

Bolivia: Ballots to Bullets

Purdue University hired Joe to work on campus with the Department of Agricultural Economics and the International Program Office program on a USAID-funded study on agricultural development in Francophone West Africa. This involved advising graduate students and collecting and analyzing farm level data from three West African countries. While the work was interesting and involved long-distance fieldwork, Joe missed the close fieldwork opportunities he had experienced in Brazil. He liked being in the field and working closely with host country nationals. Moreover, educational facilities for the children were extremely limited in sub-Saharan African countries at that time, and with six children, we felt that a return to Latin America would better meet their educational needs.

When we learned that the University of Florida was seeking an agricultural economist to work in Bolivia, Joe applied and landed the job. The Bolivian position was to be part of a multidisciplinary team to work with the Bolivian government to promote alternative crops for coca production in the Yungas and Chapare areas of Bolivia. As time would reveal, this was to be a difficult task.

Bolivia is one of the poorest countries in the Western Hemisphere. It is also one of the countries where the indigenous population is in the majority. The Quechua and Aymara Indians together constitute around 60–65 percent of the total population. These two groups are located principally in the mountainous area of Western Bolivia, called the *Altiplano* or high plain. Over time there has been some migration off the *Altiplano* and down into the Bolivian lowlands. Until 1952, the majority of the Quechua and Aymara lived on large *haciendas* (farms) owned by descendants of the Spanish conquerors or worked in mines also owned by the nonindigenous population. In 1952 there was a revolution that featured a land reform program that broke up the large farms and redistributed the land to the people living on it. The revolution also resulted in the nationalization of the mines and placed ownership in the hands of the government. In spite of the land reform and redistribution of land to the peasants, there was still a shortage of land. To meet this demand, the government built roads into the Yungas valley region east of the capital La Paz and the Chapare region in the Amazon jungle area north of the city of Cochabamba in central Bolivia. Many farm families moved into these areas seeking to make a better life for themselves and their families. Initially, they planted crops such as tropical fruits for export as well as crops they brought with them such as corn, beans and coca. The coca crop had been cultivated for many years throughout the Andean mountains. The coca plant leaves when chewed with limes that breakdown the alkaloids in the leaves serves to depress hunger and the cold of the *Altiplano*. Consequently, there was a good domestic market for the leaves, especially in the Bolivian highlands. However, with the growing popularity of cocaine use in the United States, and the resulting increase in the price of coca leaves, coca production for export developed into a rapidly growing industry. Coca was a perfect crop for farmers in isolated areas distant from markets. What the farmers needed were crops with high value and low bulk. Clearly, the cocaine market provided the value, and processing the coca leaves with kerosene reduced the bulk. Soaking coca leaves in kerosene would break down the leaves and a precipitate would form that would be skimmed off and dried. This dried product would them be picked-up by small planes and flown to Colombia for processing. The result was a rapid increase in coca production in these areas. To counter the growth in coca production USAID/Bolivia contracted with the University of Florida at Gainesville to provide a team to work in Bolivia in the Yungas and Chapare areas to identify alternative crops that could substitute for coca as a source of farm income.

Consequently, the Goodwin family arrived in La Paz, Bolivia in March 1979 to begin what was expected to be a four-year assignment. Our arrival at the La Paz airport quickly introduced us to the difficulties of living in Bolivia. The airport is 13,500 feet above sea level and many people require an adjustment to that altitude.

Ours was no different, except for my husband. Our 13-year-old son fainted, our daughters started vomiting and I experienced double-vision. Joe and Larry Janicke the University of Florida Chief of Party (COP) checked us through immigration, found our bags and got us all safely into the van to take us down to the city. La Paz is a city of steps. The airport is at 13,500 feet as was the housing of the poor, the business area of the city is located at 12,500 feet and the upper and middle class residential area was 11,500 feet above sea level. Once settled into our home, it still took a while to adjust to living at the high altitude. The humidity at that altitude is so low that the inside of your nose cracks and bleeds. It also takes your body a number of weeks to learn to live with less oxygen, so you have trouble sleeping. We discovered that food does not digest as quickly at 11,500 feet so we needed to eat earlier than normal and eat less at night.

As we became more adjusted to the geographic reality at living and working at altitudes between 11,500–13,500 feet we had an opportunity to enjoy and appreciate the beauty of Bolivia. A dominant feature of western Bolivia is the Altiplano which is a plain which lies between two parallel mountain ranges called the Eastern and Western Cordilleras, where the Andes splits into two. The two mountain ranges feature a number of snowcapped peaks that range from 16,000 to over 21,000 feet above sea level. The Altiplano stretches for five hundred miles north to south in Bolivia and eighty to one hundred miles east to west at about 12,000 feet above sea level. Because of the altitude rainfall is scanty, providing a picture of stark beauty. The beauty of the Altiplano is especially appreciated during a drive from the capital La Paz to Lake Titicaca. At the northwest end of the Altiplano Lake Titicaca is the most prominent feature of the Altiplano. Located at approximately 12,500 feet above sea level, it is larger than the island of Puerto Rico and is the largest lake in South America. On our visit there we rented a boat to take us to Sukiri Island on the lake. Suriki is known as the location where the famed explorer Thor Heyerdahl went to learn the art of building reed boats to test his theory that the Pacific islands could have been settled by boatmen on reed boats sailing from South America. While on the island we were taken on a short ride on the lake with the reed boats.

During our stay in Bolivia, we also had an opportunity to attend the pre-Lenten carnival celebration in the city of Oruro. Oruro is known for having the best and liveliest parade in Bolivia and similar to Brazil, the parade costumes are made by groups who spend weeks developing their dances and beautiful costumes. The parade lasts for hours with masks and costumes made from paper-mache and painted in bright colors.

In addition to travels in the Altiplano, Joe took three of our children, Joe, Gretchen and Jill to the Chapare for a week in the summer of 1979, on a trip they still talk about to this day. The children learned that life on the frontier was quite different from what they had experienced. They stayed in a small village in the Chapare named Villa Tunari. The village was a center for the Bolivian government coca substitution activities in the Chapare. There was a small hotel, restaurant/bar, a few shops and a small movie theater. Our children decided to go to the theater to see a John Wayne western from the 1940s. They did not stay long. The picture and the soundtrack were out of sync so whatever was showing on the screen had a twenty- to thirty-second delay on the sound track. Since the movie was in English it didn't seem to matter to the local inhabitants, but it distracted kids so they left after one reel.

However, the kids were rewarded when they were taken with their father and a colleague by vehicle into the jungle. The trip involved fording rivers as there were no bridges, with one of the adults wading the river in front of the vehicle to ensure that it did not sink or become flooded. They were able to travel sixty to seventy miles into the jungle until they reached the end of the road. There was a traditional village at the end of the road. When they arrived at the village, one of the villagers was fishing by bow and arrow. In the river, one could see large catfish in the water. It was fascinating for the kids to watch how he could hit the fish by bow and arrow without fail. Joe had taken a shotgun along and our son asked to try to get a fish by shooting into the water. After four failed attempts, they gave up.

In the village, there was a Bolivian couple who were teachers for the only school in miles. They invited the group to their hut for something to eat and drink. Our daughter Jill was the first to be asked if she was thirsty and would like something to drink. Fearing that she was going to be offered a local drink called *chicha*, she politely refused. When she discovered that they were offering Kool-Aid and they asked her again if she would like something, she said maybe a little drink. When they offered her a twelve-ounce glass of the drink, she promptly downed it in one gulp, and when asked if she would like some more, she again said yes and promptly downed another glass of Kool-Aid and then a third. She then explained to our hosts her initial concern and profusely thanked them for their hospitality.

On the return trip to Villa Tunari from the village, Joe and his group encountered a number of people standing along the track asking for a ride for themselves and their produce. Not wanting to appear as the "ugly American" and leave people by the trail miles from where they could sell their produce, people and produce were brought onboard until there was no room left. One of their passengers had a small spider monkey that he allowed our children to play with. Naturally, they fell in love with it. The man offered to sell it to them, and they convinced their father to buy it even though they had to fly back to La Paz from Cochabamba on a commercial airline. Given that the children had their winter coats for La Paz, they hid the monkey in a sleeve of their coat and smuggled him on the plane and back to La Paz, where he became a family pet.

While Joe and three kids were away on the Chapare trip and completely out of contact, I was dealing with a real crisis with Juliana. She experienced prolonged and extremely high fever. I took her to the doctor who sent us to the local hospital where we spent three nerve-racking days. Larry and Lourdes Janicke came to visit and brought her some candy. Juliana looked at it and said, "What? You want me to rot my teeth?" We all laughed, and the mysterious fever broke.

I was able to visit the other project area, the Yungas. It was a trip that I will remember as long as I live because the only way to enter the Yungas area was via one of the most dangerous roads on the planet. I am not exaggerating. Google "world's most dangerous roads" and you will find it on the list, often as number 1. Why did I take the Yungas Road if it was so dangerous?

I loved to travel in the countries where we were assigned. It helps one to better know and understand the country and its people. Joe had to travel to project sites often, but my opportunities were limited in doing overnight trips. Our team leader, Larry Janicki, mentioned he was going to visit the project site in the Yungas region of Bolivia. Since Joe was in La Paz and could watch our kids while my friend Billie Stewart was visiting, we talked Larry into letting us go along. I was blissfully unaware of how terrifying our trip would be.

The Yungas is really a series of warm subtropical valleys a few hours by vehicle from La Paz. It is a main production area for coca leaves, citrus, bananas, and coffee. Because it was a production center for coca, the University of Florida was working with farmers in the area to improve the productivity of coca, substituting products especially coffee and citrus. The North Yungas road at the time was called the death road and had earned the classification as the most dangerous road in the world.

Our destination was the town of Coroico. From La Paz, located at an altitude of 12,500 feet above sea level. The road ascends to 15,240 feet above sea level before descending to Coroico to an altitude of 3,900 feet above sea level. While Coroico is only forty-three miles from La Paz, the trip took between two and three hours each way. The problem was the quality of the road. The road was a dirt road carved out of the side of the Cordillera Mountain Range in the 1930s.

The road was only ten-feet wide with no guardrails and with cliffs ranging from one thousand to three thousand feet deep. Warm and humid winds from the Amazon bring heavy rains and fog. These result in mudslides, falling rocks, and waterfalls which seriously have a negative impact on the quality of the roadbed. The road is too narrow for two vehicles to pass, so the curves are widened to (barely) let two vehicles pass. The rule is, when two vehicles meet, the one going downhill must back up to the nearest curve and pull out to the side. Besides being very frightening, this has also resulted in a number of accidents where the outside vehicle is accidently tipped and knocked over the cliff. At the time we were in Bolivia, the estimate was two hundred to three hundred deaths per year on the road.

The combination of all the above factors caused our trip on the Yungas road to be one of mounting terror. Seeing the wrecked vehicles at the bottom of the valley, plus the muddy and narrow road, and the numerous crosses marking where a vehicle had gone over the edge led to growing anxiety as we inched along the road in fog. Even worst was the realization that when we got to Coroico, we had to return on the same road. Larry, Billie, and I made it safely into and out of the Yungas. A new road with two paved lanes and guardrails was finished in 2006 that supposedly is safer. However, once was enough for me, and I have no interest in testing the improved road or repeating that frightening experience.

Bolivia is not only one of the poorest countries in the western hemisphere, but it is also one of the most politically unstable countries as shown by the eighty (as of 2016) presidents it has had over the 191 years of its independence. The political instability was exhibited in the sixteen months we were in the country. When we arrived in March 1979, General David Padilla was in power by way of a coup d'état in 1978. However, General Padilla had seized power to ensure democratic elections in 1979. So in July 1979 national elections were held, with eight candidates. The Bolivian Constitution in existence in 1979 required that the winning candidate receive at least 50 percent plus one vote, and in the event that no one received that number of votes, rather than a runoff, the names of the top three candidates would be forwarded to the Bolivian Congress for selection. Unfortunately, the Congress vote also required the winning candidate to receive 50 percent plus one vote, and the Congress was split similar to the voters. As a consequence, after two weeks of votes within the Congress, no winner emerged. It was therefore decided that the president of the senate, Walter Guevara Arce, would assume the presidency for one year with fresh elections to be held in 1980. Hence, Walter Guevara became president with an expected tenure of one year. However, on November 1, 1979, the commandant of the military academy, Colonel Natusch Busch, initiated a coup to overthrow President Guevara. The coup was poorly organized, and the plotters did not seize control of the broadcasting facilities, and the government supporters broadcast a call to the people to rise up and fight against the coup. The call to resist was especially met by the students and a civil war erupted for a two-week period, during which we were confined to our homes. During this coup, we learned an important lesson on life in Bolivia. As soon as any political unrest erupts, take all the money you have and go to the grocery store and buy food and other essentials. Thankfully we did this and were able to have food. We lived close to the American school, and so, after several days in our house, while we were awaiting the outcome of the fighting, a group of us went to the school to play volleyball or softball. We would retreat to under the trees, if planes flew over, then resume play. After about a week of fighting, it was clear that neither side had the strength to win. Negotiations were held, and it was agreed to return to civilian control of the government. However, to save face, it was agreed that a new interim president would serve until fresh elections in 1980. The new interim president selected was Lidia Gueiler Tejada, who had replaced Walter Guevara Arce as president of the senate. Ms. Lidia Gueiler Tejada became the first female president in the history of Bolivia and almost oversaw a peaceful transition of power in 1980, but more on that later.

We had been in Bolivia around six months when we were informed that the University of Florida contract was being canceled after one more year. The growing market for cocaine and rising price of the unrefined cocoa called for a new strategy to combat the problem. The decision was made that a broad rural development approach was needed that combined market development, with investments in roads, schools and health facilities. Joe was seconded to the team to develop the new program and that became the focus of his efforts for the duration of our stay in Bolivia. While the University of Florida offered him a position in Gainesville, the short duration of our Bolivia assignment gave us pause to reconsider our future. Until that moment, we had assumed that our future was in academia working overseas. However, land-grant university work was focused on solving problems of US agriculture and not on the development problems of third-world countries, unless such work was funded by organizations such as USAID or foundations such as Ford and Rockefeller. Such funding was becoming less available. Moreover, with six children we needed a more secure future. After much thought and prayer, we decided that we should focus our career in USAID, if positions were available.

Because the American schools were more developed in Latin America we hoped to join the Latin America Bureau of USAID. However, when contacted, the agricultural office of the bureau wrote that they were looking for agronomists, not economists. Our next approach was to contact the Africa Bureau. The deputy assistant administrator for Africa, Haven North, had been the mission director in Ghana when we were there. We received a positive response from the Africa Bureau that they were in need of economists and proposed a position in Tanzania. He further advised that Joe should send in his application as soon as possible, noting the 1980 election year and that there would be a hiring freeze. Joe applied and was hired to begin in August 1980. We were happy to have a career position and prepared ourselves for an assignment to Tanzania. Complications arose when the person Joe was working with on the Chapare development project became head of Latin America Agriculture and asked Joe to work in Bolivia with the USAID mission there. Because Africa Bureau had been there when we needed a job, we felt we had to somewhat sadly turn down the offer from Latin America.

As we were finalizing our work in Bolivia and preparing for an assignment to Tanzania, the 1980 elections were held in Bolivia, in June and this time the candidates had agreed to support whomever led at the end of the first round. It appeared that we would have a peaceful transfer of power on August 6, 1980. I had invited a close friend, Billie Stewart, whom we had known from Ghana days to come to Bolivia and visit and then return home with me. We had booked and paid for a trip to Machu Picchu crossing Lake Titicaca and proceeding to Cuzco, Machu Picchu, and then Lima, Peru, and home. On July 17, 1980, our plans were disrupted by a cocaine-financed coup led by General Luis Garcia Meza and Colonel Arce Gomes. The coup started at about noon on the seventeenth, when Joe's staff returned to the office and said they had heard shooting and saw masked men while passing the headquarters of the Bolivian Labor Federation. Joe called to warn me that there may be trouble, so keep the kids inside. Shortly thereafter, I heard shooting that seemed to be coming from the house of our neighbor, the former President Walter Guevara (his yard and house connected to our backyard). I placed the children in our bathtub and had them lie down to avoid any stray bullets. Shortly thereafter, the doorbell at the gate started ringing with some urgency. I decided to check what was occurring and saw my husband standing in the street with a masked man holding a gun on him. He told the man that it was his home and he was going inside. For the rest of the day we all stayed inside. We could see from our upstairs window that the masked man was still on the small plaza in front of the house. We received a radio message from the Embassy to stay inside and they would keep us informed.

The next morning things seemed quiet, so Joe decided to walk to the little grocery next door to buy supplies as we did not know how long the martial law imposed by the new government would last. Joe was gone about twenty minutes and returned with a stranger. It turns out that he was a staff member of the Russian Embassy, who had their embassy residence around the corner from us. He had come into the grocery store just after Joe, and since there was a line of people wanting to buy things, he started talking to Joe. He asked Joe to come over for a drink of vodka. It was about 9:00 a.m. Joe, not wanting to go to his location, asked him to come to our house, thinking he would never accept. Imagine his surprise when the Russian national accepted. When they entered the house, Joe introduced him to Billie and me. The man was clearly drunk but asked for some vodka. Joe poured him a shot which he threw back, and then he passed out. We were shocked and unsure as to what to do. We finally decided to wait for him to wake up give him some coffee and send him on his way. After about an hour passed, he woke up, and we began to ply him with coffee. As he began to sober up, he became quite chatty. He seemed to know a lot about us and our family, including the names of our kids. As he became sober, we suggested that he might want to return to his home. He took the hint, went out, and drove away in a cloud of dust. We were relieved to see him go and told ourselves that it had been a bizarre experience and that we would never see him again. We were only half-right.

The following day was Sunday with a curfew from 6:00 p.m. until 6:00 a.m. We were advised by our embassy to stay close to home, but we could venture out within our neighborhood. Given that the official American families lived generally close together, in case of the need for an evacuation, we had a number of our friends close by. We decided to invite our close friends over for a visit. About fifteen to twenty responded and showed up about 2:00 p.m. We were having a good time when the doorbell rang. Joe went to the gate and returned with two men, the Russian guy from the day before with a male colleague. They came in and joined the party. They were drinking vodka rather heavily when Joe suggested that they should try Johnny Walker whiskey. As the whiskey was poured, the new Russian colleague proposed a toast to Che Guevara, whereupon one of the American guests called Che a SOB but using the full names. The proposer of the toast became upset, and he and his Russian colleague had a spirited debate in Russian before things settled down. Shortly thereafter, the new Russian colleague departed, and soon afterward, the other comrade departed.

The party went on until 5:45 p.m., when we realized that several of the guests who had arrived on foot could not get home before curfew. To avoid any problem, Joe offered to drive them home as he could return before curfew. As he was returning to our house, Joe saw several soldiers in the plaza in front of our house with rifles pointed at someone on the ground. It was the Russian man, drunk again. Joe told the soldiers that he knew this person lived just one block away, and if they agreed, he would take him home and be right back. They agreed and so Joe loaded him into the car, drove him around to the Russian compound, and rang the doorbell. Two irate Russian women appeared and took him into the compound. We never saw him after that, and when Joe informed the American Embassy authorities of the incidents, they agreed it was unusual for someone to act as he did but asked Joe to report the contact to the proper authorities when he went to Washington. He obliged but we heard nothing further from the strange encounter. The Cold War raged on for twenty more years.

Joe often says, "No good deed goes unpunished." It was a few minutes past curfew, so our family was feeling nervous about Joe.

Daughter Jenny and I were watching for his return from taking home the drunk Russian so that we could open the large metal gate leading to our driveway. It swung outward, so Jenny and I quickly pushed the doors outside and held them open for Joe to enter. Three soldiers who were stationed on the plaza across the street immediately squatted down in firing position and aimed their automatic weapons on us but did not fire.

When Joe was able to return to work, the week after the coup, he found that the country was in a state of armed conflict. The students had risen up and were opposing the coup as were the peasants around the country. The peasants had blocked the roads on the Altiplano, and it was dangerous to travel outside the city. Likewise, people were trying to depart via the airport and tickets were in short supply. After weighing our options, it was decided that the trip to Peru across the Altiplano was not feasible for Billie and me, and the money was not reimbursable. Our next challenge was how to get plane tickets. What happened next deserves an entire separate chapter. So buckle up and come along for my terrifying ride in "Trapped between Two Tanks."

Joe, Gretchen and Joe II, and Jill on a field trip visit to
a village in the Chapare jungle region of Bolivia.

Llamas surround the Goodwin family on
the *altiplano* of Bolivia in 1980.

CHAPTER 8

Trapped between Two Tanks

"Mommy they are going to kill us," the child sitting on my lap said with chilling calm as the camouflaged tank rumbled the wrong direction down a one-way main street directly toward the Land Rover in which we were riding.

Juliana was only three but world-traveled and wise enough to recognize danger. Juliana and Jennifer, her seven-year-old sister who was riding in the back seat, were too young to die, I thought. After all, this foreign service family of eight had survived five changes of government in the sixteen months since we had come to Bolivia in March 1979. Simple breathing in the high-altitude Andean country had been a challenge and daily life an exciting adventure.

I felt a twinge of resentment toward my husband for bringing the family to this forsaken place. I wondered if Joe's incredible and constant sense of humor was a cover for unspoken guilt he might harbor about the sacrifices required of his family. I have always shared Joe's noble goals, but that was beside the point. Somebody needed to pay. At that moment, Joe was at the airline office desperately seeking our safe passage out of the country. Joe was in charge of his office, so he could not leave and would remain behind indefinitely. Like Scarlett O'Hara, I would worry about him tomorrow, if we lived to see *manana*.

Suddenly a soldier popped open the hatch of the foreboding tank, stood up, pointed his machine gun directly at us, shouted in indistinguishable Spanish, and then gestured toward a one-way cobblestone street. Bruce, the friend who had offered to drive us to the airport, slammed on the brakes and shoved the vehicle into reverse with such force that Jennifer landed on the floor. We flew screeching backward down the main street with the tank barreling down closely upon us. When Bruce reached the circle, he took the first side street to which the soldier had pointed. Big mistake, as a second tank blocked the lane ahead. It was too late to reverse as the initial tank had our exit blocked. Lack of communication and being in the wrong place at the wrong time could prove fatal. I was bewildered by our predicament.

The tanks aimed their cannons at the rooftops of the tall buildings on each side and opened fire. The blasts were deafening as brick and mortar rained down on us. I laid Juliana across my lap and instructed Jenny to stay flat on the floor. Jenny complained that she wanted to see what was happening, so she could tell her daddy. As I stretched my torso to cover Juliana, I glanced out the side window. To my horror, I realized that a soldier was leaning out a second-story window pointing his machine gun directly at me. All the security briefings and all the terrorism seminars we had attended had not prepared me for this real-life threat. In fact, this was the third time in as many days that I had found myself face-to-face with a young, inexperienced soldier brandishing a machine gun. It was almost as annoying as it was disconcerting. I shrugged, raised my hands, and smiled sweetly at the soldier in hopes of conveying a message of innocence.

Bruce reached for the mobile radio to inform the marine security guard posted at the American Embassy of our perilous circumstances. Seeing Bruce with a microphone in his hand appeared to make the soldier more nervous. I felt my heart muscles tighten. Although the embassy was only five blocks away, there was nothing that anyone could do to help. The marine guard reminded Bruce that during this revolution martial law was in effect, which prohibited the gathering of more than three people in one place. He explained the snipers on the rooftops had fired at the tanks as they patrolled the university area. I needed no reminder that the army killed a number of Bolivian student protesters in the past few days. Larry Janicke, an American friend living in a high-rise apartment in the center of town with a bird's eye view of the campus, had recorded the eerie noises of that night. Larry had played them over the phone for older children Joan and Joe, who had previously rejoiced in the vacation from school which these revolutions always brought. Their carefree attitudes were transformed into disbelief as they listened to the children and to the students chanting, the sound of the planes approaching, the gunfire on the protesters, and the screams and the wailing of the survivors. Just two days earlier, I had cried from the tear gas as I had driven past a rioting crowd in front of the university.

Nevertheless, the guard on duty promised he would notify the ambassador and attempt to locate Joe to advise him that his family would arrive late at the airport. I naughtily felt a small consolation knowing that Joe would be worried for a change since I had always carried the burden in that department.

Cannon fire continued for forty-five minutes as sniper bullets danced around our helpless entourage. Although it sounds like a cliché, it is true that every second seemed like an eternity to me as my life flashed before my eyes a dozen times. I didn't like everything I saw either.

Bruce was extremely quiet except for the occasional swear word when shrapnel would hit his vehicle. The children seemed resigned to this temporary setback in their travel plans and obeyed their mother's command to stay low. They were good and very brave little girls.

I was amazingly calm as I watched one sniper squat into firing position and take aim at the tank ten feet ahead of us. The tank commander had also seen him, and in an instant, the man was blown to pieces and blood splattered the cobblestones. I have never enjoyed watching violence in the movies. In that terrible moment, I witnessed the drama of politics being played to the death.

Strange how detached I could feel as I prayed for the safety of our two youngest daughters. I wondered if the car carrying Joan and my friend Billie Stewart had made it to the airport and whether Joe been able to purchase tickets.

I vowed that if I lived through yet another crisis, I would write a book about the nightmares of the past five days, each one providing enough drama for separate chapters. I would begin at the onset of this revolution with gunmen jumping out of an ambulance, grabbing Joe, questioning him about a neighbor who was a former president of Bolivia. Next scene would illustrate me shielding the children in the bathtubs for protection from stray bullets whizzing through our backyard as the neighbor's house came under attack. Then there would be the very strange encounters with two drunk Russian diplomats who had informed Joe our house was bugged, then proceeded to name all our children and friends. I would vividly recall watching from our darkened bedroom through the slats of the blinds as bodies were dumped from the bridge near our house into the icy river in the dead of night. How could I know why these people had been killed? Were they caught out after curfew? Were they political enemies? Who knows?

I would mention the teacher friend from the American Embassy who had been shot in the arm as soldiers ransacked the commissary below his apartment. Perhaps the most dramatic and emotional chapter would be recalling the incident of the previous day when three soldiers had threatened to kill Jenny and me as we opened the gate for Joe when he arrived home a few minutes past curfew. My reaction had been humorous in retrospect, for I had just painted the walls and was indignant at the thought of having my blood splattered over the fresh paint. Who would ever believe that, so much could happen to a family in such a short time?

I thought about my precious Joe. Ours had been an exceptionally happy marriage, despite the demands of raising six kids. We had promised to be "roommates for life." But Bolivia had not been a peaceful post, and I sometimes felt a strain on our relationship caused by the antics of our teenagers. We had argued about whether it is easier raising teenagers abroad, where there are fewer temptations, or back home, where there are many more opportunities. We had agreed to disagree and dialogued about our feelings on the subject as we had learned to do one glorious marriage encounter weekend. If only I could "dialogue" with Joe now, I thought. I had once accused him of being selfish and not considering my apprehensions about living abroad. I didn't want to apologize, because those were my feelings, but I longed to feel Joe's reassuring arms around me.

I also knew that I had no wish to die in this crossfire. What good would it do Joe to have my name engraved on the list at the State Department honoring those killed in the line of duty? He needed me just as much as I needed him, if not more. Without meaning to sound conceited, I had no doubt that Joe would be absolutely lost without me. How could he possibly cope with the kids? This was an unanswered question we had faced when I dealt with cancer a few years earlier while living in Brazil.

I was so engrossed in deep thoughts that I did not quite comprehend what Bruce was saying. The tanks were backing off, the smoke evaporated in the thick mountain air, and dust was covering the aftermath of the fighting. Four snipers had given their lives in attempt to fight for freedom. Our little group huddled in the Land Rover was alive and free to continue on our treacherous journey. I noticed that Bruce's knuckles were white as they gripped the wheel. I was anxious to leave the scene, which would be forever imprinted in my memory.

The checkpoints on the way up to the airport were ridiculous. Even though there were no entrances into that section of highway, there were soldiers stopping vehicles every quarter-mile or so to check our papers and search our car. Bruce got so tired of being hassled that he decided to play a game. He bet me that the soldiers were illiterate. I suggested that they probably could not read English. He tested our theories by showing a soldier his gun permit from the State of Virginia. We knew that the soldier couldn't read when he held it upside down, studied intently, and then told us that everything was "*Muy bueno.*"

We finally reached the airport and found Joe looking weary and distressed. He had no idea what we had been through. He only knew the frustration he had encountered. His hands held no tickets. The disappointment that Joe had been unable to secure seats on the flight was slight in comparison to the apprehension I felt at the prospect of returning to our residence in La Paz.

I did not dare anger the gods by asking what more was in store for us. Indeed, I would not have liked the answer.

CHAPTER 9

The DEA Film Escapade

This chapter is a sequel to the "Trapped between Two Tanks" story. Both events occurred in La Paz, Bolivia, during the same hellish week, a week indelibly scorched upon my memory.

As noted, we had been sent to La Paz under a USAID contract administered by the University of Florida to work on a coca substitution project. It was a noble yet impossible project. Joe's work was unpopular among those who profited from the very lucrative drug trade and a bit dangerous when he would go on his field visits. The farmers would laugh at him for suggesting growing any other types of crops instead of the highly profitable coca. Cocaine was Bolivia's largest unofficial export product.

As you probably surmised from the previous chapter, Bolivia was a politically unstable country during the sixteen months that our family lived there from March 1979 to July 1980. In fact, there were five different presidents during our tenure. A couple were elected by ballot. Others were elected by bullets through various coup d'état's, or *golpes de estado* as they were called in Spanish. The joke in Bolivia is that every citizen is born to be president. That country holds the record for the most revolutions. A woman, Lidia Gueiler, had been one of the five presidents, and she actually was in power for seven months. She was the first woman elected in the history of Bolivia and she was courageous. She devalued the currency and raised the price of petrol, both steps very necessary for the good of the economy. No male leader had been that brave. Sure enough, it caused her overthrow and she fled into exile. Now figure the statistics. We averaged a new president about every three months for the remaining time of our tour. Quite often, Joe did not even have the chance to meet his new counterparts in the Bolivian government before they would be replaced.

Needless to say, this was a war in the Bolivian history and we were caught in the middle of it. It took me a long time to be able to write about my feelings and the strange events. I believe it is time to tell it from my perspective as a devoted wife, a concerned mother, and the person in my own right who wanted to make a difference in this world but was frustrated by circumstances.

As soon as anything occurs in Bolivia, everything immediately shuts down: all public transportation, every commercial business, and government and private offices. Even the airport closes. We had learned our lesson well and became champion hoarders after nearly starving during one of the two coups which took place in November 1979. There were twelve people in our household during those eleven days while supermarkets were closed. Never mind that we lived next door to a supermarket. It only made the hunger pains grow louder to even glance at the neighbors' boarded doors knowing there were food stocks on the unreachable shelves. There were two extra people visiting us and consequently became our unintended houseguests. One was a friend of our oldest daughter and the other a nervous elderly professor from the University of Florida who came for business with my husband. We were also responsible for feeding our household help and her daughter. By my calculations, twelve persons for three meals a day for eleven days meant that I had to ration equivalent of 396 meal servings based on what was available in the pantry and freezer. That was a tough challenge. It got to the point in the last two days where we only had one can of tuna fish or a can of corn, take your pick not both. The meager meal to be shared among the twelve mouths.

Okay, so we had gone through another coup. Though coups were a frequent occurrence, the one in July 1980 was different. It was led by a suspected drug dealer. Thus, began an interesting saga for me.

One of our acquaintances from church was an agent for the Drug Enforcement Agency (DEA). He was an American citizen of Mexican origin. To protect his identity, let's call him Diego. He seemed like a nice, trustworthy sort of fellow. On the day that I was expecting to escape the chaos and fly home, I received a telephone call from Diego. He asked me a rather simple question. Would I be willing to mail some film for him when I got back to United States? This was not an unusual request. People always hand-carried mail for their colleagues to be posted back home. It was a courtesy practiced for generations by diplomats and missionaries alike. Without giving it a second thought, I did not hesitate to say that I would be glad to take his film. Then Diego asked a strange question. What is my passport number? That should have been a clue that something was not right. However, being a trusting soul and very naive, I obediently reeled off my passport number. He was evasive to my question of why he needed the number. He said he would drop the film by the house and explain to me in person.

About an hour later Diego arrived carrying a small cooler. He said that it contained infrared film and that it had to be packed in dry ice for the journey. Diego asked that I take it to an express air service the moment I arrived in the States and he gave me money for the shipping cost. He said the film was very important. Diego suggested that if the customs ask me about the contents of the cooler to say that I was carrying milk and medicine for my baby. Furthermore, he presented me with a letter typed on Drug Enforcement letterhead, which stated my name and passport number and asked for special consideration to be granted to me upon entering customs in Miami. What the heck did that mean?

I realize that I was unwise not to ask more questions. I was still in a state of shock from the horrible experience trapped between two tanks and watching the snipers get killed only two days earlier. And there were so many other stresses. I just wanted to get out of Bolivia alive and never return.

I remember being a bit aghast at the size of the film he wanted me to hand-carry. I wish that I had pointed out to him that my hands were already mighty full with our carry-on bags stuffed to the limit. After all, I was leaving the country for good and I was traveling with three-year-old Juliana, Jennifer, and Joan, plus my friend Billie Stewart, who had been visiting. I should explain why I only had three of our six children with me. Gretchen had dislocated her shoulder while she and her brother were skating. She needed medical attention. We decided to send her, Joe, and Jill back home a few days before the coup took place. That was fortunate. I was very sorry about Gretchen's injury, but the absence of three of the children at the same time made the situation just a little less complicated. Somehow these three siblings tend to think that they had missed "all the fun." Fun . . . Ha!

We can't see the future. I would not have accepted that film if I had known what a nightmare awaited our escape, but I suppose my guardian angel was riding on my shoulder or else I would probably be innocently rotting away in a Bolivian jail.

When we arrived at the airport that night, it was a crazy scene: soldiers with machine guns everywhere; hundreds of jittery passengers pushing and shoving one another; airline staff screaming obscenities in Spanish; people with wads of *pesos*, blatantly trying to bribe their way onto the plane.

I do not like to fly. Never have and never will. We are in the wrong business for my delicate stomach. Therefore, I had taken the Dramamine tablet to settle my queasiness before we left home. I was feeling emotional for my husband had to stay in Bolivia to close up the project. We do not like to be separated for a length of time and not knowing how long we would have to be apart made the farewells more difficult. I imagine that Joe was probably relieved to be finally getting his family to safety. Or so he thought. We kissed goodbye and I promised to call him as soon as I got home to my parents in Monroe City, Missouri. That call got delayed by fifty-four hours due to the events that I faced. He waited and worried.

Meanwhile, Billie, Joan, Jennifer, Juliana, and I disappeared through the security doors. We most likely looked like a typical bunch of tourists with all our junk. Billie was pulling a carry-on, which was crammed with dried flowers. Yes, flowers. She and I had attended the flower show and sale and Billie had bought a bunch of flowers. I kidded her that she could probably purchase the same type of flowers in Ben Franklin back home in Tacoma, Washington, for the same price or less. But Billie is redheaded and a very determined person. Fine. I had my own silly possessions to tote in addition to the cooler, while keeping a hand on Juliana who was carrying her beloved Care Bear, named Ben, which was taller than her.

The cooler. Oh my gosh, in my sadness about leaving Joe, I had forgotten to be nervous about going through customs. I piled the cooler on the x-ray conveyor belt, glanced at the security officer who was distracted looking elsewhere when it passed through the machine. I quickly gathered all our baggage and tried to arrange other things around the cooler to make it less obvious. Since I travel under a diplomatic passport, I don't usually have to go through the body search. Normally. But these were not normal times. A short and well-built female guard motioned for our entourage to come to her table. Billie was ahead of me and traveling on regular passport. Billie had been a foreign service spouse like myself but had been recently widowed. I think she had forgotten that she no longer had any diplomatic immunity because when the guard started to search her body, Billie objected loudly. I was embarrassed by the commotion. But I later realized she did it to allow me a chance to flash my passport and keep walking. Billie caught up with me and winked. The first hurdle was over. We settled onboard.

The Eastern Airlines jet rumbled and creaked down the extraordinarily long runway in La Paz at an altitude of 13,500 feet that it is difficult to take off. The joke (almost believable) is that planes finally fall off the edge of the mountain and are airborne. I was always nervous on landing on and taking off from that particular airport. The first time we landed in La Paz, I remember being very worried about the effect the high altitude would have on Joe as he was overweight and not in great physical condition. He was absolutely fine. However, our son fainted from the lack of oxygen before we got into customs. Three of the girls complained of headaches and started vomiting. The high altitude affected my vision. It made me giggle. Joe's new boss was waiting and all I could do was giggle like a schoolgirl. How embarrassing that had been. I smiled to myself as I silently reminisced.

Just when I started to relax, the pilot announced that we would have to make a stop in Santa Cruz, Bolivia, and that we would all have to get off the plane. Hey, wait! That was not indicated on the flight pattern. Billie and I exchanged nervous glances. By the time we touched down in Santa Cruz, it was very dark. There was a soldier posted at the bottom of the steps searching each passenger and checking their passports. It was taking a long time to disembark. Juliana was getting cranky and didn't want to hold her stuffed animal after being awakened from her sleep. Our hands were full, so she had no choice. After being momentarily distracted by my youngster, I looked up and saw Billie arguing with the soldier. He had poked his rifle into her precious dried flowers and she didn't take kindly to his actions. I could not believe it. I saw her temper flare and she had the audacity to shove him back. The soldier was so surprised by the spunky little American lady that he just told her to move on. I was next. He was probably still thinking about Billie because he did not hassle me after checking our passports. Perhaps he felt sorry for me traveling with the kids and all that baggage. For whatever reason I was grateful that he did not attempt to search the cooler. We were escorted into the transit area which did not contain a single chair. Santa Cruz is in the heart of the jungle, and it was hot and humid. We were dressed warmly for the cool climate in La Paz. We waited and sweated and finally were told to board the plane again. We never learned the reason for this unplanned detour.

When we boarded, the plane was incredibly hot, and nausea swept over me before we took off. It appeared that the air-conditioning on the plane had malfunctioned. I sighed with relief when the wheels lifted off Bolivian soil. However, the relief was short-lived. About an hour into the flight—*boom!* The plane made a tremendous noise and started to experience terrible turbulence. My eyes darted out the window at the night sky. It was clear as a bell. Clouds were far below us. What was happening? *Boom!* again. And then silence. The crew was scurrying up and down the aisles and making me very nervous. Naturally, I filled another airsickness bag. After what seemed like a very long while, the pilot announced that we had lost an engine and that we would be making an emergency landing in Cali, Colombia. Oh God, not Colombia, the drug capital of the world, I thought. More customs and more chances to be questioned. Just what was the importance of the film in that cooler, I wondered?

We had a rough landing in Cali and blew out a tire. Sparks were flying as one wing scraped along the runway. But we made it. I have actually endured worse landings, so I was less upset than my friend. "*Que sera, sera*," I declared when my feet were firmly planted on the ground. What will be, will be! I would not have been so flippant if I had known what was yet to be.

Eastern Airlines announced they would bring in another plane from Panama and that we should wait at the airport. It was after midnight and we were all tired. We had to sit on the dirty floor as all the seats were occupied. I thought Santa Cruz had been hot, but Cali was a taste of hell. I sweltered. Juliana broke out in a heat rash and fussed and squirmed as she tried to sleep on top of my tote bag.

At 3:00 a.m. we were told that the rescue plane would not come until six in the morning. We were given a voucher for a motel room but told that we would have to find our own transportation. Naturally, at that ungodly hour, there were few taxis at the Cali airport and passengers were fighting over those available. Billie and I didn't secure a taxi until four o'clock, which meant we had to be back in two hours. I thought it wouldn't be worth the effort. Billie suggested we at least go and take a shower. When we arrived, I could not believe my eyes. I will put up with less than desirable accommodation much easier than my husband, but that room shocked even me. It contained two single beds with thin straw mattresses for the five of us. There was no screen or glass on the open window. The dingy, poorly lit room was full of mosquitoes. The room was on a main thoroughfare and Hell's Angels were drag racing just outside our window. Billie showered even though there was no soap and only a tiny hand towel. Under the circumstances, I decided to wait until I was safely home before I bathed. Since there was no alarm clock and no wake-up call available, we just sat there watching the kids rest a short time. Then it was off to the races again and back to the airport in an old battered taxi which had already seen better days thirty years earlier.

Six o'clock came and no rescue plane was in sight. Seven o'clock, eight, nine, ten. The benefits of Billie's shower had long since disappeared and she smelled as bad as I did again. I am a patient person, but when noon arrived, I was hungry, tired, and losing my patience too. Finally, at two in the afternoon we were told that no plane was coming. However, Eastern announced that our previous plane had been repaired. Repaired, in Cali? I was a bit skeptical to say the least and more than a little nervous about getting back onto that plane. Nevertheless, like a herd of sheep, we were reloaded onto *that* plane. As has been my custom and my comfort for years, I said a simple prayer to myself: "Jesus, Mary, and Joseph, be with us in our flight." Works every time. So far.

Did you notice that I went into and out of customs in Colombia without any incident regarding the DEA film? I started feeling smug, even patriotic, thinking now I had it made. Miami would surely be a breeze. Soon I would board another plane to St. Louis and my dear Aunt Kathleen would probably be there to meet me. If not, I would rent a van, send off the film with the ice probably melted, and drive to my parents two and a half hours away. I would not relate my experiences to them yet. I would sleep. Sleep. What a beautiful and soothing word.

"Hello, America," I cried. I always get a lump in my throat when I touch down on United States soil. Billie helped me get the kids headed in the right direction in Miami. We embraced and said farewell as she wanted to hurry through customs to catch another flight to Seattle. Billie had further to go than I did but, we later learned, she reached home over twenty-four hours before me. Why? Because I got harassed by the United States customs!

I did as Diego had instructed me and handed the letter to the customs official. He checked his computer and told me rather sternly to wait right there. He told the people behind me to go to another line as I would be delayed. Delayed? What was he talking about? I needed to catch the last flight to St. Louis that leaves in an hour and I have to get our tickets rewritten, and . . . nobody was listening.

The customs fellow had gone away with my passport and letter in his hand. He returned with two other agents who asked irrelevant questions. I thought they were accusing me of something. I didn't know what. I was only guilty of being stupid and accepting the package. Maybe I was unwittingly carrying drugs. Maybe "Diego" wasn't who I thought he was. Help! I knew I was innocent, but I didn't like the way they looked at me. I vowed to never again accept anything from any person in the future unless it was unsealed for my inspection.

The three officials then spoke to each other privately. They returned to me and changed their demeanor. They all became very nice and apologetic. They said that a civilian should never have been given the film I had in my possession. They debated whether to take it away from me. I would have gladly relinquished it and even suggested that. The head guy decided it would be better if I carried out the rest of the request and get it to an air courier immediately. Problem is, he said, it was now ten o'clock at night and every place was closed.

Ten o'clock? That meant we had missed our connection. Darn it! I didn't have a lot of cash on me. I had not expected to spend the night in Miami. Joan helped me to gather our ten suitcases—yes, ten pieces of luggage for four people. We were moving to Tanzania. Four people and ten pieces of luggage meant two taxis. Joan and Jenny took one taxi with half the luggage while Juliana and I shared the other. We went to the closest hotel which was probably the most expensive, but after not having any sleep in two days, I frankly didn't care about the price. I honestly just wanted to go home to my own mother, not to a hotel.

We all collapsed and slept relatively well the rest of that night. I called and booked another flight. Back to the airport again but this time on a bus provided by the hotel, which helped.

Lambert Field never looked so inviting. Aunt Kathleen was never more beautiful. It had been a tradition for Aunt Kathleen, my mother's sister, to meet us when we flew into St. Louis. We were sad when the day came that dear sweet lady was no longer able to meet us. Anyway, she did come, and I realized I needed to rent a van in order to take all the luggage. First, however, I asked Aunt Kathleen to drive me to the air cargo facility, so I could send off the chest with the mysterious contents. She was most gracious in helping me do that while the girls waited in the luggage area. Amen and good riddance to an unwanted task.

I could end my narrative here but maybe you are curious to know the "*rest of the story*," as Paul Harvey always said at the end of his radio commentaries.

Well, we moved to Tanzania and I gradually put this incident out of my mind. Months later, I received a letter from Diego asking me to return the difference in the cost of the freight and what he had given me. I don't remember the exact amount. It wasn't much. Actually, it was a fraction of what it had cost me to spend the night in the hotel as a result of his "favor." That made my blood boil to remember. I sweetly answered his letter and told him the whole story. I did not include a check for a refund. About six weeks later, I received another letter from Diego. He apologized for all the trouble and told me to "keep the change." Big deal. However, he went on to say that the United States Department of Justice, the Central Intelligence Agency, and the Drug Enforcement Agency were extremely grateful to me. I had provided a service to my country and to Bolivia. It turns out that the film this Missouri "mule" was packing was evidence of criminal drug-related activity being carried out by the then current president of Bolivia. It had been sufficient to force his resignation and prosecution.

I tried to comprehend how my assistance had been so powerful as to topple a corrupt government official. Only I did not feel a sense of accomplishment. I felt betrayed and used. I had trusted this person. He obviously had trusted me or, because I looked so innocent, thought I was a perfect decoy.

When I realize the possible repercussions, which would have occurred if that film had been detected in my possession while I was still in Bolivia, I felt resentful toward the government for which I have made so many personal sacrifices. I might not have lived to tell this tale. The experience made me a stronger person. I have learned when to *just say no*.

CHAPTER 10

Mood Killer

Remember, dear, when our six kids were small how we longed for quiet, quality time alone? I remember one week when we had made a date to share some intimate Sunday evening *hours*.

You planned to drop the dears at the theater while I slipped into something comfortable. I anticipated the night like a blushing bride. You sent me a lovely bouquet of *flowers*.

It all sounded so romantic and enticing. You chilled champagne in a silver ice bucket. The logs in the fireplace eluded a special glow, akin to the flame of desire I felt in my *heart*.

When the appointed hour to take them to the movie arrived, our son declared he would not go. Said he was worried that we would be lonesome by ourselves. What a precocious little *fart!*

I suspect that he was simply curious to discover why his folks were so flirtatious with one another. He didn't appear convinced by your protestation that he had to go, to protect his *sisters*.

When you finally managed to pack the whole gang into the cumbersome old station wagon, I bounded up the circular staircase so fast it's a wonder that I didn't get *blisters*.

Donning a sheer black lace negligee with its lovely matching opaque gown, and dousing myself with my most expensive perfume, I felt sensual as I turned out the *light*.

Then the doorbell rang, and I was a bit annoyed that you had forgotten your key yet again. "Oh well, what the hell," I thought aloud, "give my man a thrill and let him hold me *tight*."

Reaching the front door, I closed my eyes. After striking my sexiest pose, I flung the door open with great flair, and seductively uttered a suggestive *word*.

Silence. I waited . . . to be swept off my feet. Instead, the voice of the parish priest inquired, "Do you always greet your guests in this manner?" I opened my eyes in disbelief. Incredible! *Absurd!*

Who was more embarrassed; was it me, *Father Keller* or you, when you returned to your scantily clad wife wearing little more than rosy cheeks pouring tea for the Reverend? Oh, what a mood *killer!*

CHAPTER 11

Assignment Tanzania

Background

In August 1980, after a very abbreviated stay in the United States the Goodwin family flew to Tanzania, where Joe was assigned as deputy agricultural development officer. We were happy to be back with USAID. The time working for USAID as a member of a contract team rather than in USAID had provided Joe with valuable field experience and would prove to make him a better USAID officer. Joe had joined USAID just as they had changed from implementing development projects directly to managing the process. His time with Purdue and Florida had not only given him field experience in implementing projects but also insights into how to improve the working relationship between the contractors and USAID. Our three years in Tanzania resulted in major changes for our family and me.

Tanzania is a large country, more than twice the size of California, located on the East African coast and is bordered on the east by the Indian Ocean, on the north by Kenya and Uganda, on the west by Rwanda, Burundi, the Democratic Republic of the Congo and Zambia, and on the south by Malawi and Mozambique. The area known as Tanganyika was conquered by imperial Germany in the late nineteenth century before coming under British rule after World War I. Tanzania at the time of our arrival was a relatively young nation, having become independent as a member of the British Commonwealth in 1961 as Tanganyika. In 1962, it became a republic. In 1964 the Republic of Tanganyika merged with the neighboring island nation of Zanzibar and was renamed the United Republic of Tanzania.

In the briefing in Washington, before departure Joe was told that Tanzania was budgeted to become the biggest program in Africa by 1982. President Nyerere of Tanzania had just completed an official visit to Washington coming away with increased support from President Carter and his administration. President Nyerere was a world-respected leader who was committed to reducing rural poverty in his country. While this reputation was deserved, unfortunately, the implementation of his vision was not working well. After a promising start, the Tanzanian economy had faltered. An important reason for the economic problems was the push to implement socialism, Tanzanian style. The government had nationalized a number of firms and industries which had discouraged private investment. Neither did the government have the technical and managerial capacity to implement its policies. The government instituted a policy of pan-territorial pricing, which decreed that the same price would prevail for a product over the entire country. The intent was to try to ensure that people in distant rural areas did not have to pay more for a product than people in the capital where it was produced. What the policy meant in reality was that people in distant rural areas did not receive the product since there was no incentive to ship it to those areas and absorb the transport costs. The result was most people in rural areas had to depend on the black market to buy products at higher prices since that black market was officially illegal. Agricultural exports had fallen as people in rural areas were moved into villages away from where their crops were grown. This was especially important for tree crops such as coffee and cashews, two of Tanzania's principal exports.

The effect of the government policies were exacerbated by the deterioration of the international economic situation in the late 1970s and early 1980s. At the time of our tour in Tanzania, the government maintained an unrealistic fixed exchange rate, of approximately seven schillings to the dollar while the black-market exchange rate was seventy schillings to the dollar. This disparity between the two exchange rates was reflected in the economy. Scarcity was the rule.

The Americans were fortunate to have a small commissary. The commissary was tiny, with limited stocks and items on the shelves were often outdated but we bought anything we could find. At least

Joe could buy beer there for $17 a case instead of paying the hundred dollars a case price on the local market. Some products arrived in the commissary infested with insects. For example, the flour we imported often was infested with weevils during shipment. I learned to freeze the flour, then sift out the dead bugs, and pretend it was premium grain. When the kids would ask about the little black things in their bread, I would tell them it was poppy seeds. In those days, one either learned to overlook a lot of things while living abroad or else one perished (or considered another line of work).

When we arrived, we were installed in the USAID guesthouse. It had been necessary for USAID to open their own guesthouse because of the condition of the hotels in Dar es Salaam at the time. At the Kilimanjaro Hotel, then the best in the city, when guests checked in, they were issued lightbulbs and toilet paper and were requested to return them when leaving the hotel as they may not be in the room when the guests returned. Because we were a large family, it was difficult to find a house large enough. The search was made more difficult by the shortage of housing, caused by the government nationalizing houses if an individual owned more than one house.

Schooling Situation

Our children went to the International School of Tanganyika (IST), as there was no American school in the country. The teaching methods were different from the American school system the children were used to and they experienced adjustment problems. Our oldest daughter, who was beginning her junior year of high school, was especially unhappy with the quality of education she was receiving. Because of concerns about the schooling in Tanzania, the State Department included boarding school as an option for those assigned to Tanzania. After six weeks in IST, we and our daughter agreed that she needed to go to boarding school. We examined boarding school options in Europe and the United States before finally deciding to send her to St. Mary's Academy, a Roman Catholic Benedictine girls school in Nauvoo, Illinois, where she would be only a two-hour drive from her grandparents in our home town of Monroe City, Missouri. It was a difficult decision to make, but we tearfully bid goodbye to Joan and sent her to boarding school. While she was able to return home for Christmas, spring and summer break, we knew that it would never be the same again, as our family was starting to separate. The night that Joan left for the United States, I found Joe sitting in her room in complete darkness with tears in his eyes. It was hard on all of us.

A year later, we faced a similar decision with our son, and he went to the Abbey, a Benedictine boys boarding school in Canon City, Colorado. Both received an excellent education at their respective schools, but we still look back at the pain of having our children leave home at such an early age. This is a problem that many foreign service parents still wrestle with today and is one cost of choosing a life in the foreign service.

My own career with USAID started the same day that Joan left for boarding school. I was hired to take a temporary position as administrative assistant to the director. It was to be for two months but turned into a more permanent job in the Office of the Controller for fifteen years and two years in the Health Office. The financial reward was sparse, but job satisfaction was plentiful.

Changed Priorities

As noted, when we arrived in Tanzania in August 1980, Tanzania was projected to become the largest USAID program in Africa. However, after the November 1980 US election of Ronald Reagan, the priority ranking of Tanzania dropped. Like all the other sectors, the agricultural budget was reduced drastically. Joe worked on development of a National Agricultural Research Project, until in 1982, Joe became the mission senior economist and worked closely with the mission director, the ambassador and other donors on economic policy issues. While this involved drafting a number of economic policy papers and participating in workshops and conferences, limited impact was made on changing the GOT's economic policy, although the groundwork was laid for some change.

With the reduction in the USAID/Tanzania budget, we had more free time on the weekends. Luckily, we had a number of wonderful colleagues with which to socialize. One of our favorite memories were the Sunday afternoon parties held at our friends Ed and Eve Sprague's house on the beach. Their house had a wonderful patio facing the ocean about fifty feet away, plus the flat roof of their house offered another viewing platform where we could sit, admire the ocean and discuss the problems of the world. We had a great group of friends with which we shared these wonderful Sunday afternoon parties. These included Ron and Vivien Harvey and their daughters Ronda and Lynette; Patty and Alberto Ruiz de Gamboa and their kids Isabel and Alberto; Ivan and Annie Peterson, Art and Anne Handley, and Tim Miller; John and Iona Anania and their boys JJ and Darius; Mike Fuchs-Carsch and Rose Marie Depp; and Larry Johnston. We would all bring drinks and food to share and made lifetime friends and memories.

My Most Memorable Christmas

The time: Christmas 1980.

The place: Dar es Salaam, Tanzania

The characters: The Goodwin gang consisting of six youngsters who eagerly anticipated the special season

Catalog orders were placed in late summer in response to Jenny and Juliana's letters to Santa. However, Santa was unable to deliver a single thing thanks to an unreliable sea pouch system hampered by a dock strike in New York which delayed shipments to that isolated post on the Dark Continent.

It is noteworthy that during those years there was not anything to buy in the city of Dar es Salaam, not even essential food so there was no option to purchase locally. Oh, what to do? Nothing less than create the most meaningful Christmas in memory!

I practiced what I had been preaching for years about the "true meaning of Christmas," being to honor the birth of baby Jesus and I disavowed commercialism entirely. I fashioned homemade gifts with love. For my dear husband I filled photo albums with several years of family pictures. Joe relished them with pride, and by eliminating the clutter of boxes, I also gave myself a gift. I used my sewing skills to create something special for each child such as stuffed animals, toss pillows, and clothes for the teenagers. The kids caught the fever and made their own contributions, such as IOUs for breakfast in bed, back massages, car washes, etc. We were blessed to have Eve Sprague, a thoughtful commissary manager who, realizing the dilemma of the parents, sent out an SOS to neighboring posts. Through Eve's persistence and an expensive airfreight scheme, we were able to obtain a few toys and some candy from another African post.

The happy result was not really the fact that we improvised for gifts, but rather it was the community spirit at the post. We became one another's families—loving, caring, and sharing. On Christmas Day, many friends came by our home bearing cookies and homemade gifts. A couple of our daughters still possess the most thoughtful gift from the USAID director's wife, Maria Williams. Maria had created a treasure chest by painting colorful tins with the child's name on the lid and had filled them with tiny items: seashells, rocks, notepads, costume jewelry, campaign buttons, etc. A gift from the heart and accepted with the joy and enthusiasm that only children can produce!

And now for the rest of the story. The ship finally came in on Valentine's Day 1982, carrying our Christmas gifts. We had an impromptu party to celebrate with the same wonderful community who had been there in our time of need. It was a fun evening, but I maintain that the children received greater gifts the first time around when they accepted and gave gifts from the heart rather than the pocketbook.

Tanzania is a beautiful country with many natural wonders to see. There were the wild game parks, the Selous, and Mikumi close by, and then the wonderful Lake Manyara, Tarangire, the Serengeti Plains, and the Ngorongoro Crater in the Northern Highlands. The game park lodges suffered from the same deficiencies as the hotels in Dar es Salaam, namely lack of drinks and toilet paper but we solved that problem by bringing our own supplies.

Finding food on the open market was a challenge, especially meat. Hunger drove us to do dangerous things as related in the following "Lion in Camp" chapter.

CHAPTER 12

Lion in Camp

When I recall the hunting safaris our family made during the years we lived in Tanzania (1980–1983), I believe we had more guts than brains! Feeding our big, growing family was an everyday struggle for the entire three years and I contend it was hunger pains that affected our rationale. The serious lack of food during those years drove us to take such drastic measures in the pursuit of protein.

Times were very difficult for Tanzania during that period. Julius Nyerere's brand of socialism, imposed upon the country for many years, had clearly not worked. Tanzania collapsed economically, and people had returned to a system of barter.

We had to make all our own bread as there was a shortage of wheat in the country. I should clarify that the "we" who baked the bread was Matola, our cook. He was a tiny little Muslim who giggled constantly and called me Mama, much to my chagrin, as he was my elder by at least ten years. Nevertheless, he looked to me for guidance and I suppose I was like a mother to him. Matola would break dishes, giggle nervously, and inevitably say, "No problem, Mama." He and I might have parted ways, but I was working and needed him as finding ample food was a full-time, exhausting, and necessary job. The salvation was a tiny American Embassy commissary though it limited what we could buy.

All this lack of food led up to the idea of hunting. Now, I am not talking about shooting a rabbit, squirrel, deer, duck, or wild turkey like my father. I am talking about going on a real hunting safari. I mean *big game* hunting, not for the sake of taking trophies but rather for the sole purpose of feeding our family. Sometimes we felt like pioneers moving westward into the unknown.

Joe was in charge of the agricultural program in Tanzania, and through his work, he met some ranchers. One day the ranchers told him they had a serious problem with lions killing their livestock and solicited his help. They invited him, and any friends, to hunt on their vast land and said they were welcome to kill any wild game that grazed there as they were in competition with the livestock for feed. Joe bought a hunting license and paid a fee for each specific type of animal that he expected to hunt during the season, which lasted six months.

During the initial weekend hunting trips, only the men ventured out into the savannah. They would arrive home late Sunday night feeling tired, looking dirty, wearing bloodstained clothes, with meat to be dissected and packaged for the freezer. Joe would very enthusiastically relate their experiences and made me a little jealous not to be sharing those times with him. Perhaps he read my mind as he suggested that the kids and I should consider joining them. All he had to do was ask! Thus, began our adventures into the wild as a family unit.

Joe and I had never actually been the camper types before, so this was a new experience. Pitching the cumbersome eight-person tent was a major operation. The tent collapsed on us several times before we got the hang of it. Cooking over the open fire was a challenge for me, but the kids' appetites seemed to increase in the fresh air and they appreciatively devoured anything I fixed.

The particular trip, which was most exciting and memorable, took place during the Christmas holidays in 1981. Joan and Joe were home from boarding school as were some of their friends. The community had heard about our adventures and thought it would be fun to go on a hunting trip in a large group. The more the merrier, right? Wrong! Twenty-six excited and very inexperienced diplomats set off together, including fourteen-month-old Lynette Harvey. Shortly after we arrived, while each family was getting settled, I heard the baby's mother scream and looked up in time to see her drop the baby and run. Vivian had seen a snake and freaked out. As much as I hate reptiles, I could've had the same reaction. Her husband, Ron, wanted to drive back to Dar es Salaam to take the baby to the embassy nurse. Frankly, the frightened and remorseful mother needed attention more than Lynette who was flashing her lovely smile and enjoying the extra attention. Everyone calmed them down, and thank goodness, they didn't leave as Ron figures prominently later in this story.

The men went off hunting. Late in the afternoon, the hunters returned with a small antelope that they gutted and hung in the tree right close to our tent. My son had bagged this prized meat, and he was delighted. He proceeded to tell me how his dad had shot at a warthog and had wounded it in the leg. It was obvious that my husband did not want him to relate the whole story, but Jody thought it was too good to keep. Apparently, father and son and the guide decided to track down the injured warthog. When I expressed my disapproval of them getting out of the vehicle and wander off on foot, they sheepishly explained that they didn't want the animal to die and the meat to be wasted. Yes, they agreed; I was right to be concerned. They had not gone far when a seven-foot-long spitting black cobra reared up into their faces, eye-to-eye level. The guide had yelled "shoot" but they stood like statues mesmerized by the scene unfolding. Inexplicably, the snake started slithering backward, without spitting in their eyes. They took that as their cue to retreat to the safety of the Land Rover.

That night I was not feeling as festive as the rest of my family. I had been bitten by a poisonous spider on my bottom while setting in a folding lawn chair and was running a temperature. The kids were having a great time dancing around the campfire and roasting marshmallows and hot dogs on bamboo sticks, so I excused myself and went inside the tent to attempt to rest.

Suddenly . . . *Roar!* Impossible! The roar of a lion, just ten feet outside my tent, is one of those eerie things that are never forgotten. It reverberated like the inside of a drum. Was the lion reversing the roles of the hunters and the hunted or had he simply caught the smell of fresh animal meat hanging in the tree and figured on a bit of shoplifting? Were there other lions lurking in the periphery of our campsite? Everyone had laughed at me earlier in the day when I had suggested fashioning a thorn fence around our camp, a practice used for protection by the Maasai people. I had thought it was a good idea but wasn't in the mood to gloat now.

A thin green canvas tent is not much in the way of psychological reassurance, when confronted by a lion. The tent, with me inside it, was the only thing standing between the lion and the campfire where my beloved husband and children and our friends were sitting, totally exposed. The four teenagers, visiting from boarding school during the vacation, had cranked up the volume on the boom box so loud that they did not hear or recognize the sound of the lion roar. I screamed "Lion in camp!" at the top of my lungs. No immediate response or acknowledgment came from the group of twenty-five as they continued to chatter, watching the logs burn down to glowing ember coals. I frantically let out a bloodcurdling scream loud enough to shatter a chandelier, had we been in more-luxurious surroundings. Fear was closing my throat. All I could manage to scream was "Lion, lion!" This time Ron Harvey heard me above the din of the music and the crowd. He hushed the group, grabbed his powerful gun that he had kept at his side, and shot off several rounds of ammunition into the air in hopes of scaring the lion away. It was a moonless night and pitch dark except for the glow from the dying fire. There was no way to know if the lion had retreated. I unzipped the flap on the front of the tent and was knocked down by my family as they scrambled inside to join me. Some others in our hunting party were more intelligent in their choice of sanctuary and crowded into a Chevrolet suburban vehicle for protection.

Joe fumbled in the darkness as he loaded and cocked both the shotgun and .300 Magnum Winchester rifle. He handed the shotgun to our son and instructed him to use it if the lion made any attempt to swipe his mighty paws across the canvas. Jody was shaken, and he told us that he had gone to the bathroom five minutes earlier in the area where the lion had roared.

We put the five daughters in the center of the tent with the youngest, Juliana, age four, curled up in the middle. Everyone obeyed our whispered commands without question. A guilty feeling more powerful than the fear that gripped me, was gnawing my insides. I had wanted to come along so badly that I hadn't fully considered the dangers to which we might subject our children. For the record, I must say that I was extremely proud of every one of them. They were truly brave. Real troopers! Not one squeak, not one tear, not a single outburst that would make the situation any more volatile. Their complete cooperation allowed us to keep our wits.

We listened and waited, listened and waited. The sounds of the bush at night were both scary and beautiful. Howls from the hyenas sent chills up my spine. The song of the birds, on the other hand, brought me solace. Finally, lions began to roar at each other in the distance, fortunately not just outside our tent but perhaps a half mile away. It was a strange serenade.

I could not relax even though some of the children had fallen asleep from sheer exhaustion. Joe and I debated whether to move the family to sleep in the station wagon. We agreed that it would be uncomfortable but safer. The negative side, we realized, would be that we would suffocate if we kept the windows up, and we would be eaten alive by malaria toting mosquitoes or tsetse flies if we kept the windows down. In addition, I didn't relish the idea of making a break for the Chevy located twenty yards away, still uncertain if that lion stalked nearby. Images flashed before my eyes of some grotesque photos I had seen in a magazine years earlier of a German man being attacked and eaten by lions right in front of his wife and two young sons. It was too horrible to imagine. In the end, I vetoed the idea of abandoning the tent.

My husband told me to lie down and try to sleep. Joe said he would set up and stay on guard with the guns ready. He was strong and brave, as always a hero in my eyes. I lay down, but sleep eluded me. Suddenly, I heard strange noises that sounded like a lion snarling and growling. I bolted upright and listened. The sound was closer. Good Lord! I realized it was only my "hero" sitting straight up, leaning against his gun, and snoring. My dearest sentinel was sound asleep. I was angry and amused at the same time. It occurred to me that his snoring might sound like a mating call to the lions. I was sure he could be heard from a distance. In fact, our colleagues confessed the next morning that his snoring had also frightened them, and we had a good chuckle. Nevertheless, at that moment, I didn't feel much like laughing.

I woke him up and he swore that he wasn't even asleep, much less snoring. Next morning eighteen people begged to differ with him. Obviously the only thing to do to ensure that he was alert all night was to stay up and talk to him. So I did. We sat close together despite the stuffiness and heat of the tent. We spent the rest of the wee morning hours counting our blessings while recalling many happy times in our past. We spoke softly so as not to disturb the kids. We realized one of them was listening intently to our stories when she interrupted and told us to speak louder so she could hear. Jill always was the nosy one in the family. It made us laugh and realize that things were normal and that we would probably make it through the night.

Indeed, we did survive not only that night but numerous other hunting trips before our Tanzania tour ended. I prefer the photographic safaris we do now.

Friends tease me about the time I accidentally jumped into bed with our Tanzanian guide. Mosquitoes were devouring every exposed part of my body as I tried to sleep on the hard ground. Lions had been roaring in the distance, so Joe and Alberto Ruiz de Gamboa decided to set up with their loaded guns across their laps. I was listening to Joe as he was relating frightening lion stories from a book entitled *Death in the Long Grass*.

Suddenly the heavens opened, and the rains poured down. Not wanting to get wet, I ran to the suburban and jumped in the back seat. The seat moved beneath me, I landed on the floor, the other door opened, and a man rushed into the night. Lightning struck, revealing the outline of our startled guide. Guess he thought it was better to take his chances with the lions in a rainstorm than sleep with this crazy American woman who had just leapt on top of him. I am not sure which one of us was more surprised but at least I was dry the rest of the night.

Our kids have great memories of our safaris and I wonder what things they will tell their children. Perhaps for Gretchen the two things which will stick out most in her mind are skinning an eland and picking up the toilet tissue with a stick and putting it in plastic bags. Much to our surprise, fastidious Gretchen did the former without blinking an eye while the latter disgusted her immensely. Jill is likely to remember being attacked by a huge baboon or her severe allergic reaction to tsetse fly bites. Our son especially loved the expeditions, but malaria racked his body and hospitalized him back at boarding school after our final trip.

In the summer of 1983, we left Tanzania and moved to Quito Ecuador. I thought I had died and gone to heaven the first time I walked into a bountiful, modern supermarket in Quito with an abundance of food and packaged meats and realized I would not have to forage for food—at least not during that tour. *Amen!*

CHAPTER 13

Home Leave at Last

In the foreign service, overseas assignments for USAID staff are typically tours of two years. For each tour overseas, the employee and his or her family receive three weeks of "home leave" per year of assignment abroad, which can only be utilized if an individual is reassigned to the same or another overseas position. The home leave can only be taken in the United States and not for any foreign travel. In our previous assignments, because we changed employers or returned to the United States, we had never received home leave. We had been in Tanzania three years and had been assigned to Ecuador, so we had accumulated almost nine weeks of home leave.

We were excited about our assignment to Ecuador. Because of the educational situation in Tanzania, we wanted to return to Latin America for our next tour. Joe had the support of the new head of Latin America Agriculture, Scaf Brown, and we were assigned to Ecuador in 1983, where Joe was named the director of the Office of Rural Development. At that time, the Ecuador rural development program projects had been recently developed and Joe expected to focus on implementation of the current program, not developing new projects. We anticipated a less hectic life and hoped we could have more family time. That would hold true for a year, then life would become hectic again. I did not have a job when we arrived in Ecuador but that too would change.

As we were leaving Tanzania in June of 1983, we used some accumulated annual leave to travel to Ethiopia, Egypt, Israel, and Belgium on the way home. Two of my aunts had lost their husbands while we were in Tanzania and knowing that they had long wanted to visit the Holy Land, we invited them to come to Tanzania for a week before our departure and then travel home with us. I also invited my mother to join us and her two sisters on the trip, but she elected to stay home and take care of my father. She always regretted that lost opportunity.

Wildlife Safari in Tanzania

Upon the arrival of my aunts Lil and Kathleen, we took them on a four-day safari to the Serengeti Plains and Ngorongoro Crater in Northern Tanzania. Joe and I and a good friend Patty Ruiz de Gamboa shared the safari. In addition to the Serengeti and Ngorongoro Crater we visited the Lake Manyara and Tarangire Parks in northern Tanzania. We had a wonderful time. We saw four of the big five—elephants, rhinos, lions, and buffalos, but no leopards. We saw hundreds of wildebeests, zebra, and Grant's and Thomson's gazelle. My aunt's enjoyed the chance to do a safari and experienced the problems of safari trips at that time. They especially enjoyed our stay at the Ngorongoro Crater Lodge. The lodge is built on the lip of the rim of the Crater, and when you enter the lodge, there is a wall of glass that lets you see into the crater about 1,600 feet below. The dining area is situated such that it appears that you are suspended over the crater.

Ngorongoro Crater is an extinct volcano, formed about two million years ago. The volcano collapsed in on itself and formed what is now known as Ngorongoro Crater. A single dirt road leads into the crater and a separate dirt road is used to exit the crater. We have visited Ngorongoro Crater a number of times and it is one of my favorite places in Africa to see wild game. There is a large lake in the center of the crater that provides the animals with water, and because of this many animals stay in the crater. We had a most unforgettable safari experience while we were in Ngorongoro Crater in the midst of a herd of Cape buffalo, one of the more dangerous game animals, when our Land Rover died. We tried to get it started, but no luck. After considering all the alternatives, we decided to try to push the vehicle to get it started. Keeping our hands on the vehicle and our eyes on the buffalo, we, including my aunts, pushed the vehicle, and after several tries, it started, and we made sure that it didn't die on us as we made our way up the exit road out of the crater.

Ethiopia

A couple of days after our safari, the ten of us, Joe, our six children, my two aunts, and I departed Tanzania for a nineteen-day trip home. Our first stop was a one-night stay in Addis Ababa, Ethiopia where we did a tour of the city. We drove by the former Royal Palace where Joe had attended a cocktail party and met Emperor Haile Selassie. Our tour van was involved in a fender bender and a large crowd surrounded the vehicle. An Ethiopian child asked Jill for her comb, and she regretted giving it to him when an older boy took it away and the kids started fighting over it. We were fascinated by the tour of the city market in Addis.

Egypt

The next day we flew to Cairo, Egypt. The flight was supposed to stop in Khartoum, Sudan, but we were delayed three hours in Asmara, Ethiopia, now the capital of the Republic of Eritrea, due to a sandstorm. The sandstorm had diminished somewhat by the time we reached Khartoum, and it took several tries before we could land. The temperature at the airport when we landed was 120°F, and we wondered how anyone could live there, not realizing that in about thirty months we would be arriving for an assignment. After an exchange of passengers, we took off and landed in Cairo in the evening.

Because we were a group of ten, we qualified as a private tour group and were met at the airport and taken to the Nile Hilton. We were excited to be back in Egypt and have a chance to see the pyramids, the sphinx, the antiquities museum, King Tut's treasure, and then continue south to see the Valley of the Kings and take the Nile cruise in southern Egypt from Luxor to Aswan. There are two principal tourism areas in Egypt and they are separated by around four hundred miles. In Northern Egypt (also known as Lower Egypt) around Cairo is located the first center of Egyptian civilization as evidenced by the pyramids and the sphinx and the destroyed city of Memphis. The second location in Southern Egypt (also known as Upper Egypt) is located outside the city of Luxor, and includes the ruins of the ancient capital, Thebes including the temple of Karnak, and the Valley of the Kings and the Valley of the Queens. Our plan was to visit both areas.

After a restful night, we were met by our tour guide for a tour of Cairo. Our first stop was the Antiquities Museum, followed by a visit to the pyramids and sphinx as well as a visit to nearby Memphis, the capital of the Old Kingdom. There we saw the statue of Ramses II and the alabaster sphinx. We also visited the step pyramids at Saqqara, the first pyramids built. In 1983, access to all the sites was easier. We had our own tour of the Antiquities Museum, including the treasures from King Tut's tomb. At the pyramids and the sphinx, we rented camels and could ride around them and even climb the pyramids. In fact, at the largest, the Great Pyramid of Cheops, we entered an opening to the inside of the pyramid. The entrance sloped upward and while the adults were climbing the tunnel stooped over, our youngest, Juliana, scrambled ahead and having reached the end of the tunnel and seeing a sarcophagus, shouted down, "No need to come up, there is only a bathtub up here." We all laughed. After the pyramids, we visited Islamic Cairo.

Following our whirlwind tour of Cairo, we were deposited at the train station, for an overnight train trip to Luxor, in southern Egypt where we were to catch the Hilton Hotel boat, Osiris, for our Nile cruise. It is about 420 miles from Cairo to Luxor and takes about eleven hours, so we booked the train that had air-conditioned sleeper compartments and a lounge car. The food was excellent and we arrived rested in Luxor.

We were met at the train station and taken to the Hilton boat only to find that we could not board until 11:00 a.m. We were able to leave our baggage at the boat and hired two horse drawn carriages for a tour of Luxor. We were able to check in upon our arrival back to the boat. The Osiris was one of two Hilton cruise boats doing the Nile tour in 1983, and while it was very nice for its time, the river cruise boats of today are significantly more luxurious. The boat had a canopy covering the main deck and a small pool on the deck, so after unpacking, we went on deck and began our relaxing Nile cruise.

The ancient capital of city of Thebes is on the outskirts of Luxor and was the focus of our first tour from the boat. We were taken by bus to Thebes where our guide led us to the remains from the city that was destroyed in the last century before Christ. Thebes's period of fame and prosperity began around 1500 BC, and it was the capital of both Northern and Southern Egypt. In Thebes, instead of building pyramids the pharaohs in Southern Egypt built elaborate tombs in the sides of the hills close to the city. One of the most impressive of the ruins was the temple at Karnak in honor of the god Amon. The massive columns remaining were thirty-three feet around and sixty-nine feet tall. Observing the columns, it was difficult to believe that these sandstone temple columns could have been put in place over three thousand years ago. We were even more impressed when our guide informed us that the columns came from a quarry more than a hundred miles from where the temple was located. To this day there is disagreement among experts as to how the columns were transported from the quarries and put into position at the temple.

The next day, our floating hotel crossed the Nile for a visit to the Valleys of the Kings and Queens. With the movement of the capital of Egypt to Thebes, beginning about 1600 BC, the pharaohs, beginning with Thutmose, began a tradition of carving their tombs into a mountainside in a valley that became known as the Valley of the Kings. The burial chamber for the pharaohs was carved with an elaborate tunnel system that had false passages to distract anyone trying to enter the main burial place. However, the burial places were almost always found, and the valuables taken by thieves. To date, only one pharaoh's tomb has been discovered that had not been robbed. In 1922, the tomb of King Tutankhamen was discovered by an English archeologist, Howard Carter. In 1983, we were able to visit the tomb with our guide and spend as much time in the tomb as we wanted. Since the growth in numbers of tourists, restrictions have been placed on the number of tourist entering the tomb per day, limited to four hundred per day in 2008, and it is expected that entrance to the tomb will be prohibited soon. We were fortunate to have visited when we did. In addition, to our visit to the Valley of the Kings, our tour included a visit to Deir el-Bahari an impressive funerary complex built for Queen Hatshepsut, only the second woman pharaoh and the most famous.

After our tour to the Valley of the Kings, we returned to our floating hotel and started our trip toward Aswan. On the trip to Aswan, we stopped to visit the Temple of Horus and the twin temples at Lon Ombo. Upon arrival in Aswan the next day, we were supposed to fly 190 miles south to see the Temple of Abu Simbel. The temple was built by Ramses II and is famous for two reasons. The first, because of the magnitude of the temple, 125 feet wide by 215 feet long with four statues of the pharaoh seated on his throne on the outside of the temple, each statue being 66 feet tall. The second reason for its fame is the relocation of the temple to prevent it being flooded when the Aswan dam was constructed. To do this, the entire front of the cliff into which it was built, and the temple were removed to higher ground and reassembled. Unfortunately, we were informed the evening before arriving in Aswan that the plane we were to take had mechanical problems and the trip had been canceled. Because we had an onward flight to Israel the following day, we had to forego the trip to Abu Simbel, a trip we still hope to make one day. Upon our arrival in Aswan, we had a crazy taxi ride to the airport when the driver turned off his headlights "to save gas." We caught a flight to Cairo and then connected to Jerusalem, Israel.

Israel

We had included Israel on our itinerary as we wanted to visit the Holy Land and did not know when we would have another chance. We arrived in Jerusalem on the Sabbath and learned that keeping the Sabbath is taken seriously in Israel. Our room was on the seventeenth floor. The elevator automatically stopped at every single floor so that nobody broke the Sabbath by pushing the button.

My aunts had also always wanted to visit the Holy Land, so we had arranged a private six-day tour for just our family and it was wonderful. Our guide, David, was Jewish and he made certain we understood the history and the religious values to Jews, Christians, and Muslims alike at each place we visited. On the last evening in Israel, David likely saved all our lives. as he changed our reservations from Haifa to a Kibbutz near the Lebanese border. That very evening a bomb exploded in the restaurant of the hotel where we had reservations in Haifa killing four people. Meanwhile, we learned all about community living in Israel.

Belgium

From Israel, we flew to Brussels, Belgium, for two days. We arrived in the evening and were taken to our hotel in the center of town via bus. The route selected by the driver was through the red-light district, where at that time, the working girls advertised their fare by sitting in windows scantily clad. The trip raised several questions from our younger travelers as to why the girls were sitting in the window. We arrived at our hotel about 10:30 p.m. To help us unwind from our trip we went to the large plaza in front of the hotel where there were tables and chairs and only a couple of waiters. It took us about thirty minutes to be served, so my husband decided to order two beers rather than go through another long wait. Joe was quite shocked when the waiter told him that he could only have one beer, and after he drank that one, he could order another. This led to a discussion between Joe and the waiter on quality of service, but he only received his one beer. The next day we toured Brussels and did some shopping for Belgium lace before departing the next day for our homeland.

Travel in the USA

Our anticipated arrival in Ecuador wasn't until the end of August so we scheduled a road trip with the children to let them experience the United States. We planned to spend several weeks in Missouri and then to drive through Iowa, South Dakota, Montana, and Wyoming before returning to Missouri. When we arrived home in Monroe City, Missouri, we learned that my father-in-law and his wife, Mary

Ellen, had bought a large used RV. We invited them to join us on our trip out west, with us taking our car and they agreed to follow in their RV. The first stop on our trip was Sigourney, Iowa, where we spent the night with a college friend and her husband Sara and Dean Horras. On the drive to Sigourney, the RV had some problems with the gas line but then it seemed to clear up. Because we were concerned about finding hotel space for our family of eight, we had made reservations for our first three nights in the different cities we would be visiting Mitchell and Rapid City, South Dakota.

We left Sigourney, Iowa the morning of the second day of our trip heading for Mitchell, South Dakota. On the drive, their RV began having problems and we stopped several times. About sixty miles from Mitchell, my in-laws stopped at a campsite for the night. Since we had reservations in Mitchell, we proceeded onward, with the understanding that they would drive in the next morning and we would spend the day in Mitchell. The next morning, we waited at the hotel for them until 10:00 a.m. Since this was before cell phones we had no way to know what had happened to them, but we assumed they were still having problems with the RV. Joe decided to drive the sixty miles back to the campsite to see what had happened. Upon arriving at the campsite Joe discovered that they had left, and assuming that he must have passed them on the interstate he returned to Mitchell. They were not at the hotel nor was there any message from them. We became concerned that because of the problems with the RV they had decided to return to Monroe City. We called Joe's siblings to find out if they had heard from them. No one had any news, so we decided to continue our trip but to give our families in Monroe City phone numbers of the locations we would be for the next several days once they had news from Joe's dad and stepmother. We visited the Corn Place and several other sites in Mitchell before heading to our next destination, Rapid City, South Dakota. On the way to Deadwood, we drove through the Badlands National Park. The Badlands consist of an area of around 244,000 acres of eroded rocks and soil formations that provided an amazing array of cones, ridges, gulches, and pinnacles that take on different hues of color due to the layered mineral deposits and the movement of the sun as the day progresses. We found ourselves constantly stopping to admire the natural beauty of the park. When we arrived in Rapid City and were checking into our hotel we were told we had a telephone call. Sure enough, it was Joe's dad and stepmother. They were in Rapid City at a campground. We had a happy reunion, and learned that they had stopped at our hotel in Mitchell, while we were there and told we were not there. We decided to stay together henceforth. The RV problems seemed to have been solved and we had no further vehicle coordination problems.

The rest of our trip went smoothly, with visits to Mount Rushmore and Deadwood, South Dakota, Devil's Tower, Yellowstone Park, and the Grand Tetons in Wyoming. It was the first opportunity for the children to see some of the beauty of our western states, although we had much more we wanted to see. Upon arrival back in Monroe City, we made our purchases of items to take with us to Ecuador and bid farewell, to our two oldest children, who were remaining in the United States for studies. Our daughter Joan was beginning her freshman year at Truman State University, while our son Joe was returning to his boarding school in Colorado for his senior year. While Ecuador had appropriate high school education facilities, our son really liked his boarding school and friends in Colorado, and wanted to finish his high school there. Even though we had to pay out of pocket for the difference in cost between the two schools, it was worth the extra cost for him to thrive.

Goodwin family riding camels around the pyramids
of Giza in Egypt with aunts Lillian Hagan and
Kathleen Montgomery in June 1983.

CHAPTER 14

Exciting Ecuador

To love what you do and feel that it matters—
how could anything be more fun?
—Katherine Graham

In late August of 1983, we arrived in Quito, Ecuador, to begin what we expected to be a four-year USAID assignment. Ecuador became one of my favorite countries and I was sad when we were transferred after only two years there.

Arrival in Quito introduced to us the challenge of landing in a city surrounded by mountains. The airport is on the edge of Quito and it is necessary to circle around doing almost a corkscrew landing, often in thick clouds, always unnerving me.

Darell McIntyre, who was Joe's deputy in the Rural Development Office met us at the airport, took us to a temporary guesthouse and then to his home where his wife, Xochilt, had prepared a wonderful dinner. Thus, began a lifelong friendship.

Ecuador is a small country (approximately the size of Colorado), but it has an amazingly diverse geography. Western Ecuador has tropical beaches and a tropical climate, while the center of the country includes the Andes Mountains, snowcapped peaks, and active volcanoes. Cotopaxi at 19,347 feet is the world's highest active volcano while the eastern third of the country is part of the Amazon River basin. In addition, the Galapagos Islands lying 600 miles off shore are also part of Ecuador. That was a wonderful place to visit too.

Our twentieth anniversary / my fortieth birthday occurred while staying in the guesthouse. Unbeknownst to us, our four youngest children decided to host a surprise party, inviting the McIntyres to join us. Knowing how their dad enjoys champagne, our thirteen-year-old daughter Jill went across the street and bought a bottle of bubbly. No questions asked by the storekeeper. The champagne gave me a memorable headache, but the idea was appreciated.

It was lovely to move to our permanently assigned home which was neat and full of character and eloquence—six bedrooms on six levels, two fireplaces, and a dramatic fountain under the stairwell in the foyer. There was practically no garden area, but the house was great and centrally located.

Having returned to the work force in Tanzania, I was hoping to find employment in Ecuador. Shortly after arrival, I was offered a job in the USAID Finance Office as project accountant for a disaster relief project that was assisting Ecuador to address the damages caused by the 1983 El Nino that resulted in tens of millions of dollars in damages in western Ecuador due to flooding that destroyed roads, bridges, crops, and schools. Afterward, agricultural production alone fell 14 percent.

While I worked on the El Nino project, Joe kept busy as head of the Rural Development Office. The agricultural sector in Ecuador at the time was suffering not only from the results of El Nino but also from economic policies that negatively affected the sector. As a consequence, in addition to rural development and forestry projects in Joe's portfolio, Joe began a small economic policy project that analyzed the impact of government policies on the agricultural sector. A well-known Ecuadorian economist, Dr. Francisco Swett, was contracted to lead the work.

We were excited to see and experience as much of the beautiful country as possible. We loved to visit the Indian markets on weekends where one could buy many local crafts. It was fun to share the country with our family visitors, such as Joe's sisters Jean and Carol, his niece Ann, my parents, and Aunt Kathleen.

We developed a large circle of fantastic Ecuadorian friends. As a family, we shared many good times and travels with Darell and Xochilt. During our frequent travels around Ecuador, we created many happy memories while visiting the snowcapped mountains, the seaside, the plateau, and the jungle.

As for our kids, Joan and Joe were away at college but visited during the summers and holidays. Gretchen was a senior in high school and had fallen in love with Sgt. Scott Merrill, her future husband, who was serving as a marine security guard at the US Embassy. Admittedly, there was a rabble-rousing coming from Jill's corner, but generally she had seemed content with her close friend, Tori Moffett. Jenny and her sweet friend Ladna were twelve-year-olds and were interested in books and various projects. Juliana had a pet chicken named Andrea (who met a sad ending in the cook's pot) and a darling pug-nosed, bug-eyed friend named Katie Garst, who we lovingly nicknamed ET after the movie character.

One terrific experience none of our family and Joan's college friend Teresa Emmanuel will ever forget is the weeklong trip down the Amazon River. We flew to Coca, a town that has since been leveled by an earthquake, and boarded motorized canoes to carry us to the larger wooden floating hotel the *Orellano* anchored on the Napo River, a tributary of the Amazon.

The jungle setting was like being in an adventure movie as we cruised under branches with snakes draped over their limbs. Occasionally we caught sight of beautiful tropical birds, such as toucans and macaws and a few monkeys. One day we took a hike through the dense jungle and ate lemon ants, which exploded in our mouths from interacting with saliva. We saw some of the most beautiful florescent butterflies in the world. We fished for flesh-eating *piranhas*, caught, and ate them after the kids had taken a swim in the middle of the river. One night we took a smaller boat and watched the guide catch a baby alligator with her bare hands. She also submitted herself to the sting of army ants to show us how their pinchers were used in place of sutures in the jungle. We visited a museum in the middle of the jungle in which a missionary priest displayed his collection of spears taken from the backs of human victims. Certain tribes did not trust foreign intruders. The flotilla stopped at night for safety reasons.

The Amazon cruise was an almost perfect trip until six-year-old Juliana came down with a jungle fever the day before our trip was to end. Her body temperature measured 106°F for more than twenty-four hours, and we truly feared we would lose her. No doctor was available, and we had no way back to civilization. Joe and I sat together by Juliana's feverish body all night, rubbing her with ice, and desperately praying for her salvation. The disco dance floor was directly above our room and the noise of the music and the stomping of feet reverberated through our ceiling.

About midnight, Juliana broke the tension and made us laugh heartily for a brief moment when she asked indignantly: "Don't they have any respect for a dying woman?" Indeed, at six Juliana already considered herself a woman. Three other children on the cruise had similar fevers and the embassy doctor could not identify the cause when we returned. He simply named it jungle fever.

The flights to Quito were scheduled to arrive in late afternoon just as the clouds formed over the city, which meant that often you were circling downward in the clouds, praying that you didn't hit a mountain as you were doing so. Once I was driving to the airport to pick up Joe who was returning from a field visit on a day that cloud cover was especially thick. Suddenly the wheels of his plane dropped out of the clouds and then disappeared. Joe said that the pilot said he would try to land and if they didn't make it they would fly back to the coast and spend the night in Guayaquil, Ecuador. Joe was wondering, if we didn't make it, how did the pilot know that Guayaquil would be an option? As they were circling down in the dense clouds, becoming more and more concerned about whether he would make it, when the clouds disappeared, the pilot realized they were close to the ground, too far down the runway to land. The pilot accelerated and pulled up. That moment is what I had witnessed. Joe was relieved not only that he didn't crash but that at least he would go back to Guayaquil and return the next morning, when the clouds would be less. Instead, the pilot said he would try one more time. Again, they descended, circling and bumping through clouds. After what seemed like an eternity, he broke through the clouds, still only about two hundred feet above the ground but this time, on target to land, safely. Thanks be to God.

As you might visualize life in Ecuador was treating us well after two years of intensive involvement and none of us were ready to leave our dear friends, especially not Gretchen who had to be dragged onto the plane after darting back through customs to give Scott another tearful hug before departure. She then headed for Barry University in Miami while Scott remained in Quito to complete his assignment.

Fortunately, true love prevailed, and they survived that forced separation as well as subsequent long periods apart which they have endured during Scott's seven months duty in the Gulf War (1990–1991) and his five months attendance at Warrant Officer School (1995) across the continent from his family.

The picture cannot be completed without reference to our faithful maid named Maggie whose baby, Jessica, was also a part of our extended family. Maggie didn't cook a large variety, so entertainment always fell on my shoulders. And entertain we did—frequently and formally! I got tired—extremely tired physically and mentally, at times. So did Joe. But we believed in the cause. The proud moment I knew that our sacrifices meant something to the people of Ecuador was when the minister of agriculture, Marcel Laniado, pinned a beautiful medal on Joe's lapel, naming him the recipient of *El Merito Agricola* award, an annual award for the person who has made the largest contribution to Ecuadorian agriculture each year. Joe is the only foreigner who had ever received that coveted award which is typically reserved for Ecuadorians. Having worked beside him, I am fully aware that Joe deserved it. I know Joe would have given me credit for my part in helping him earn that special recognition if he had been able to speak. For once in his life, Joe was absolutely speechless! It was a total surprise to him and he was overwhelmed by the honor. I was and am so *proud* of him.

In early 1985, we were informed that Joe was being considered for transfer to the Sudan, as the associate director of economic policy and program. Sudan at that time was our second largest program in the world, and a political priority. There was a need for a senior officer with strong economic skills and Joe was selected. Joe had worked closely with the ministers of finance and agriculture and both wanted Ecuador's president, Febres Cordero, to send a letter of protest to Washington, requesting cancelation of the proposed transfer. When we were informed of the plan, we said that while we appreciated the offer, we had to allow the USAID to decide our fate.

One thing that also influenced our decision to accept the transfer without much resistance was something disconcerting that Joe and I had learned and kept secret from our children for the last six months in Ecuador. We did not want to frighten our kids by telling them their father's name had been found on a list of people targeted for assassination for being too close to the Ecuador government. That scary list was found in a briefcase of one of two terrorists who were arrested in early 1985. We both worried about kidnapping and encouraged the kids to vary their routines without telling them the reason behind our advice. So now, our kids know why their parents sometimes seemed overly protective.

In fact, we later realized we should have been even more protective as we were totally unaware of one of our daughter's secret. It was during home leave, when we learned of Jill's pregnancy, that we knew our timing had been auspicious in departing Ecuador. God always works in mysterious ways. It was a test of faith and love and I believe the happy results show we passed both tests.

Farewell Ecuador

I received a gorgeous emerald and diamond ring from my kind and thoughtful husband as a consolation for leaving Ecuador. After enduring tearful and touching farewell parties given for us in Quito, Joe departed the country first accompanied by Jill, Jenny, and Juliana. They stopped in Panama where the girls had a memorable time watching the ships slowly pass through the locks of the Panama Canal in sweltering heat. They visited prospective boarding schools in Florida. I had to remain in my job for another two weeks and finally left with the older three children.

Terrible Home Leave

The home leave of 1985 was the worst time. The weather was unbearably hot, setting record highs. Everyone was in personal turmoil. Frankly, none of us had wanted to leave Ecuador or go to the Sudan. That may not be noble, but it is the truth. For various reasons, our medical clearances were delayed which meant we had to put Jenny and Juliana into school at Holy Rosary for six weeks. Then we were dealing with where Jill would live and her future.

Gretchen was missing Scott and nervous about college. Bravely, she insisted on flying alone to Miami. I still regret that I didn't go with her as the school left her stranded for hours at the airport which made my heart bleed for our shyest daughter when we learned of her plight. She was really gutsier than we expected and that was a time of growth for her. Gretchen aspired to being a pilot and we admired her for enrolling in the ROTC and taking two buses through rough parts of Miami to go for training. In the end, however, she found her niche with chemistry and has been highly successful as a clinical lab specialist.

Anyway, home leave did finally end in late October after getting Jill settled at St. Monica's maternity home in Springfield, Illinois. We were heartbroken to leave Jill, but she was so brave for her young age.

The Emerald Isle

En route to the Sudan, Joe, Jenny, Juliana, and I treated ourselves to a stopover in gloriously green Ireland. We stayed at beautiful Dromoland Castle. While sipping Bailey's Irish cream in the castle's dungeon which was converted to a pub, we enjoyed harp music and sang Irish folk songs to our daughters. We rented a car and traveled around the beautiful country for five days. We took an interesting tour of Waterford Crystal factory and ordered a set of wine glasses in the Kathleen pattern, in honor of our favorite aunt. We purchased a beautiful hand crocheted tablecloth near Blarney Castle where we kissed the famous Blarney Stone. We went to a medieval banquet at Bunratty Castle and were chosen to represent the royal family which was so much fun sentencing fellow diners to the dungeon for the slightest offense. The diners then had to sing for their supper. It was a hilarious evening.

Ireland was a relaxing and much-needed break before going from fairytale castles to the reality of Khartoum. What a weather and cultural contrast.

I am proud to share this beautiful poem written for our anniversary by our teenage daughter Jill. It nicely depicts her struggles and our everlasting love.

To My Parents
By Angela Jill Goodwin

My parents try to **understand**. Throughout the good and bad, they offer me a helping **hand** and give it all they have.

In the first seventeen years that I have **grown**, they have helped me live and learn. Their love for me was always **shown**, when I thought I'd nowhere to turn.

There were times I had to get **away**, and they would set me free, and even though I made them **gray**, they still had faith in me.

When my life got very tough, they helped me stick it **out**. Though life's battles can be rough, they helped me through my **doubt**.

And when we aren't together, there is always **love**, a bond that lasts forever, thanks to the Lord **above**.

And next year as we **part**, remember how much I care, the love for you that's in **my heart**, a love we will always share.

Joe receiving a medal by the Ecuadorian Minister of Agriculture Marcel Laniado for his contribution to Ecuadorian agriculture through his work with USAID in 1985.

Goodwins chosen to act as "royalty" at Bunratty Castle dinner in Ireland in 1985.

CHAPTER 15

Surviving Sudan

Courage is resistance to fear, mastery
of fear—not absence of fear.
—Mark Twain

It took more than a decade for me to cope with the trauma of being evacuated and subsequent consequences. On April 17, 1986, we were evacuated from Khartoum, Sudan. "Flight from Terror" read the headlines of the *Washington Post*, which greeted us evacuees. It is not an anniversary date we wish to celebrate or commemorate.

Ironically, on April 17, 1995, Joe departed our Virginia home to live in Cambodia where April 17 is a date with horrible memories for its people. On that day twenty years earlier in 1975, the Khmer Rouge rebels conquered and evacuated Phnom Penh and all its citizens following the Communist victory in neighboring Vietnam. The genocidal repercussions from that event will forever haunt Cambodia.

As I first wrote this segment in 1996, television news stories featured the evacuation of Americans and expatriates from civil war in Monrovia, Liberia. As I sat glued to the unfolding story, empathy welled up inside me forging a bond and understanding shared among those comrades with similar experiences. Seeing the visible fear in the faces of the evacuees running for the planes and helicopters prompted me to write and attempt to express my own feelings about that dark period in our lives when we personally dealt with forced evacuation. Writing helped heal the wounds and erase the scars inflicted upon my mind from all my negative experiences in the Sudan.

Happily, the gripping terrorist nightmares that plagued me for many years after our evacuation now invade and disturb my sleep only on rare occasion. I have learned what stress points usually trigger these nightmares and how to cope with the unwelcome intruder by jolting myself back to reality. Joe also deserves much credit for the improvement as he is so attuned to my nightmares that he often wakes up when, subconsciously, he senses a change in my breathing pattern, even though he is normally a very deep sleeper. He gently awakens and reassures me and massages the tight muscles caused by terrible dreams. In the beginning, the nightmares were so horrible that I would wake up hyperventilated, in a cold sweat, tears staining my pillow, feeling paralyzed, unable to move even a finger. What dirty tricks the mind can play on the body!

Joe's favorite phrase "No good deed goes unpunished" is a good description of our assignment to Sudan. It seemed to be doomed to disaster before it began.

For the first six weeks after our arrival in Khartoum, our family stayed across the Nile River from the office in a "suite" at the Friendship Palace Hotel which was fairly new at that time. It has since closed. The furniture was really sparse and the round bolster pillows felt like sleeping on cement blocks. The view of the river was nice, and the service was friendly in the restaurant although the menu was extremely limited. Sometimes we would venture down the dusty road to buy pita bread filled with a smashed bean mixture. We were woken daily by the loudspeaker call to prayer at the nearby mosque.

Expatriate housing was scarce in Khartoum although we were shown a few from which to choose. Most were too large even for our family requirements. We settled upon an unfinished seven-bedroom house and turned down the ten-bedroom monstrosity, which the Sarhan family accepted. There was nothing smaller available. Then on December 12, 1985, six staff members and families were "voluntarily" evacuated in a designated drawdown of staff. That freed up some houses and apartments, so our family moved to the huge former Lyver's home where we became acquainted with a great cook, Gabriel, a Christian man from Juba, in Southern Sudan. He had six children he had not seen in years due to the civil war. It was in that house that we spent Christmas with Joan, Joe, and Gretchen visiting for the holidays. I fashioned a Christmas tree out of green tinsel wrapped around a support pole in the living room. One absurdity I remember about that house was that it had originally had a swimming pool that had been filled with sand so as not to be "ostentatious." A pool would have brought welcome relief from the hot desert wind.

We acquired Louie, the beloved Rhodesian ridgeback breed of dog from the controller who was retiring. The girls loved that handsome dog who came with his pedigree papers. We also picked up a poor puppy who we discovered nursing from its dead mother along the road, but we promptly found a home for it. The Sudanese neighbor women routinely beat the skinny dog which was tied to a stake. Our kids would protest loudly, and the women would scream back but continue to whip the dog. A different culture!

A few days before our young folks returned to college, I had an unpleasant experience while riding home from work in the office car pool van. One of Joe's staff, Sachicko Sidhu, was in the front seat with the driver, but she was turned talking to me where I sat in the second row. As she spoke, I noticed that the car in front of us carried four men sporting afros and large sunglasses. We had been taught to read the Arabic license plate, which read PLO. Sudan had a deserved reputation for being a haven for terrorists and the Palestinian Liberation Organization compound was quite large and foreboding. We passed it every day of our way to work. I observed the driver was watching us in his outside mirror. Their car started going slower and slower. The USAID driver said nothing but began to drop further behind. Passengers in the car started staring at us and laughing. All of a sudden one of them pulled an AK-47 automatic rifle up to the back window and flamboyantly pointed the gun directly at us. Being extremely alert to the threat, our driver immediately took a sharp right turn, and we bounced across the sand in a hasty detour. I feared we would bury the heavy Suburban in the sand, but he was going so fast that we only skimmed the surface. That driver's alert reaction won him an award for which I had written the recommendation. Our son was very disturbed about this incident, but my husband, ever the optimist, minimized the danger, which caused me some resentment.

After that fright and feeling that I needed to take my safety into my own hands, I signed up for a security seminar the Department of Defense offered on the banks of the Nile. For three days a group of us were trained in self-defense measures, which we could use as a last resort if a terrorist was about to exterminate us. On the first day I was used as an example (since I was the smallest in the class) of what they expected me to achieve by the end of the third day. The instructor declared that before the end of the training that I would be able to throw the largest man in the class (Bill Caulkens, an embassy communicator) to the ground. Everyone roared with laughter—especially big Bill and me. But on the third day, Bill did not laugh when I gripped him, grunted like a charging marine, maneuvered my hips, and decked him flat on the ground! I cried with triumph and joy. Remember his name because, sadly, my nice "victim" Bill became a real-life victim to a PLO bullet three months later, an event that prompted and hastened our evacuation from the Sudan.

By mid-January 1986, our own house was ready at last. Joe was in the States on business during the move, so I received and unpacked our sea freight. Much to my chagrin, this was not the first time Joe managed to be away at such a time. The consumables shipment, which we needed badly since food was so scarce, was delayed and only received the week before we were evacuated. What a shame!

On January 29, I returned to the United States to assist Jill in her time of need, leaving the youngest two girls with Joe. When I boarded the plane in Khartoum, I picked up a copy of the *Herald Tribune* and was horrified by the full-page picture of the *Challenger* spaceship explosion, which occurred the previous day, killing all seven astronauts including a teacher who was the first civilian space passenger. That was so tragic and added to my stress. I hate to fly, especially alone. It was such a long journey and I had a lot of time to worry about Jill. The temperature was 115°F when I left Khartoum and snowing when I arrived home in Missouri. *Burrr.*

I am so grateful that I was there on February 8, 1986, when our first grandchild, Angela Hope, made her miraculous appearance. Jill had complications as she had developed toxemia and had extreme fluctuations of blood pressure. The umbilical cord wrapped around the baby's neck, but fortunately, her doctor realized the problem in time and untangled it before delivery. Angela Hope was a carbon copy of her mother, ironically weighing and measuring the exact same as Jill had at birth. Her lovely olive skin was darker than her mother's pale complexion but otherwise she was the spitting image of the child I delivered less than sixteen years earlier. I would have known her anywhere. If Jill had not already decided to keep the baby, I know that I could not have let her go either. It was love at first sight and bonding at first touch. Her doctor told me that Jill might not have made it through the labor without me being there to keep her calm, but I think Jill's inner-strength deserves most of the credit as she was a marvelous sport throughout the difficult labor. I am grateful to Joe, Jenny, and Juliana for making the sacrifice of letting me go for three weeks, which most certainly passed more quickly for me than for them. After coming home from the hospital, we spent two weeks at my parents and Angie slept in a makeshift cradle which her great grandma Gander fixed from a dresser drawer. Then Jill and Angie moved to her Aunt Mary Jean and Uncle Bob's home and Jill attended Monroe City high school. She had been tutored at the maternity home, so she didn't miss school.

I returned to Khartoum laden with pictures of the grandbaby to share with the family. I went back to the job at the controller's office which was not great but filled my days. The only day diversion Khartoum offered from the heat and boredom was its mystic intrigue.

Political tension in the country and in the Middle East region escalated over the next few weeks. Wild rumors abounded and hints that another "voluntary" evacuation was pending floated around the post. It was not a particularly happy or relaxing time.

On April 8, Joe left for Zambia with a team of six Sudanese officials to study the foreign exchange auction system in place there. The following Sunday afternoon while Joe was away the girls and I went to the American Club for a swim. The club was the only respite available. While relaxing by the pool, one of the marine security guards made a strange statement to me. He said that if I were wise, I would pack up my girls and get on the next flight out of the country because in a day or two it would no longer be safe to be in the Sudan.

He would not comment further but left me to ponder what inside information he possessed.

That very night came the answer. President Reagan ordered the bombing of Tripoli, Libya, in retaliation for terrorist acts allegedly committed by the Libyans in Germany against American military. Do two wrongs make it right? I wondered. Although the Libyan leader Muammar Gadhafi's home was targeted and struck during the bombing raid on April 15 he escaped injury. The action set off a furor in the Arab world. American diplomats were shot in three countries. We became victims of American policies which we didn't necessarily support. Just happened to be government workers in the wrong place at the wrong time in history.

Around noon, the next day Gretchen telephoned me from her dorm room in Miami. She was concerned as she had heard on television that we were being evacuated and that one of our Embassy people had been shot. That was news to me! As I spoke with her, I heard the mobile radio screech an "all stations cell call." I ran upstairs to the radio and listened to Ambassador Hume Horan's calm message. It was true! Bill Caulkens (the good-natured fellow who was my partner in the security seminar) had been chased by a PLO vehicle as his car left the embassy the prior evening. Bill was shot in the head and crashed into a wall in front of the Russian Embassy compound. The Russians notified the American Embassy. Bill was medevac'd to Saudi Arabia for surgery. I will mention now that Bill survived although he remained in a coma for a long period. The happy ending is that Bill returned to work after almost ten years in recovery. Miracles do happen.

During that same day, there were three more near victims in the Sudan. We were told to stay home. Mel Van Doren, the USAID acting director, thought that he would make a quick trip to return a videotape to a store near his house. He was walking home when a drive-by gunman opened fire, killing a cat a few feet away from Mel. Two other USAID women were chased in their cars by gunmen. I was unaware of those incidents until we came together that night.

Ambassador Horan announced that we should prepare to depart during the night. We could only take one suitcase and no pets or large items. He said we would be taken to Nairobi for safe-haven to wait out the situation and would likely return to Khartoum in a month. Thinking that I might want to buy things in Kenya that I could not get in Sudan, I only packed my suitcase half-full. That was a mistake. It was eighteen months before I saw my possessions again.

The ambassador also told us that the children were being picked up from school by security guards and brought home early. What he neglected to do was inform the superintendent that the Sudanese security guards were being sent to the school. So what happened when they arrived was that the Sudanese demanded that the school gather up all the children of the American diplomats. At first, the superintendent did not know it was for their protection but thought they were being taken hostage. He quickly radioed the embassy and was given instructions to release the kids. Again, there was a break-down in communications. Poor flustered school officials were scurrying around with the men in uniform to collect the diplomatic kids but failed to explain what was happening to either the children or their teachers. Juliana and Jenny's reaction was that it was an exciting adventure. It never crossed their young minds that they might be in any danger. They simply obediently followed the uniformed strangers toting guns. When the girls arrived home, they were singing and in a festive mood. When I told them, we were leaving they were actually excited about a trip to Nairobi. The circumstances for our unplanned vacation from school didn't mean much to them at that point. Their only worry was leaving their dog and friends.

Meanwhile, Joe had originally been due to return to Khartoum that day. His office knew that he was transiting in Nairobi where he spent the previous night. They sent a cable to the USAID office in Kenya asking them to locate Joe and stop him from returning to Khartoum. Unfortunately, Joe had changed hotels so that he could remain with the Sudanese officials who wanted to stay in a less expensive hotel than the office had reserved. That meant USAID/Kenya was unable to locate Joe before he left. It was only during his flight that he read in the *Tribune* about Bill's shooting but did not know about the evacuation. He arrived at the airport in Khartoum and thought it odd that no office driver met him. He took a taxi and went to the office and found it locked and vacant. He took another taxi home. I did not hear him enter the house. I was in the bedroom packing when Joe found me. Being the eternal kidder he is, he got down and looked under the bed and then asked if he had been gone so long that I had decided to leave him. We laughed heartily and fell into one another's embrace.

My relief in seeing him was short-lived as Joe called the Embassy to add his name to the roster of evacuees and was told that the plane was already full, and he would have to wait for the next flight. I didn't want to be separated from him again so soon and asked for a recount. They said that the only chance he had to accompany us was if the Jim Sarn family did not return from their trip to Eastern Sudan before the flight. That brought mixed feelings. We were all worried about Jim and Leslie and their four beautiful children who happened to be away, out of radio contact, and unaware of the potential danger. In the end, they returned safely the next day and caught the second flight which was another scary story. An explosive in plastic was placed at the airport in an open bag carried by one of the unsuspecting missionary women. Fortunately, the bomb was discovered by security as she was about to board the plane which carried 350 people, many of them being our friends and colleagues. I shudder to even imagine that close call.

Late in the afternoon of April 16, we realized that our income tax information was at the office. Yes, I know we were told to stay home, but Joe and I thought we should go fetch our important papers. While we were there, a guard came running in and announced that there had been a bomb threat at our office. We exited quickly! No bomb was found nor detonated but it was not funny to us.

We ate leftover lamb for dinner and tried to have a family meal as peaceful as any other night. However, this was not any ordinary night. Our minimal bags stood ready by the door. We were told that we would be picked up around eleven o'clock in the evening. We sat in the darkness of our two-story living room with its balcony full of plants blooming overhead. We felt very small, alone, and extremely apprehensive. Juliana clutched her doll and yawned sleepily while Jenny petted Louie, who sensed something amiss. Joe told amusing stories to distract us all. Me? I prayed silently.

Twice the doorbell rang, and we expected to see our rescuers but were surprised to find first a Swiss Red Cross ambulance with Jenny's friend and father and the second visitors were Juliana's Libyan/Sudanese friend with her father. All of them had taken a great risk by being seen saying goodbye to an American, a dirty word in the country. They came under the cover of darkness. None of them lingered but their efforts were very much appreciated.

Midnight came and went. At about one o'clock in the morning, we saw headlights streaking across the empty desert lot in front of our house. Suddenly the doorbell was ringing frantically. Joe ran to the front gate and was briskly greeted by two US Marines and two Sudanese special forces in combat fatigues, all four with their fingers on the triggers of their menacing automatic weapons. They dashed into the house, grabbed the bags, ran them to the bus, and returned in a flash. We were then taken to the bus individually with a marine on each side and the Sudanese soldiers in front and back. At the pace they moved, we must have all four been escorted to the bus within one minute's span. I vividly recall the sad look in the dog's eyes as I brushed past Louie, sitting regally at the front door. His eyes signaled his knowledge that I would never see him again. Sadly, he was right.

Silently the caravan snaked through the city picking up other Americans. Every time a vehicle would approach us, a scout truck of fully armed Sudanese soldiers in front would race up and stop the other vehicle from getting close to us. That seemed a bit like overkill, even to me, but I appreciated their caution.

When all the vehicles in the caravan were filled to capacity, we were taken to the home of the US agricultural attaché for staging. Travel orders were distributed. Passports were collected. Papers were to be signed. Other nationals signed agreements to repay their portion of the cost for the evacuation plane. Tired and nervous people milled around aimlessly. Coffee was available although people's adrenaline kept them alert. Friends hugged and found comfort in one another. The sleepless children, running on nervous energy, scampered around. We were asked to be very quiet as there was a tall apartment building next to the house and they did not want to arouse any suspicions. Our evacuation plans had not been public knowledge despite our kid's friends knowing about it.

At 5:00 a.m., we were loaded back into buses and hastily driven to the airport which was fairly close to the attaché's house. We were taken directly to the chartered Lufthansa 747 sitting on the tarmac. Our bags had already been delivered and x-rayed before we were moved to the airport. The loading was accomplished rather quickly even with the heavy security set up at the ramp of the plane where our bags were thoroughly searched. That safety precaution saved the second planeload of evacuees the next day from being bombed as I mentioned earlier.

At 5:45 a.m., we taxied out to the runway. My heart was racing. Joe was yawning, acting very nonchalant as usual, but smiled, winked his understanding blue eyes at me, and squeezed my hand to acknowledge my apprehension. It is funny now as I remember thinking what burley and clumsy crew the Germans had for stewards. It had not dawned on my innocent mind that these were not airline personnel at all. The crew was actually a German-trained SWAT team.

We sat on the runway waiting to take off for an unusually long period. I sensed something was wrong. The pilot then said that our clearance to take off had been withdrawn by the Sudanese. The silence on the plane was deafening. One could've heard a pin drop above the snores of my husband who was already asleep. Tension does strange things to people. The man seated behind me started panicking and rambling out loud. We all wanted to choke him for the thought, which he shared. He said, "They want to wait until daylight so they can shoot us down with the ground to air missiles at the end of the runway." His point was as reasonable as any other explanation but none of us wanted to hear such a thing. I glanced around at the strained faces of my companions. I looked at my husband who was sleeping like a baby and wished I could join him and forget about our predicament. We taxied back to the terminal and the engines were shut down, which caused Joe to wake up and inquire if we were already in Nairobi. We waited and fidgeted while the pilot negotiated with the control tower. The morning sun dawned over the desert horizon. My mind kept racing back to that guy's point about waiting for daybreak to shoot us down and I mentally made my act of contrition.

At 6:15 a.m., we were given authority to take off. Statistics show the first twenty minutes of a flight is the most dangerous. But I was most worried about those first twenty seconds after liftoff until we got past the cannons. Wheels up with my spirits down, we did indeed take off and soared easterly toward Nairobi. The dire prediction did not come to pass. I could not sleep although all my family passed out the whole way to Kenya.

USAID/Kenya and US Embassy folks were at the airport in force to greet us. We were taken to the Hilton and told that President Moi was concerned about possible retaliation attacks against Americans and did not want us to stay in Kenya as had been planned. They had already arranged for more charter planes to take us to the United States within three days. Meanwhile we could detox. Some of our friends took a Safari one day, which we had planned to join but I got sick the night before, so we had to cancel. It might have been food poisoning, but it most likely was a severe case of nerves coming untwisted. We stayed at the hotel and the girls swam with their friends. Once the mission got its thoughts together, they decided that Joe was one of four people who would stay in Kenya and hope to return to Sudan from there. That news did not set well with me. I certainly did not want him to return to the Sudan. Foreign service is akin to the military. One takes and accepts orders whether you like it or not. I definitely did not like it.

The three days flashed by and it was time for the girls and I to join the buses for the airport. It was drizzling rain which did not cheer our moods. Through my tears, I waved goodbye and blew kisses to Joe who ran alongside the bus, smiling bravely, his beautiful blue eyes looking pitifully sad, to the end of the block. I remember thinking that our lives would never be the same. I was right. The terrible long separation had begun.

Leaving Nairobi on a Pan Am chartered flight was uneventful. One thing different and nice for us was that since I was the highest-ranking USAID spouse, the girls and I were put into first class along with Ambassador Horan's wife and kids. I was also charged with going around the plane gathering addresses and contact numbers for all the USAID personnel. We later compiled a list for distribution and formed our own support network. Good thing we did as our support from Washington headquarters was sporadic at best.

The flight stopped to refuel in Germany at an American airbase. That day, April 22, happened to be the twenty-fifth wedding anniversary of our colleagues, the Lammerzahls. So when we made our refueling stopover, I ran and bought a bottle of chilled champagne for their big silver day. Back onboard, six of us shared the champagne from paper cups. That was the only champagne ever consumed on that flight. However, I was absolutely furious with the headlines of the *Washington Post*, which stated, "Champagne Flight from Terror." That was misleading. The article unfairly implies that we were all given free champagne at government cost. It criticized the government for housing us in "luxury hotels" both in Kenya and the United States. We were in fact in evacuation status and not given a choice of hotels. A cheap group rate was worked out in advance. If I ever felt I deserved a bit of" luxury," it was then.

I must not skip the arrival scene at Andrews Air Force Base in Maryland. When we reached Washington, DC, after the long flight from Kenya, a thick fog had descended upon the entire area and we circled the city endlessly. I worried that they could not locate the base in the fog. After forty-five minutes of circling and experiencing heavy turbulence, the pilot finally explained that the dignitaries and news media who wanted to greet us had not been able to reach the base airport due to the fog. So that was the reason for our aimless wandering in space. I got claustrophobic and airsick as I often do on planes. I felt annoyed that this exhausted group of evacuees would be further inconvenienced.

When we finally touched down, we were told to remain in our seats until the assistant secretary of state boarded the plane to address us. An old friend, Larry Saiers, was among the dignitaries who boarded the plane. We were happy to see one another. He was surprised at how big Jenny was and told her that she used to cry every time she saw him when she was a baby in Ghana. In the eyes of a toddler, tall Larry had been a giant.

We did not want speeches. We did not want to talk to any news reporters. We simply wanted a clean bed to rest our weary bodies. I wasn't alone in this desire. One woman fainted coming down the ramp. We couldn't see where we were stepping between the fog and the spotlights set up with cameras flashing. My family in Missouri witnessed live coverage of our getting off the plane in a daze.

Inexplicably, we were bussed across the metropolitan area to a hotel in Bethesda, Maryland. Again, the cameras were intrusive. By that time, I was so traumatized from our ordeal that I was unable to sign my name to pay the credit card charge for the room. The desk clerk was understanding and told me that I was the tenth person from among the evacuees who was unable to write their name. He said he trusted me to pay when I left. Only God knew when that would be! I needed to pull myself together before making decisions about our future.

My dear little girls had already attended two different schools that year, and I wasn't keen on making them adjust to a third school in mid-April. I called my folks but told them nothing significant. After a long night's sleep, the girls and I went out to search for a McDonald's; those arches in the sky still represent heaven to kids and adults living overseas. I will never forget that cold spring breeze. We did not have any sweaters and it was freezing. We trudged on to McDonald's nevertheless. I remember the tulips and daffodils in bloom. It was so beautiful after barren Khartoum.

Next day we went to visit Patty Ruiz de Gamboa and her kids. I made the decision to go to Missouri to wait out the evacuation after Patty talked a lot about the advantages of being close to family. She noticed my hands shaking and advised me to wait a few days before I went. It would not be fair to my mother to see me in that condition. I waited until I felt calmer.

Our evacuation was big news for about three days. Then a much bigger world event occurred—the nuclear plant explosion at Chernobyl, Ukraine. Our story suddenly was truly insignificant by comparison.

Eventually we went to Missouri and Jill and Angie joined us at my parents. Jenny and Juliana reenrolled in Holy Rosary School to finish the school year. I adored caring for my granddaughter. Dad and Mother were marvelously understanding about the invasion of their privacy. They were so supportive, and I am still so grateful.

Meanwhile, Joe spent six weeks working in the Kenya mission. In June, he was sent to Washington and the kids and I went to join him. The reunion only lasted two weeks before Joe was requested to return to the Sudan by the minister of finance. Joe was flattered but I was not happy about it. We bought a used station wagon from our friends and Joe drove us back to Missouri. We moved Gretchen to the University of Missouri branch in Kansas City as her fiancé Scott Merrill had been reassigned to a recruitment station in the area.

The rest of us all temporarily moved in with Joan while looking for quarters in Columbia, Missouri. I had decided to go back to college, and since the kids didn't want to stay in Monroe City indefinitely, we moved again. I rented a three-bedroom condo, which was so crowded for the eight of us. And across the world were Joe and the dog in a seven-bedroom house. Not exactly equitable! Joan and our son Joe moved back home after being on their own for five to six years. That was hard on them I realize.

Joan slept on the sofa in the living room. I sat up an office in the garage, which had no heat, so my studying was in brief segments. Joe, being the only male, had to occupy one of the bedrooms. The master bedroom housed me, Juliana, Jill, and Angie. Jenny and Gretchen shared the third bedroom.

By midsummer, Gretchen and Scott announced their engagement. Their wedding date was set and changed several times. Gretchen was determined to have her father walk her down the aisle and his return kept changing as he was acting director. All his family wanted was for him to come home safely.

On an unusually hot fall day, September 27, 1986, Joe proudly escorted his beautiful daughter, Gretchen, down the aisle of St. Stephen's church and entrusted her into the hands of handsome Sgt. Scott A. Merrill, resplendent and sweltering in his marine "dress blues" wool uniform.

In December 1986, we moved to a five-bedroom condo, which we had purchased in Village South in Columbia, Missouri. That was much nicer to have space. Joe returned to Columbia the night before I took my final accounting exam. All the family were together for Angie's first Christmas. Scott gave Gretchen a diamond ring and she cried with joyful surprise. Joe left for the Sudan on New Year's Eve.

The following month Joe was named the deputy director in Zaire, which meant he had to return to study French at the Foreign Service Institute in Virginia.

The children remained in the condo, so they would not have to change schools again. I drove from Missouri to Virginia accompanied by Aunt Kathleen and we met Joe on February 7. We were readjusting to life together when my father had an aneurysm break between his heart and stomach. I flew to St. Louis on February 22 and was met by my dear cousins, Roy and Anne Schurwan, and driven to the hospital in Hannibal where dad had just barely survived six hours of surgery. His surgeon, Dr. Burton, had warned my mother and brothers that dad's chance of making it through that surgery was only 10 percent. I did not recognize my father. Apprehensively, I approached his tube-filled body, and Mother insisted I speak to him even though he seemed unconscious. I whispered for him to hang in there, so we could celebrate their fiftieth wedding anniversary (later that year). I gingerly took Dad's hand, he squeezed mine, and a tear rolled down his cheek and I knew he was aware of my presence. I spent the next three weeks with my family at dad's bedside in Intensive Care.

The day Dad was moved to a private room, four of our kids and I drove back to Washington to visit their father for a week during their spring break from school.

It was very hard to leave Joe again, but I had to take the kids back to school. Jill and I took turns driving while the others slept on a mattress in the station wagon and we made the trip to Columbia in a record eighteen hours straight. Just one week later, I flew back to rejoin Joe in Virginia and I began my French training. We spent a lot on plane fares and road trips during that difficult period. Juliana was only nine at the time, but she became very independent. She and Jenny did well in school despite not having a parent there to prod them. Of course, there were lots of telephone calls and disputes to settle long distance. Big brother Joe was resented by the girls for being overly protective because he was trying hard to take the place of both parents. Jill was on a roller coaster as a new young mother. It was not an easy time for any of us! Joe and I were also coping with our own feelings about the evacuation, the subsequent separation, and trying to shed the extra thirty pounds that each of us gained while we were so unhappily living apart. We exercised daily after our intensive days in French classes at the Foreign Service Institute and managed to drop twenty-five pounds each that summer.

At the beginning of our reunion, Joe and I attended a marriage encounter weekend and learned not to be afraid to express our feelings. I discovered that Joe had felt "abandoned" after the evacuation and Joe learned how much I had "resented" being forced to be a single parent. We both realized that neither one was to blame for our situation. However, it helped to be able to admit our feelings and to accept one another's feelings for their value. We started over. When we renewed our marriage vows at the end of that weekend, it was the most touching moment of our lives! Much deeper, richer, mature, and more meaningful than the first time we entered blindly into married life.

Fear of political upheavals and terrorists acts still hang over my head, but I feel I am stronger, more courageous, and the master of my fears if not my fate.

CHAPTER 16

In the Midst of Gorillas

Happiness lies in the joy of achievement
and the thrill of creative effort.
—Franklin Roosevelt

The day we were leaving Missouri to drive to Washington, DC, before flying out to Zaire, our second granddaughter was born. Jennifer Linn Merrill made her debut on September 24, 1987, and our family were thrilled to visit the new baby in the hospital in Kansas City before going back abroad.

Joe had passed his French proficiency exam at the Foreign Service Institute in Northern Virginia in August and the USAID/Kinshasa mission was anxious for him to arrive at post. Moreover, the school year had begun at the American School of Kinshasa (TASOK) and the girls needed to catch up. We had been delayed by the wait for medical clearance. The silver lining is that delay allowed Joe to meet his granddaughter Jennifer.

Joe, Jill, Jenny, Juliana, and our granddaughter, Angie, departed for Kinshasa, Zaire. I stayed behind to help Gretchen and Scott with their newborn and then attended my parents fiftieth wedding anniversary on October 13, 1987.

Three years of living in Kinshasa, Zaire, passed so quickly because we were so busy. Joe worked very hard as deputy director while I accomplished the enormous task of computerizing fifteen years' worth of USAID financial records while installing the MACS system. It makes me sad to realize that all our work went down the drain when the USAID mission closed within a year after we left. Actually, the political situation was always tense, and we expected it to blow up long before it actually happened. Some of our best friends were evacuated following terrible riots when the pot boiled over. President Mobutu's reputation for corruption and decadence is well deserved. Meanwhile, the good people of Zaire continued to suffer at his expense. Greed is a terrible evil.

Chaos and poverty were the only certainties that the majority of Zairians ever knew under the harsh Mobutu dictatorship. We truly tried to ease their burdens, despite the obstacles. It was a crazy economy. Government-owned Mercedes lined the wide boulevards. French foods were stocked on the shelves. People drove too fast and terrible accidents occurred within the city limits. Traffic jams were exhausting. The city police force called *gendarmes* was notorious for shaking down people. Gangs of thieves roamed the streets. It was wild when we lived there but I understand that was tame compared to the situation after we left. I received letters from former Zairian colleagues who related the desperation of their lives. I think of them often and pray for their good health.

When we arrived in Kinshasa, the physical infrastructure in the country had deteriorated badly. The road infrastructure was so bad that travel by road to project sites was often impossible. Nor was there reliable air transport between cities. As a consequence, USAID was forced to charter small planes in order to visit project sites. This could be dangerous as the planes did not have GPS technology and pilots had to fly low enough to use visual landmarks to reach final destinations. At times pilots would attempt to use short cuts, and that could be dangerous. One such incident occurred when a pilot was flying four USAID staff from Lubumbashi in southeast Zaire to Kinshasa a distance of over 1,500 miles. The pilot, instead of following the rail line to his next geographic marker, tried a short cut by which he could save time. Unfortunately, the pilot ran into cloud cover and missed his marker and became lost. The mission was notified that the plane was missing. Joe and the director spent two anxious hours waiting for word. Finally, just as they were going to notify the spouses of the USAID staff that they were missing, word was received that they were safe. They were lucky! The pilot was lost, ran out of gas, but was lucky to find an open field in which to land. The passengers started walking, and came upon a missionary station that had a short-wave radio which they used to inform our Lubumbashi office that they were safe. These were some of the risks we encountered while working in Zaire.

Driving within the city was not easy either. We have never seen larger or deeper potholes in any country. I witnessed a pedestrian get killed by a car swerving to miss a pothole. It was awful.

We were accompanied to post by our granddaughter, Angie, and three youngest daughters. We will always cherish the years we spent with Angie in Zaire.

Being first-time grandparents was an undertaking for which we were ill-prepared. Having our delightful granddaughter living at post provided a new twist to our lives. However, it could not have been a better encounter. Angie charmed the community as well as her Mamaw and Pawpaw, as she nicknamed us.

From the time she was born, we all spoke to Angie as if she were an adult which might explain why she went through a rather precocious period. We were often astounded by her adult like declarations. One Sunday afternoon we were enjoying a Texas barbecue at the home of our friends Ron and Vivian Harvey. Ron jokingly offered four-year-old Angie a Primus beer. She took a look at the bottle of Zairian brew and said, "No thanks, Grandpa and I only drink Heineken." Embarrassed, Grandpa Goodwin explained that when he was barbecuing, he let Angie sample his beer in a shot glass so she would know it tasted bitter and not be curious about it. To our surprise she had liked the taste and would ask Pawpaw for a sip sometimes when her mother was not looking.

Our beautiful hillside home had a swimming pool and the expansive arched balcony provided a magnificent view of the Congo River, down which we took several pleasant cruises.

Many Sundays in Kinshasa were spent with the girls and often their friends and ours having a late brunch or a barbecue on our big balcony, followed by a relaxing swim in our "water reservoir," as it was classified by USAID. In fact, that was an appropriate designation. Frequently we did not have electricity or water, so the toilets were flushed with chlorinated water from the pool.

Zaire and Rwanda had become famous for the mountain gorillas after the filming of "Gorillas in the Mist." Joe and Jill realized the dream of being in the midst of gorillas. Fast forward to 2013 and I was able to experience the gorillas in Rwanda with Joe and Gretchen. Both experiences were surreal.

As a Christmas present, I gave Joe a trip to Goma in eastern Zaire to visit the mountain gorillas along with Jill who paid her own way. It was not an inexpensive adventure, but both claim it was worth it. I had planned to go also but my job and caring for the girls kept me from accompanying them. Good friends Bill Anderson and Kate Delaney joined the expedition even though they had not seen the gorillas on a previous visit to Goma. Their group of six trudged through the dense jungle four hours with an armed guide tracking the gorilla spore. Suddenly, a loud snort gave a warning signal. They spotted a big silverback male who had heard their approach. He was surrounded by a number of other gorillas, members of his family. The tourists froze in their tracks, not daring to speak or move. Mesmerized, they were privileged to watch the activity of those wondrous creatures from a very close distance for about ninety minutes before the guide signaled for them to retreat. Not having enough, they returned to the mountains a second day and were again successful in locating a larger group of gorillas. Being in the midst of powerful gorillas was a humbling and unique bonding moment for Joe to share with his daughter.

Jill remained with us for two years after graduation so that she could work and earn money to provide furniture and things that she and Angie would need when Jill started college. We are grateful for having shared that time and space. Angie did not realize what a good life she had until they moved back to the United States. Jill related how Angie went crazy the first time she took her to Toys R Us. She wanted Jill to buy everything she saw. Jill said she could not do that because she was poor. Disappointed, Angie told her mother, "I don't like being poor. Let's go back to live with Pawpaw and Mamaw." The other change which was tough for Angie was adjusting to life without her beloved nanny Dionga. When Jill fussed with Angie to be more helpful, Angie suggested that they hire a maid. Jill explained that they could not afford a maid. Angie thought for a minute and said, "I've got an idea—why don't you be my maid?" The humor escaped Jill.

Joe was named the Country Director for Ghana effective in September 1990. Ghana was the country of our first posting in 1971. We were excited as we had loved Ghana and the Ghanaians, and we looked forward to returning as the director of the USAID/Ghana program. The name Zaire no longer exists as the country is now called the Democratic Republic of the Congo, or DROC for short.

CHAPTER 17

Return to Ghana 1990–1994

In September 1990, Joe, Jenny, Juliana, and I arrived in Accra, Ghana, to begin our new assignment. We stopped in Paris on the way to visit with my sister Alice and her husband, Joel, who were engineers with Michelin Tires at their headquarters in Clermont-Ferrand in central France. We arrived in Paris on September 1, the end of the August vacation period in France. When we arrived at the Charles de Gaulle Airport, there was complete pandemonium as thousands of people were returning to Paris from vacation. That situation compounded the problem we faced in obtaining our luggage and clearing immigration. We planned to stay in Paris for several days, so we had to claim all our luggage. Since we did not expect the majority of our clothes to arrive in Accra for several months, we had brought two (overweight) suitcases each. There was a shortage of luggage carriers. After finally securing a cart, we then had to wait for over an hour in line at immigration. In the end, after more than three hours, we emerged from the airport just as my sister and her husband were preparing to leave, thinking we had missed our flight. Once outside the airport terminal, our next problem was finding a taxi. Given the large number of arriving passengers, the waiting line for a taxi stretched around the terminal. It took another hour of waiting before we were able to get two taxis and go into Paris. Once in the city, we had a wonderful time as Alice and Joel were terrific tour guides and took us to all the highlights.

On September 4, we departed Paris and arrived in Accra in late afternoon. We were taken to the residence of the mission director where the resident cook had a meal prepared. The USAID director's residence was at the same location as it was during our first tour in the 1970s. It was a large old home with a screened in porch overlooking a couple acres and beautiful old trees.

Our first week was bittersweet. Juliana entered eight grade at Lincoln Community School, but there was no American high school in Accra. Jenny was a senior in high school and had to leave for boarding school at the American School in Switzerland (TASIS) alone. That was a difficult situation for everyone.

Ghana had undergone a number of changes since our departure in 1974. The military coup in 1972 had overthrown the civilian government. The period of military rule was a period of economic mismanagement that severely damaged the Ghanaian economy. Corruption and economic mismanagement combined with an overvalued exchange rate had resulted in a destruction of the export sector. Ghanaian cocoa exports were the principal foreign exchange earner, which had been over 400,000 tons per year in the early 1970s had fallen to around 160,000 by 1980. As a consequence, a military coup led by Flight Lieutenant Jerry Rawlings in 1979 overthrew the existing military government with a promise to restore civilian rule.

The elections were held in June 1979, but the civilian government lost credibility and on December 31, 1981, FL Jerry Rawlings again assumed power. Initially the new government approached the Soviet Union for support, but the request was met with a recommendation that the government instead approach the International Monetary Fund (IMF) for support. After some delay the IMF was approached and an agreement was negotiated and signed that included a number of policy reforms. Many doubted that the government would stick to the agreement, but it did. By the time we arrived in September 1990, Ghana had established a reputation as a leader in economic reform in sub-Sahara Africa. In response, the United States and other major donors increased their financial support.

When we arrived, USAID was still a smaller program with a small staff. However, with support from Washington the program and staffing increased. USAID/Ghana became a leader in promoting private sector development and was instrumental in encouraging a more outward growth strategy focused on increasing exports, especially nontraditional exports. To accomplish this noble cause Joe and I worked tirelessly in hosting lunches and dinners where public and private sector leaders were brought together to form a Team Ghana concept. At the same time, I was employed by USAID as senior project accountant in the Office of the Controller and for a year as a financial analyst in the Health and Population Office.

I am very proud of the accomplishments of the USAID/Ghana team on which I was a member while Joe was the respected mission director. Joe managed growth of the mission's portfolio from annual program budget of $10 million to over $60 million during that four-year period. The principal achievements related to economic policy and private sector growth included:

- Design and implementation of $80 million Trade and Investment Program that supported growth of nontraditional exports from $62 million in 1992 to $400 million by 2000. It has continued to have a positive domino effect on the entire country.

- Supported creation of following private organizations to promote private sector led growth and public/private sector dialogue: Private Enterprise Foundation-Apex organization unifying principal private sector organizations for conducting policy dialogue with Government; Federation of Associations of Ghanaian Exporters, organizing individual export crop associations into a Federation to address common policy and program issues for the export sector; Center for Economic Policy Analysis, an economic think-tank staffed by Ghanaian economists to conduct policy related research for public and private sector.

- Created a sustainable donor luncheon group where principal donor organizations meet monthly to review developments in Ghana and share information on programmatic and policy concerns.

- Negotiated approval with AID/Washington for creation of endowments to provide core financial support for creation of three organizations: Center for Economic Policy Analysis, an independent economic think-tank; Ghana Social Marketing Foundation, an NGO that provides leadership in addressing family planning and HIV/AIDS issues in Ghana; and Ghana Heritage Conservation Trust, an NGO responsible for preservation of historical monuments such as Elmina Castle and nature conservation like the Kakum National Park where Joe suggested the canopy walkway be built over the rain forest. This successful tourist attraction continues to provide needed revenue for Ghana. Until one loses a family member through despair, it is impossible to understand how such tragedies affect a family. My oldest nephew Joseph Paul Gander died at age thirty-three on Good Friday, April 9, 1993. My niece Teresa wrote this poem on the first anniversary of our sadness while we were working in Ghana.

A Yellow Ribbon
By Teresa Gander Hettinger, April 1994

I've avoided thinking about today.
It's been a year since you passed away.
My heart aches, as I still ask why.
You were taken from us, too young to die.
Your birthday came, and we sang to you.
We brought balloons and a yellow ribbon too.
"I love you," Leah wrote in the snow.
As she cried, "Mom, I want my Uncle Joe."
I wish I could just talk again to you.
Do you see how much the kids grew?
Most everything around here has really changed
Some cherished memories we hold, they remain.
You were with us just a brief year ago.
Before the angels called, we were whole.
If I could, I'd tie a yellow ribbon to every star.
So you would know our love isn't very far.
Every time it rains, I know the angels care
I place my trust in God and I say a prayer
May God bless this family saddened with pain
Through His grace, our tears are not cried in vain.

Ending this chapter on a happier note, I will share our daughter's poem.

My Papa's Cocktail Parties
By Juliana L. Goodwin (Age Thirteen)

From underneath the table I would peek out,
to see what adulthood was all about.
I saw actors with plagiarized smiles and perfect hair
and preconceived laughter that danced in the air.
My papa's cocktail parties were always precise;
his guests regarded everything as "lovely" or "nice."
No one got wild or had too much to drink.
It was a time to relax but to cautiously think.
A time to play the role of society's best,
with expensive handshakes, they hoped to pass the test.
Falsely they regarded each other with the utmost respect
and no one dare say anything that wasn't politically correct.
Men always drank whiskey while women sipped wine.
In the eyes of a child hiding, the scenery was divine.
But it didn't take long before I recognized their game
and realized my father's guests always acted the same.
Yes, I remember the cocktail parties where I soon found out
I'd be a child forever, if that's what adulthood was about

CHAPTER 18

Peace Corps Family

*It is one of the most beautiful compensations of this life
that no man can sincerely try to help
another without helping himself.*
—Ralph Waldo Emerson

Peace Corps volunteers provide the greatest humanitarian service and the best value for taxpayer dollars in my opinion. Joe and I had planned to join the Peace Corps after college. Our ideological dream to serve as PCVs was postponed due to having kids but we have never lost interest in that terrific program.

Since we could not become volunteers, the next best thing has been to befriend volunteers. It has been our practice abroad to volunteer our home as a place of refuge for many volunteers over the years. The benefits that we have derived from becoming friends, substitute parents, and mentors of PCVs are enormous.

Emerson's quotation above fits the bill for this subject. Peace Corps volunteers substantially benefit from their many sacrifices to help the less fortunate. Our family has been highly compensated by our efforts to help make their jobs easier and their lives less difficult. We have extended our large family and gained lifetime friends of whom we are exceedingly proud.

The most productive and fun group of volunteers we have ever met arrived in Ghana the summer of 1992. However, at that stage of our career, we were so heavily involved in the design of the $80 million Trade and Investment Program for Ghana that we had little time to devote to PCVs or other interests.

Credit belongs to our son, Joe II, for diverting our attention back to meeting the needs of PCVs. Joe, then almost twenty-seven, came to visit us in Ghana that fall, interviewed for a position as manager of the American Club, and was selected the day before his scheduled departure. We were delighted to have him stay longer in Ghana as he had left home for boarding school at age fifteen, and we always felt cheated by the lost opportunities to share good times. It was a fantastic opportunity to become acquainted on an adult level. He also made us proud with his professional performance. Joe was named as the Outstanding Manager of the Year for all American Embassy recreation associations worldwide. He was also runner-up for the coveted award after his first year on the job, which suits his friendly personality. Our son inherited my sensitivity and his father's sense of humor, a nice combination.

One morning shortly after he arrived, I found Joe singing away in the kitchen as he cooked his breakfast. Not being an early morning person, I asked what made him so chipper. "Mom, I met two girls with the most beautiful smiles in the world at a bar last night" were his exact words. He was referring to two beautiful Peace Corps volunteers from South Dakota, Renae Adam and Christie Harter, who were later assigned to our family for a "home stay" during the Christmas holiday. That marked the beginning of lasting relationships. Through Renae and Christie, we soon became acquainted with their fellow PCV friends, including two fantastic Minnesota volunteers, Kristin Johnson and Karol Kosec; charming Lora Baker from Ohio and her fiancé, Dave Dixon; handsome and funny Tony Malay from Chicago; sweet and thoughtful Noel DesMarteau from South Carolina; easygoing Doug Schuster from New York; Sharon Malone, who grew up in Papua New Guinea; and adventuresome Dave Brown.

I found myself delighting in playing the part of mother hen to these six adopted daughters and five new sons. It may sound strange for me to refer to all of them as my friends, considering the age difference, but that is exactly how I view all of them. In fact, I received letters from most of these great young adults more frequently than I did from my own flesh and blood who also complained about my lack of letters after they left home.

My own mother faithfully wrote to us weekly despite my being an infrequent respondent. Only a mother's love could keep her from giving up on me as the daughter who seldom writes home. When we first moved abroad, I wrote long descriptive letters about the country and events. I am not certain what made me stop those epistles. There were many times I did not want to worry my parents about the dangers of being abroad, so I avoided writing. My biggest regret is never keeping a diary. Joe encouraged me to do so. Writing this book would have been easier with the aid of a diary rather than my fading memories. Mother kept all my letters tied up with yellow ribbons by year. These would have been a good resource if they had been available to me when I started this book.

My memories of the wonderful times we shared with our Peace Corps family, especially in Ghana, have not dimmed with time. I have a box filled with treasures from our association with them. It contains beautiful poems, songs, homemade cards, which are great pieces of artwork and creativity, and thank you letters written by all of them and their parents. Included in this chapter is their own rendition of "Kisses Sweeter than Wine," which they knew was our favorite Jimmie Rogers song when we were dating. In honor of our thirtieth wedding anniversary, Renae Adam, Kristin Johnson, Christie Harter, and Karol Kosec made up new lyrics and performed a dance routine to the tune of "Kisses Sweeter than Wine." It was hilarious, thoughtful, and very touching. Their cute performance remains one of my favorite home videos. These clever ladies made another video for us as a joke which reflected how much they appreciated having a hot shower and American food whenever they were in Accra. All our family relished their visits and we also visited their sites to offer encouragement.

Each and every one of "our kids" accomplished a great deal in Ghana. Most notably, Renae and Kristin cofounded Women in Progress, which later become known as Global Mamas, and is hugely successful. They have devoted their lives to the work of helping woman help themselves and their families.

It was difficult for our son that we left the country at about the same time that the PCV tours ended. Only Kristin extended an extra year. That was ironic, considering she was voted the least likely to finish her Peace Corps tour after she showed up at staging with the most luggage of all the PCVs. We reunited with Kristen when she visited us in Cambodia while she did a semester in Thailand.

The attitudes and ethics of our offspring and of our wonderful PCV family give me great hope for the future of our world. With leaders like them, peace and justice will come.

MOM
By Joe B. Goodwin II
Written by my son in honor of Mother's Day 1992

Mom, your soul is as pure as a white dove
You amaze me with your unconditional love
I take pen in hand to salute you
For who you are and the things you do
If life is one long test
You get an A because you're the best!
When I'm down, you give me that maternal smile
That gives me the courage to go that extra mile
I hope that these words will let you know
That your presence is with me wherever I go.
I think that my best traits you've endowed,
So to call you Mom makes me proud.
I am ashamed that I don't write when we are apart,
It doesn't mean that I don't love you with all my heart.

Kisses Sweeter than Wine
Rendition composed and performed by
Renae Adam, Christi Harter, Kristin Johnson, and Karol Kosec

When I was a young girl as a PCV,
I had to think it over; how lonely it could be.
So I got me a family and they took me in,
And I kept coming back, again and again.
**Because they had kisses sweeter than wine. Oh, oh, kisses sweeter
than wine.**
Well they asked us to move in and make ourselves at home.
So we brought our dirty laundry and used the telephone.
With a fridge full of food and time on our hands,
Oops, oh Lordy, we're busted again.
**Because they had kisses sweeter than wine. Oh, oh, kisses sweeter
than wine.**
Well we worked really hard to do well at our sites.

We had classes to teach; digging wells really bites.
We tried, and we tried to be good PCV kin,
But oops, oh, Lordy, we're back at the Goodwin's again.
**Because they had kisses sweeter than wine. Oh, oh, kisses sweeter
than wine.**
Now that we're old, looking back on our time,
The laughs at the Goodwin's were really divine.
I never can replace that special family,
'Cuz, oops, oh, Lordy, they meant so much to me.
**Because they had kisses sweeter than wine. Oh, oh, kisses sweeter
than wine.**

CHAPTER 19

Our Thirtieth Anniversary

One man has enthusiasm for 30
minutes, another for 30 days,
but it is the man who has it for 30 years
who makes a success of his life.
—Edward B. Butler

Achieving our thirtieth wedding anniversary seemed like a big mile-stone. Since the same day also marked a half-century of my life, Joe and I decided to really celebrate in style. We took a fantastic and romantic Greek cruise and visited Turkey. It was a dream come true for both of us.

Before we left Ghana for Athens, our son arranged a lovely birthday luncheon for me at the American Club. What we did not know was that he was also scheming with the deputy director, Dawn Liberi, to cohost a surprise party to celebrate our anniversary on our return. Actually, we were so unsuspecting that we almost missed the party in our honor. Joe had come down with a fever that day and asked me to attend what he thought was a business dinner alone. But Juliana insisted that would be rude and that he should at least go for a drink. Reluctantly, he got out of bed. What a great surprise and shock when we walked in the door at Dawn's house! She had removed the furniture and decorated the house with balloons and streamers, creating a festive atmosphere. The congratulatory messages of our friends were very touching. One colleague, Gordon Kunde wrote a beautiful poem which was a terrific tribute for us. The food, which our son had prepared, was fabulous. We danced half the night and Joe ignored his fever.

Another fabulous thirtieth anniversary party was hosted by Peter and Teetee Weisel and Cleveland Thomas to which many of our Ghanaian friends came to share our joy. A banquet of delicious Ghanaian food was impressively served in black pots. They hired a live band who had terrific musicians. We were entertained by a troupe of Ghanaian dancers. The huge cakes were gorgeous. We had a ball. Cleveland gave a humorous speech and was a suave master of ceremonies. I offered the following vote of thanks, as ending speeches are called in Ghana:

> I am not very experienced at public speaking but since you have all had many opportunities to listen to Joe give speeches, on this very special and happy occasion I have asked for the privilege of offering the Vote of Thanks.
>
> First, saying mere words of thanks to our hosts Peter, Teetee, and Cleveland, seem inadequate to express our deepest appreciation for their thoughtfulness in giving this lovely party. Joe and I are deeply touched and grateful for their efforts on our behalf. We love them and thank them from the bottom of our hearts.
>
> Second, distinguished ladies and gentlemen, we feel extremely honored by the presence of each one of you who have gathered here tonight. Thank you very much for coming to help us celebrate your friendships which have made our lives in Ghana so wonderful.
>
> I am uncertain whether in the Ghanaian tradition it is the custom to make such a big deal of a thirtieth wedding anniversary. But it is sad to think that long-term loving relationships are unfortunately becoming rare. I would like to thank my own parents for setting such a good example for us. My parents have just returned from a trip celebrating their fifty-sixth anniversary and in all those years they have never once missed taking a trip to honor their love, to renew

their commitment to the sacrament of marriage. Our parents taught us that marriage is the longest, and the most challenging and important career two people can share. Happily, I chose wisely!

Next I would like to thank our six children and our two granddaughters for the enrichment and joy which they have brought into our lives. Often when paying the debts caused by raising a large family, Joe and I have asked ourselves why we took literally the blessing to "go forth and multiply." But the rewards have been tremendous while the many crises created by our children have only served to strengthen our unity.

Last, but certainly not least, I would like to thank you, Joe, my dear husband who is not only my partner, my roommate for life, but also my lover and my best friend! I thank you for your devotion to our children and myself. Life with you these past thirty-three years since we first fell in love can only be described as an adventure. Having the same goal of trying to make a small difference in the world was our first attraction to one another. Actually, our love for all the wonderful people of Ghana is a reflection of our love for one another as we share a vision. Joe, I am proud to live and work by your side. You may not resemble the same eighteen-year-old farm laborer who won my heart, but in my eyes you will never age.

I realize that I no longer look like the seventeen-year-old girl who was determined to be a missionary nun when we met. But I hope that I have maintained a missionary spirit. Thank you for making the commitment to a continued exciting lifetime of shared experiences.

Joe, you are what makes the good times memorable and the bad times bearable. Thank you, my dear Joe.

Happily, the good times far outnumber the bad times. What marvelous memories we have made together.

CHAPTER 20

Timbuktu or Bust

In November 1993, our son, Joe, and Renae Adam, a friend of the family who was a Peace Corps volunteer in Ghana, took an adventuresome and rather dangerous three-thousand-kilometer trip from Accra, Ghana, to Timbuktu, Mali, in a tiny Tico car.

Despite the fears for Renae's safety which we shared with her parents, Renae rode her bicycle across Africa for six months upon finishing her Peace Corps stint in Ghana. Not surprisingly, Renae not only achieved her goals but she also met her fun-loving husband, Dave, while visiting Zanzibar where he was a PCV also.

The following Mali trip had whetted Renae's appetite for high excitement.

Joe and Renae arrived back from their twenty-day drive through West Africa with the wild tales of adventure and intrigue. I only wish that we had recorded the recanting of their saga, which kept us mesmerized for two hours as they related their experiences, both horrible and humorous.

That night I lost sleep as it sank in that we came so close to losing our son and felt guilty that I had not worried more while they were gone. Actually, I had made a supreme effort to minimize worry because Renae had chided me for being overly concerned about my kids. Joe said that during their tense moments Renae would say, "Your mother should be worried now." They would laugh and that would relieve the pressure.

They did achieve their two main goals which were (1) to visit Dogon country in Mali (which ranked as the highlight of cultural experiences) and (2) reach and explore Timbuktu (which was a tremendous disappointment to them).

Joe and Renae were hassled everywhere they went, partly because they didn't speak French, and shelled out a fortune in bribes to get through the roadblocks even though their papers were in order. At one point, in Dogon country, they walked fifty kilometers through the desert sand, ran out of water, and thought they would die of dehydration. Fever, chills, and diarrhea followed.

But the worst was yet to come. Joe drove for eleven hours one day from Mopti to Gao, through a tribal war zone without realizing that crossing this area without a military escort was not permitted. They saw two truckloads of rebels on the way who seemed very surprised by the sight of Joe and Renae in such a tiny car, but they were not bothered by them.

Upon reaching Gao they were fined a large sum for having driven alone and told that they would have to wait there for three days before they would be allowed to continue their journey with the next military escort to Niamey, Niger.

In Gao, they were shown newspaper articles about the tourists who had been murdered by the Tuareg warriors who were in revolt. It was very sobering, and even though they described Gao, Mali, as a "hellhole," they wisely decided to wait for the military convoy. It was a long, hot, miserable three days of waiting and sleeping on a hot parking lot in the desert.

When the caravan gathered, the truck drivers decided that Joe's little car (which is the Korean equivalent of a Geo Metro) could not possibly make the trip to Niamey, Niger. There was no highway to Niamey, only tracks through the desert sand. However, not wanting to spend another moment in Gao and not wanting to backtrack, they took off with the convoy. They quickly became stuck in the sand, were pushed out, and became stuck again and again. The caravan continued on without waiting for Joe and Renae. Joe and Renae continued but had a number of times that they were stuck in the sand and had to dig the car out. Once after digging out the car yet again and realizing they had been abandoned they were frightened by the headlights of a truck that seemed to be in pursuit. Thinking that it could be a band of rebels, Joe drove as fast as the Tico would go, but the headlights steadily approached closer. Much to their relief, it was a military truck who then accompanied them until they caught up with the convoy that night. Because of the activities of the rebels the convoy did not travel at night but stopped on the way to Niamey until daylight.

That night at the convoy stop, Joe and Renae met a Ghanaian who was a mechanic on one of the trucks going to Niamey. He suggested that Joe empty all the contents from his car to make it lighter and put them and Renae on the back of one of the trucks, while he and Joe would take a shortcut through the desert. Joe agreed and that proved to be a wise choice. Although Joe was hesitant to leave Renae with strangers it was fortunate for her that he did as she was spared the frightening experience which awaited Joe further across the desert.

Taking a route separate from the one followed by the convoy, Joe and his new Ghanaian friend started for Niamey. They crossed numerous dry riverbeds and trudged along for several hours, getting stuck only occasionally. Suddenly, as they came over a sand dune and landed in a dry riverbed, Joe found himself smack in the middle of the camp of rebel Tuareg warriors. The Tuareg let out a bloodcurdling scream, grabbed their AK-47 automatic weapons, and charged toward the car, which Joe realized was stuck in the sand. Joe quickly counted 15 men around the car. Although he could not speak their language, their weapons and gestures spoke for them. The dark-skinned self-appointed guide with Joe turned white and admitted he only knew a few words of Tuareg. Using those words and what French he knew the guy pleaded for their lives and told the Tuareg that Joe's traveling companion was with the caravan, that she would report Joe missing and that the military would come back and wipe out the rebels if they killed them.

After much bantering, the rebels said they did not shed blood on Fridays, so they would let them go unharmed. Joe and his guide managed to talk the rebels into helping dig the car out of the sand, which they did, but immediately surrounded the car again demanding cigarettes. Joe obliged and when the rebels started fighting over the cigarettes, Joe took the chance to make an escape although he anticipated they would open fire. Praise be Allah, they did not. Joe and his guide made it to the border ahead of the convoy and were waiting to greet them when they arrived. The trip from the border into Niamey, the capital of Niger, was uneventful. As a result, those same drivers who had ridiculed the little car now wanted to buy it. The drivers raved about how brave Joe had been. Foolish seemed like a more appropriate word to his parents.

Tragically, just one week after Joe and Renae crossed the Mali-Niger border, a land mine planted by the Tuareg exploded killing several Italian tourists.

"God is good, God is great!" is a slogan that can be found on signs all over Ghana. Let's just say that we had a great deal for which we were thankful that Thanksgiving day. We were especially grateful that our son and our friend were alive and safely home.

It had been our tradition every year to host the American community for Thanksgiving dinner. That year the large numbers anticipated seemed overwhelming to me personally, so I passed the baton to our son who put on a marvelous Thanksgiving feast at the American club where he was manager. Joe served 182 people with such grace and ease that both amazed me and made me proud. Everyone had a wonderful time playing games watching football or the Macy's parade or just getting acquainted. The food tasted almost as good as if it came from Mom's kitchen, and in fact, he even used my mother's recipe for dressing. Thus, a new tradition began.

It was the first time I enjoyed Thanksgiving in many years because I did not have to do anything but buy tickets and relish the compliments, which our son received for a big job well done. Raising kids is a daunting task but the reward comes at times like those. Joe and I are very proud of all our offspring and think they are very good world citizens.

CHAPTER 21

Honorary Law Degree

The following excerpts were taken from the acceptance speech delivered by my husband before an audience of seven thousand people at the University of Ghana graduation ceremony on March 19, 1994, on the occasion of being conferred an honorary doctorate of laws degree. It was one of the proudest moments of our lives abroad.

> Honorable President of Ghana, Mr. Chairman, distinguished faculty, Nananu, members of the diplomatic corps, graduands, ladies and gentlemen . . .
> It is an enormous privilege to be at the University of Ghana receiving the great honorary degree of doctor of laws today. I humbly accept this overwhelming honor on behalf of myself and my very distinguished fellow recipients . . . My family and I will treasure and cherish this honor forever. Ghana will always be a special country because Ghanaians and Ghana are such a special people and place . . .
> It was Ghana in 1957 that lit the lamp of freedom for sub-Saharan Africa and paved the way for the fight for freedom and independence, a fight which is coming to a close with the first independent multiracial elections in South Africa next month.
> Today Ghana is still providing leadership in Africa, this time on the economic front. Ghana's record of economic growth since 1985 is the envy

of many nations, not just within Africa. Ghana has shown that sustained economic growth is possible in Africa. It is leading the way in the development of a public and private sector cooperation and collaboration strategy necessary to continue the growth process. . . .

It is you, the graduates of the class of 1994 that are the leaders of tomorrow . . . Please accept my challenge to go forth and make your wonderful country proud of your accomplishments.

Hope and Joe holding the diploma after Joe received honorary doctorate of laws degree from the University of Ghana in June 1994.

CHAPTER 22

Royal Enstoolment

It was a momentous occasion when royal status was bestowed upon us in Ghana, on June 25, 1994. On that magical day, Joe and I were deeply honored and greatly privileged to have become an honorary Development Chief and Queen Mother of Atiavi, a village of Ewe tribe, located in the Volta region on the eastern coast of Ghana. This fishing community of ten thousand people executed our ascension to the throne stool in the grandest, most glorious style imaginable. The event was instigated by the most prominent Atiavi citizen His Excellency Dan Abodakpi, deputy minister of trade and industry, with whom Joe had worked closely during four years of collaboration on changing trade policies.

We were thrilled to share the cultural experience of a lifetime with three of our kids, thirty-two friends, and all ten thousand smiling, friendly, and lovable citizens of Atiavi.

This is a difficult chapter for me to write because I still get a huge lump in my throat when I recall the unexpected honor. Words are inadequate to capture our feelings about the event that ranks highest in our memory bank. I have great respect for the tribal lineage and customs of West Africa, which are rich in history, tradition, and culture. I would love to describe the significance of every ritual performed and each piece of clothing we wore, but I could not do justice to the dignity of the throne. The reason for my lapse in information is that I was in a state of shock while being briefed of each action. It was an astonishing surprise to me when I was enstooled alongside of my husband.

In fact, I was horrified when a Queen Mother ordered me to take off all my clothes after Joe had been led away to be dressed and briefed on the seriousness of the occasion. I wondered what in the world was the fate of the wife of a chief? Why had no one warned me what my role would be? I was truly bewildered by her request to strip. Equally baffled by my resistance and look of panic, the Queen Mother asked the Peace Corps volunteer whose home we were visiting to translate. He asked why I appeared to not want to become a Queen Mother. What? Me a Queen Mother? Preposterous! Why had Joe not warned me? Later I learned that he only knew that I would be recognized but had not realized the extent. He had not even mentioned it for fear of bringing on a migraine. Joe knows how stress produces my awful headaches. In his attempt to spare me worry, it nearly caused heart failure on my part. My innocent reaction seems funny now.

I had not focused on the beautiful piece of handwoven kente cloth or the lovely antique trade bead necklaces laid out on the table. Obediently, I followed three women to an alcove with a cloth curtain for a door. Trustingly, I disrobed and allowed them to dress me. The first item wrapped around me was a heavy kente skirt. The ladies had difficulty getting it to stay on me and searched for a piece of string to secure the waist. I suggest that we used the strip of kente cloth that I had worn that day as a belt. They graciously accepted it even though the weave of the kente belt was a pattern of the Ashanti people. They took great pains to make certain that not a fragment of the Ashanti cloth was visible. Next came a delicate white eyelet blouse that was a bit too transparent for my taste. Heavy strands of beads were ceremoniously hung around my neck and matching bead bracelets tied onto my arm. A matching cape of kente cloth was draped over my left arm, and I was shown how to carry it regally. Another piece of kente was tied around my head. The grand finale was the royal slippers which were about twice the size of my feet. Ghanaians have a wonderful ability to laugh and we all burst out laughing at the sight of my small feet trying to clamp the thick leather strap between my toes. These had been specially made for me and were gilded with silver decorations worn by Queen Mothers. Wearing ordinary thongs was out of the question so alterations were made. A man came in with a hammer and renailed the toe piece. Satisfied, they all hugged me and gave me the traditional Ghanaian finger snapping handshake.

And when they had finished weaving their magic spell, I felt fit to be a queen!

By this time, Joe had also been dressed and crowned by a chief and the village elders. I was led to join him. We were seated onto blond wooden stools covered with gold satin brocade pillows. A lengthy explanation of what would occur that day was given to me and included instructions on how to act including how to wave the sword of authority. When Joe was told that he should not smile as chiefs should be serious and command respect, I knew we were in trouble. Both of us were grinning from ear to ear at that moment. They asked us to look sterner. Well, we tried to wipe those grins off our faces. Instead, we started to laugh aloud and the whole room joined us. Here we were breaking tradition before we were even sworn in.

Just when I thought the good people would realize their mistake and call off the enstoolment, we were asked to raise our hands for the swearing in ceremony. Suddenly, we were struck with awe and became very serious indeed. Tears came to my eyes as I repeated the promises we made to the people of Ghana. On Joe was bestowed the title of Togbi Godwin Atiavi I while I became known as Mama Atiavi I. Stoles of kente with these new titles woven into them were placed across one shoulder and attached at the opposite side. I could imagine how Miss America feels when she receives the stole, and this was far greater than any beauty contests.

A hushed crowd of about three hundred people had gathered silently outside the teacher's home waiting for our ceremony to end. When we appeared in the doorway, the drums began to beat, and everyone began to chant, cheer, and dance. I was overwhelmed by their warm smiles, their sense of dignity, and obvious pride. Joe was ushered to a palanquin and hoisted upon the shoulders of six men. The man assigned to the front right side was much taller than the other five, which created an imbalance and nearly caused Joe to tumble out backward. Again, we all laughed, and they sat the new Togbi back down on the ground to discuss this problem. He was a thin but obviously a strong man and wanted to be a bearer. After much chattering in Ewe with everyone shouting their opinions, it was resolved that the gentleman simply leaned backward to make himself shorter.

What back pain this must have caused but he carried Joe with grace. I was shown my place which was to walk directly in front of Joe's carriage. On one side, I was accompanied by the other Queen Mother who gripped my arm tightly. On the other side was a lady assigned to fan me the entire day. How her arm must have ached, but she refused to stop when I suggested that it was not necessary. She understood her role better than I did and she was very sweet but insistent. A lovely young schoolteacher named Ellen walked behind me to carry my possessions. Directly in front of me was a young girl wearing only a loincloth and cowry shell necklaces. She was in the midst of the puberty rites and her body was streaked with chalk. She carried a basket full of shells on her head which I was told symbolized wealth. Cowry shells had been used as currency in West Africa many years ago. I was struck by how regally this young woman walked with her head held high and no embarrassment whatsoever about being topless. It made me forget my self-consciousness about wearing the thin blouse. A young boy carried a large umbrella to provide shade for all of us. Two other fellows carried our stools on top of their heads.

We inched along a dirt path at a snail pace. Joe was waving his sword in the manner in which he was shown. But he could not obey the request not to smile. Actually, he was radiant, and the crowd responded warmly. I was smiling happily despite the pain caused by the sandals. Blisters appeared, and blood oozed from between four toes. So I was grateful that we were walking so slowly. Besides I was thoroughly enjoying the crowd. Their joy was contagious. Our numbers swelled until we reached the town square where ten thousand people were gathered.

While the community and visitors awaited our arrival, they were entertained by various dancers and drummers. Being short and surrounded by people, my children were not able to see me until I was seated on my stool under the umbrella with tanned animal skins under our feet. Our kids were surprised to see me wearing the robes of a Queen Mother and gave me a thumbs-up signal. I wished the rest of our family could have shared that moment.

The program which followed was very interesting. There was more entertainment, followed by speeches, including Joe's vote of

thanks speech and a presentation of gifts from the community association. We received a wooden map of Ghana, some statues, and a
staff or walking stick with our names engraved on it. Following those
ceremonies, we were escorted around the square and introduced four
times on each side of the square. Our escort would repeat our chiefly
names and present us to each group. We could not stop smiling and
I think we were forgiven by the crowd as they were so receptive as
we paid our respects. We curtsied and bowed to all the chiefs, which
had gathered from other regions. I admired the gold bracelets which
adorned their upper arms. Then we were allowed to sit with the
chiefs under the tent. Our stools had been moved to that area while
we were being introduced and placed in the front row. Sitting on the
tanned hide of an antelope in front of us was the topless young girl
who constantly wove her hands through the cowry shells.

Next pledges and donations from the crowd were solicited for
the village. When it came our turn, we had to dance across the square
to contribute to the basket. It is customary to announce the amount.
Pledges were made, and the funds were slated to go toward electrical
lines. We are delighted that Atiavi now has electricity.

Dancing and gaiety followed the collection of money. It was
then noon and the hot African sun baked the earth, but that did not
dampen the spirits of the people. I marvel at the stamina of people
whose diet is not as high in calories as our own. I was wilting from all
the excitement and the heat but reluctant for the wonderful moment
to end.

Our whole entourage was invited for a delicious lunch of traditional Ghanaian dishes at the home of Dan and Mary Abodakpi. The
setting provided great camaraderie among the Ghanaians and the
Americans who have always been such cordial partners and nations.
Bonds were strengthened as we passed a delightful afternoon. After
much hugging and sad farewells, we got into our vehicles to head for
Accra which is a two-hour trip. Lo and behold, we were escorted by
sirens screaming all the way through the village lined with people
waving fan palm leaves. Joe and I were deeply touched. We stopped
when we reached the main highway for one final embrace. Within
one month, we were scheduled to leave Ghana and we knew our

lives would never be the same. We later learned that a busload of our friends attending the enstoolment got bruised when the driver lost control in loose gravel and landed in a ditch. Everyone was exhausted but exhilarated from sharing our happiness with wonderful Ghanaians. We are forever grateful for such terrific friendships.

The newly crowned Togbi Godwin I with his
queen mother Mama Atiavi I surrounded by
citizens of Atiavi, Ghana in June 1994.

CHAPTER 23

Washington Assignment

*The future belongs to those who believe
in the beauty of their dream.*
—Eleanor Roosevelt

After witnessing the wedding of our daughter Angela Jill to Michael Sorensen on August 20, 1994, we headed to the Washington, DC, area.

Our assignment to Washington was one of the hardest, most foreign of all our postings for Joe. But after twenty-four years of working abroad, Washington decided it was time for us to come home and declined our request to stay a fifth year in Ghana. Joe accepted the position of director for Southern Africa Region, which sounded exciting. We loved the Africa Bureau and were interested in continuing our service in that area. However, the job turned out to be more paper pushing than policymaking. In Joe's opinion, too much time was spent contending with lobbyists and congressional concerns.

Thinking that we would be in Washington for at least three years, we purchased our dream home in Ashburn, Virginia. Located thirty-two miles from his State Department office, Joe left every morning at 6:00 a.m. and arrived home after 8:00 p.m. Days were long, but once he arrived home, he felt the drive was worth the effort. We bought furniture on weekends for two months. I reveled in fixing up our home and trying to blend all the artifacts from our life abroad.

Being closer to our families was a wonderful new experience. Many friends and relatives came to visit. I adjusted instantly to the conveniences provided by life in the United States. Life was great for me and I could have stayed in our great home forever being blessed with such wonderful neighbors. Juliana, on the other hand, was a senior in high school and it was a hard transition for her. In addition to her high school courses, we both enrolled in creative writing courses at Northern Virginia Community College. Dr. Melody Ziff was our marvelous teacher. It was a fun diversion for me. Juliana also worked three jobs despite having no driver's license. Guess who was chauffeur? I put twenty thousand miles on our car in seven months. No matter. I was happy to be back in the country we had left in 1971, despite some negative changes.

Before long, however, Washington made Joe an offer that we could not refuse—a chance to return overseas. He was quite frustrated with his job and morale was low. I could not visualize him continuing in that rat race without much feeling of accomplishment. He accepted the position as mission director for Cambodia and Joe left in mid-April 1995. Juliana and I stayed on until she graduated from high school. I was tasked with the job of purchasing consumables to ship to Phnom Penh as well as supervising all the pack out of airfreight, sea freight, and all the furniture sent off to storage. Juliana left to visit her brother in Ghana and I loaded the car and drove to Missouri to bid farewell to our family.

It broke my heart to rent out our beautiful home and move halfway around the world, but it was wonderful to be back with my husband. "Whither thou goest I will go" and all that stuff seem to be the motto of us foreign service spouses. It is sometimes easier said than done.

The Washington area home did not have a happy ending either. Our dream home became our nightmare home. The family who rented it offered to buy it but would never sign a contract. Then they stopped paying rent for eight months until we evicted them. We spent $40,000 to repair their damages. Another couple made an offer to buy it and moved in as renters in anticipation of our return for settlement. This was followed by a lawsuit by the original renter, so the second couple moved out. It was a year-long saga, which cost us a net loss of $220K in the end. Unbelievably, we lost the legal battle over the house on September 11, 2001. Our world collapsed along with the Twin Towers that horrible day.

CHAPTER 24

Cambodia Clips

> I do the best I know how; the very best I can; and I
> mean to keep on doing it to the end. If the end brings
> me out all right, what is said against me will not amount
> to anything, If the end brings me out all wrong, ten
> angels swearing I was right would make no difference.
> —Abraham Lincoln

Many books have been written about the history of Cambodia and its traumatized society. I have nothing relevant to add to these volumes. However, when I visited the Killing Fields or the Genocide Museum, it was impossible for me to understand or imagine how genocide could have occurred in this country of such gentle and kind people. It is incomprehensible!

Visiting the eleventh-century temples of Angkor Wat three times made all the difficulties of living so far from home seem worthwhile. What a rich cultural heritage these wonderful Khmer people enjoy. It is a precious commodity which should be marketed to the world. Tourism should bring in a great deal of needed revenue as long as a reasonable amount of safety can be insured and services provided. Cambodia has come a long way in the short time since the democratic elections in 1993. Progress is made one faltering step at a time. Cambodia deserves peace and stability.

I chose Lincoln's quotation above because it captures the enormous frustration of what I felt as the wife of the USAID director in Cambodia.

Dealing with the hand which had been dealt in Cambodia was a truly tremendous task for both the country and for me personally. I am the only person qualified to understand what obstacles my husband encountered in his position there. Likewise, Joe is the only one who witnessed the depths of my disappointments and shared the highs of my elations. It is great to be married to my best friend.

Joe's vision, his constitution, and his fortitude never cease to amaze me. His incredible sense of humor and humility have been our salvation throughout the years but even more important during the Cambodia posting. Many impressive accomplishments are never accredited to USAID staff or the sixty-nine NGOs funded by USAID. One seldom reads about their many successes. Instead, the local press relished negativity, innuendos, and discourse. This tendency bothered me much more than it did Joe, but I grew a thicker skin.

Hard decisions Joe made reflect what he believed is best for Cambodia, regardless of opposition from various sources. I am proud that he never compromises his principles or yields to pressure from Washington headquarters or lobbyists or worries about the negative tone of the local press. He just does the best he can, and I know he will keep right on doing it right up until the end.

Residing in Phnom Penh was like living in a small town. Rumors and gossip were rampant. Political uncertainty and security threats were part of the daily diet, which is not very palatable. What I personally found equally distasteful was the amount of jealousy among the NGO community there. Whatever the cause, whether it be a turf battle, a fight for resources or just plain pettiness, it was a new and unpleasant experience for us.

The needs of Cambodia are enormous. The demands are mind-boggling. There is more than sufficient work to go around but some organizations or individuals feel that glory shared is glory lost. It saddens me that a minority of "do-gooders" does no good by being distracted from the real job at hand and cause bad publicity.

On the other hand, we met some of the most productive and committed people in the world working in Cambodia and making a tremendous difference in the lives of many Khmer people. We applaud the joint efforts of Khmers and other nationalities who were attempting to bury the bloody past, determined not to repeat history and to move forward. A special salute to a very dear friend, Linda McKinney, UCC/Kampot, for the enormous efforts and sacrifices made on behalf of landmine victims and disabled. Linda and her very capable staff brought hope to so many unfortunate people by giving them marketable skills. I marvel at her energy, creativity, and dedication. Also, we tip our hats to Catherine Geach for sharing her musical talent with disabled children in Kampot and using traditional Khmer music as a means of healing their wounds.

A very special thanks to Paula Bryan, who was the sharp eyes and keen ears advocate for Cambodia back in Washington. She eased the burden of all the staff of USAID/Cambodia. Paula and I shared a hearty laugh during one of my husband's business trips to Washington regarding Joe being on "body time rather than clock time." Paula wrote, "I used to think that it was my duty to get Joe to meetings on time, but I slowly concluded that I would need a leash, and he would have to go to obedience school first, both of which are impossible. I have begun to realize that being on 'body time' rather than 'clock time' is an admirable quality . . . however irritating to others!" I responded to Paula that indeed Joe had been to obedience school, but I was a dismal failure as his teacher. As for the leash idea, well, I gave that some consideration. I vowed to adjust my attitude about this problem, which could save both my sanity and my marriage. Joe has improved with age and I have raised the threshold of my annoyance.

To Caroline Harley, I expressed my sincere appreciation for trying to keep Joe on track and always keeping me informed of official functions I was hosting more than a day in advance.

Motorcycle Mama

Never in my wildest dreams did I ever imagine earning the term of endearment Motorcycle Mama. I had never ridden a motorcycle in my life before I went to Cambodia. Necessity is truly the mother of invention.

Prior to our assignment to Phnom Penh, I had been whipping around Virginia in a beautiful ice-blue Mercedes. Having been advised not to bring our car to Cambodia due to the high risk of carjacking and not wishing to become a target, we sold the car. I would be dishonest if I did not admit how much I missed my wheels and my independence during that assignment.

Finding a job in Cambodia was problematic. It was no reflection on my own achievements during my prior thirteen years of experience with USAID. Rather, it was a combination of factors, the largest disadvantage being my husband's position. Just when I was ready to return to school, four job offers came at once. I accepted the first offer which was made by Judd Iversen, senior academic advisor for the University of San Francisco School of Law project. The job was cleared through the highest legal authorities in Washington to avoid any conflict of interest problems. There was no question of impropriety since I was not involved in policy decisions. Joe signed a recusal anyway. The job was a perfect fit for both sides. Some of the finest people in the world worked for the University of San Francisco/ Cambodia program. I enjoyed my job immensely. I obtained a new perspective from an NGO point of view. We avoided discussing business at home.

To get to and from work at the Faculty of Business located across the city, I rode on the back of a big Honda motorcycle. My faithful driver, Roat, took good care of me, drove slowly, and tried to miss the numerous potholes in the streets while dodging the traffic.

Our motorcycle rides always reminded me of an ant colony nearly bumping into one another constantly. We witnessed six collisions as they occurred. The good-natured Khmers simply picked themselves up, brushed off their clothes, and got back on the motorcycle without a harsh word being spoken. It is an example of their resiliency. There has been too much conflict in their lives. Their patience and tolerance are admirable qualities.

Children of the street vendors amuse themselves in simple entertainment. They love games and compete by seeing who can throw an old thong shoe the greatest distance. They kick socks filled with rocks. They roll old tires with a stick. When it rains the gutter-less streets become rivers and the children delight in playing in the muddy water. Kids were always smiling, too young to have appreciation for the past tragedies.

My ride to work took me past such a variety of scenes. In the morning women bent over hot pots of boiling oil while frying various foods or boiling the noodle dish which is the favored and delicious breakfast choice. Soup kitchens and impromptu cafes sprang up like mushrooms in the early mornings and then disappeared at night. Portable generators and air pumps along the street provided needed services. Shops on wheels sold many things, including keys, cigarettes, fake name-brand watches, and gemstones fashioned into jewelry and set in gold or silver, among other items. The street curbs had stacks of local and imported fruits and vegetables, bottled water, and the fascinating grilled chickens which appear to have been dipped in either red or gold plate. We passed shop after shop of colorful floor tiles made in Cambodia.

Most enjoyable was watching the beehive of activity around the huge central market. The beautiful flower arrangements were especially pleasing to the passerby. For a moment, it made one forget the plight of the many beggars throughout the market. The number of schools offering to teach English or computer courses increased significantly during our tour. The Khmer were anxious to join ASEAN and recognized the importance of learning English. In fact, the desire to learn English was so strong in Cambodia that students at the Faculty of Business often visited my office for the sole purpose of practicing their English. They were very delightful and charming young folk and I was honored that they felt comfortable enough to practice English with me. It was a wonderful association and I missed the 1996 graduating class, especially Sivutha.

Motorcycle Mama was not ready to rush out and purchase a Harley Davidson or a black leather jacket. However, I came to love the feeling of the wind on my face as we rode past tree-lined boulevards. It helped blow away the gas fumes, which I attempted to avoid inhaling. The amount of pollution that hung in the air was worse in certain areas, so I learned where and when to hold my breath for long periods. My clothing stank with the smell of petrol. I am grateful that we did not live in Bangkok where the pollution and traffic are much worse.

The skies above Phnom Penh were generally clean and clear as industrialization had not reached the city at that time. A unique phenomenon occurs when rain clouds hover. It would appear that every household possesses firearms. They indiscriminately fire into the clouds every time it rains. Different explanations for this behavior have been given, but I failed to ever understand the logic. It was not legal and falling shells posed a serious threat to everyone. Our upper balcony was pierced by a stray bullet. That was one custom that I did not miss when we left.

Unexpectedly, USAID requested Joe to transfer to Haiti for a bigger challenge. In 1994, the United States had led an intervention to force the military-led government to resign and permit the democratically elected government to return to power. As a consequence, a large development assistance program was put into place. Joe was asked to go to Haiti as the deputy country director with the expectation that he would replace the existing country director who was expected to retire within a year.

While we hated to leave Cambodia so soon, the move to Haiti would allow us to be closer to home and family and to participate in implementing an important development priority. So in August 1996, Joe departed once again for a new assignment while I remained working in Phnom Penh until October in order to train my replacement at the University of San Francisco program.

Birth of Third Granddaughter

During our tour in Cambodia, I was able to return to Missouri for the birth of our third precious granddaughter, Taylor Marie Sorensen, on February 7, 1996, and to help Jill and Mike for a week after she was born in Columbia, Missouri. It is a very special memory for me.

Visitors during Cambodia Tour

We took advantage of opportunities to tour many places of interest in Cambodia such as Angkor Wat several times. We also ventured over to Vietnam and Thailand during visits from our daughters Jennifer and Juliana and friends Kristin Johnson and Nicole Dial. Nicole was fascinated by Joe's work and subsequently joined the International Rescue Committee. Sadly, she was killed by the Taliban in Afghanistan while doing the work that she loved.

Hope, Joe and Jennifer visiting the temple of
Angkor Wat in Cambodia in 1996.

Joe met King Sihanok
Phnom Penh, Cambodia

CHAPTER 25

Another World (Juliana)

This antiracism poem was beautifully written by our daughter Juliana for her poetry class at Temple University in 1996. It brought her professor to tears. He told the class he had been waiting years for a student like Juliana. I think it is very important to comprehend her point that we are all created equal, especially during this era of terrible division and hated in our country.

Another World
By Juliana Goodwin

If I met you in another time, another place, another world, could we
    be friends? Perhaps even lovers?
If you did not judge me on pigmentation, could you love me? If we
    did not judge each other by the color and honesty of our hair,
    would we laugh together?
If name brands would not separate our place in society, would you
    break bread with me?
If music we listened to, or groups we know, did not sever our friends,
    would you sing with me?
If our shoes did not separate us into cliques, would you walk a mile
    beside me?
If I did not wear a cross and I lay dying in your arms, would you pray
    for me or let my soul go unnoticed?
If my accent took a different tone, would you listen to me? If I was
    educated in the projects, would you take my mind seriously?
If my legs were paralyzed, would you take a leap of faith and believe
    in me?

If I was blind, would you see me? Or are you already blind to me? I wonder, if we roamed the world deaf, dumb, and blind, would you manage to find yet another difference between us?

Do I not laugh with equal joy as you?

Don't I feast upon the earth as you do?

Does my voice not soar, and crack at times, as does yours?

Am I not human? Can I not cry? Tell me, are my tears a different color than yours?

Do I not pray? Can I not die like you?

Perhaps in death we will find peace.

Maybe our souls will soar free, free, free of prejudice, free of ignorance.

So until our souls have a chance to meet, walk this world blind to the differences that our bodies reveal, the differences that our hypocritical eyes critique, then, perhaps, one day we will meet as friends, even lovers, in another time, another place, another world.

CHAPTER 26

Help for Haiti

August 1996–April 1997

Joe arrived in Haiti in August 1996 to work in a country with some of the greatest development challenges in the world. Haiti is one of two countries located on the island of Hispaniola, the other being the Dominican Republic. Christopher Columbus on his first voyage to the New World claimed the island for Spain in 1492 and he and his crew were the first Europeans to land on the island. In 1697, Spain ceded three-eights of the island to France. The French possession with the labor from African slaves producing sugar, indigo, and cotton in the eighteenth century became one of the richest French colonies in the world. By advent of the French revolution, there were five hundred thousand slaves and thirty-two thousand whites in what is now Haiti. In 1791, the slaves revolted and there began a period of insurrection and unrest, until 1804, when independence was declared and the first black republic in the world was officially named Haiti. The initial republic was short lived as the leader of the republic declared himself emperor. This began a period of fighting among leaders of the rebellion that continued throughout the history of Haiti. In fact, it was only in 1996, that there was a transition from one democratically elected president to another, from President Jean Aristide to Rene Preval.

After I arrived in Port-au-Prince, I read the most fascinating eight-hundred-page history book about Haiti called *Written in Blood*. It would be difficult to summarize it in one paragraph, but I kept thinking about poor, poor Haiti as I read and experienced it firsthand. Haiti has probably had the most turbulent history of any country in the world.

Shortly after arriving in Haiti, Joe learned that the current country director would not retire but would be continuing on as director. Joe was disappointed as he would have preferred to remain in Cambodia as country director than be the deputy director in Haiti even though the Haiti program was more than ten times larger than the one in Cambodia. However, he and the country director worked well together and there was much to do. Joe worked closely with the economics team on implementation of the economic reform program and the agricultural and private sector office on addressing the constraints to development in those sectors.

I finally landed a position at the US Embassy in the Commercial Section. It was a nice change of pace. American companies were vying for access to the cell phone market. Business exploded with increased cell phone usage. My colleagues were very nice to me and I enjoyed the job but hated the ride to and from the office. The streets of Port-au-Prince were very narrow, and traffic was horrific. The sides of the streets were strewn with trash. It was not pleasant. And this was prior to the devastating earthquake. I heard from friends who survived the earthquake how bad it was afterward. Poor Haiti truly needs help.

Trip to DR with Joan, Ann, and Karen

Thanksgiving 1996 found us enjoying the company of our daughter Joan and her friends Ann Buckman and Karen Kassen. We drove them up to the Citadel in northern Haiti, built by the Haitian Emperor Henri Christophe and they got a taste of the poverty along the way. Then we drove across the island to Santo Domingo, Dominican Republic, which was like another world in terms of goods available and things to do. We had lots of fun. The ladies took a day trip to an island and loved the rum punch for which the DR is famous while Joe met with colleagues in the Dominican Republic for business.

In March 1997, Joe was contacted by Dr. David Franklin of Sigma One Corporation, in Raleigh, North Carolina. Sigma One had a contract in Ghana working on trade and investment issues and wanted Joe to become the Chief of Party for the contract. As Joe and I were on the way to the airport to pick up Dr. David Franklin, who was coming to interview him for a position with Sigma One, Joe kept patting his head and saying, "My hair hurts." The whole weekend Joe was in pain and he hardly would answer Dr. Franklin's questions so sometimes I would respond for him. I didn't realize that he had contracted a nasty case of shingles until his right side of the head was totally broken out. He suffered for several weeks with the nerve pain and it is something that I hope to avoid.

Amazingly, despite his poor interview due to the pain of having shingles, Joe was offered the job with Sigma One. It was an attractive offer as we both loved Ghana. Joe was eligible to retire from USAID, so the timing was right. Moreover, with the fall of the Berlin Wall, the foreign aid budget was declining, and country programs were being cut back. A final favorable factor in the decision was the position gave the opportunity to return to Ghana.

The chance to expand his career by working for the private sector was too tempting so he accepted the challenge. God certainly opened a window as we ended up going back to work for the third time in Ghana, which was like a second home to us.

CHAPTER 27

First Grandson

Our first grandson, Trevor Michael Sorensen, was born October 20, 1997. Naturally we were very excited to get a boy since it had been thirty-two years since we had a male heir in our immediate family. I was able to be there for Trevor's birth. Joe was working in Durham, North Carolina, at Sigma One Corporation at the time. He was also overseeing the final construction of a new home we were having built in Durham. I also hated being so far away from that new grandbaby. Jill suffered from migraines for eighteen months after Trevor was born, but he was a happy child.

I returned to North Carolina for closing of the house and we moved in on Halloween. We were surprised at the number of trick-or-treaters who came that evening and welcomed us to the neighborhood. It was a beautiful suburb and we had designed the home to our liking. So we set about getting settled and furnishing the spacious and wonderful library and buying other pieces of furniture that we were missing. Alice and Joel and Jenny and Juliana came for Thanksgiving. We hired a landscape artist for suggestions of what to do with the large yard.

Alas, I never had the chance to plant trees or flowers. By Christmas, we realized that we would be moving back to Ghana by mid-January. In all we spent less than ten weeks living in the home we had designed and spent five months building. It was time to pack out before we were truly settled.

Joe had been named as the chief of party for the contract that Sigma One had been awarded by USAID. Dutifully, off we went and spent another five years in our beloved Ghana.

We rented the house to a couple who ultimately bought it. That was a tough decision as we had poured our hearts into that abode.

We loved the friendly people of North Carolina and our daughter Jennifer was living in Charlotte. We had planned to settle there after retirement. The best made plans always seem to go astray when one chooses international development work as a career.

CHAPTER 28

Private Sector Experience

April 1997–September 2002

The day after retiring from USAID in Haiti, we moved to Durham, North Carolina, where Joe had accepted a position with Sigma One Corporation. We were there nine months during which time we built a home we had designed.

We only got to live in the new house for ten weeks before leaving for nearly five years in Ghana. Joe was chosen as the chief of party for Sigma One's contract with USAID's Trade and Investment Program.

It was Joe's first experience to work in the private sector and this was under an institutional contract, so it required some adjustment. However, Dr. David Franklin and Lou Harrell had assembled an excellent team, and they worked well together and accomplished a great deal of policy reform and increased trade. Two members of the Sigma One team became the vice presidents of Ghana.

This tour was our third time to work and live in Ghana which was our favorite African country. Why? Because Ghanaians are genuinely friendly and open.

I was able to secure a job in the Controller's Office at USAID where I worked for a couple years before transferring to the Health Office, which provided a nice change for me.

Our son was living in Ghana as the manager of the American Club, so it was great to be able to spend some time with him. Juliana visited periodically from college. In 1999, Joe II started working at a gold mine in Western Ghana, so we got to visit him there too. Eventually he moved to Tanzania and then to Uganda where he now lives with his daughter, Chloe. After fifteen years, he left the mining sector and bought Priceless Farms on the banks of the Nile River in Northern Uganda.

Even though I was working full-time, we spent a lot of evenings and weekends entertaining the public and private sector in Ghana because we felt it was important. I wish I had a dollar for every person I fed at our table. But I did and do believe in the cause. It wasn't always easy, but it was worthwhile.

The major problem was that my parents were getting fragile and we were living so far away and unable to help them. In the end, we decided to move closer to home. It was the best move for the circumstances and we have no regrets about that choice.

Even though it was difficult to leave Ghana for the third time, we could proudly reflect on many accomplishments in helping Ghana in the quest of alleviating poverty through policy changes. As chief-of-party for USAID's policy component of the Trade and Investment Reform Program, Joe directed the Sigma One team working with public and private sector officials in providing economic analysis support to USAID, the Minister of Finance, Minister of Trade and Industries, Minister of Human Resource Development and Employment, and the Bank of Ghana on various policy issues. This included policy analysis on specific program issues addressed included—exchange rate policy, competitiveness, labor market reform, financial sector reform (including the need for new financial instruments), trade and tariff policies, tax revenue issues and social security/pension reform.

They assisted the government of Ghana with organizing and implementing a national economic dialogue process where government, labor, private sector, and NGOs meet annually to review the state of the economy and formulate policy recommendations for action. This process was initiated with a series of predialogue meetings with individual groups that often ended around the Goodwin dining table. These meetings resulted in the development of policy briefs, formalized recommendations emerging from the Dialogue Conference, and provision of implementation support.

This work supported the adoption of policy changes completed prior to our departure in 2002 included: new labor law promoting greater labor market flexibility; the creation of medium term bond market; reform in management of free trade zones and bonded warehouses; reduction in tariff dispersion, recommendations on elimination of loan programs by social security system; proposals for development of private pension savings system; and reporting of real as well as nominal exchange rates in Bank of Ghana bulletin. All of these policy changes have had a positive effect on the lives of Ghanaians.

New Mercedes

Joe surprised me with a brand-new Mercedes C-Class salon car so that I had transport whenever I went back to visit my parents. Joan met me at the Columbia Airport with the keys on an icy December day. We had a dangerous ride to the Lake of the Ozarks. The roads were slick, and it was snowing. I was jet lagged and stunned by his generous gift. I loved that beautiful blue car and kept it ten years.

CHAPTER 29

Nicaragua Spanish School

When Joe was awarded a contract to work in the Dominican Republic, we felt nervous about our rather rusty Spanish. It had been seventeen years since we had lived in Ecuador and last spoken Spanish. So we decided to take some time to relearn at our own expense and wanted total immersion.

We found what fit the bill perfectly in Granada, Nicaragua. We lived three months with a lovely Nicaraguan family and spoke only Spanish while taking classes eight hours a day at the Nicaraguan Spanish School.

It was really difficult at first and extremely tiring. The host Nicaraguan family were very kind to us and gave us their only room with an air conditioner. On weekends, they took us around Nicaragua.

One weekend we flew to Costa Rica to visit Frank and Meg Hicks, friends from our days in Ghana. That was a lovely R&R while Frank drove us around the beautiful country.

We returned back to Missouri in time to attend Juliana's graduation from Missouri State University with a degree in journalism. It was the first time we actually were able to witness any of our kid's college graduations as we were always abroad.

Ten days before Christmas, we flew off to the Dominican Republic for an assignment that lasted three and a half years, so we regained fluency in Spanish. The experience in Nicaragua had helped to save us from lingual embarrassment.

CHAPTER 30

Dominican Republic

December 2002–February 2006

Joe never applied for the senior economic advisor position at USAID in Santo Domingo. Truth be told, I applied on his behalf. I wrote his cover letter to explain the willingness to accept a huge annual cut in pay so that his wife could spend time with her ailing parents. I forged his signature. I filled out the necessary application form and emailed it from my computer in Ghana. Joe didn't even realize that I had sent the application. He had decided that nobody would consider hiring him because he had not worked in a Spanish-speaking environment in seventeen years. After receiving a rejection email two days later, I assumed that Joe was right, and I had wasted my time.

Months passed. Then Joe received an email which made us laugh. The contracting officer stated, "After much consideration, we are offering you the position." What we suspected and later was confirmed was that the number one candidate delayed and didn't take the job. The entire hiring committee was against hiring Joe because they could not believe that he was genuine in his desire to sacrifice for his wife. They assumed that he had a big ego because of his previous career background and that he would not be able to work in a lesser job. They presumed he had been a problem or not performed well as chief of party.

But Joe proved them wrong as he worked diligently as a great team member from December 2002 until February 2006 in the Dominican Republic.

Juliana and Joe II came to visit us the first Christmas. There had been an ice storm in Missouri and it took Juliana a harrowing nine hours to drive from Springfield to St. Louis airport. Joe II was flying in from Africa where he had purchased his ticket and was due to arrive on Christmas Eve. Joe I went to the Santo Domino airport to pick him up while Juliana and I stayed at the apartment to prepare a lovely meal. I got a call from Joe I, saying our son had not arrived. Then I got a call from Joe II asking if his dad was coming to get him and I assured him that he was there. Another hour passed and finally Joe returned to the apartment alone. It turns out that Joe II had flown into the wrong airport and was at Santiago. He hired a taxi to bring him to Santo Domingo. The driver was intoxicated already and wanted to stop to buy more beer. The driver wasn't familiar with the capital city, so we agreed to meet on the main square. At 1:00 a.m. Joe and I went to receive him and saw a car parked. A pair of legs wearing white socks was sticking out the window. Assuming it was our son, Joe I went up to the car and said, "Howdy, big boy. Would you like a place to sleep tonight?" Lo and behold it was not our son, and the guy drove away quickly. We laughed and laughed and thought what a pervert that fellow must have thought Joe was. Shortly afterward, the taxi did arrive with Joe II, and he was so relieved to see us. The turkey dinner was ruined, but we celebrated the next day with lobster tails.

Separate Maintenance

The whole point of accepting the tour in the DR, giving up my job, and taking a huge pay cut for Joe was so that I could spend time with my parents, who were starting to show their ages. Both were in their eighties. So we made the decision that I would go on separate maintenance which meant that I could not spend more than thirty consecutive days with Joe, or I would lose that little allowance. That was the best decision we ever made, even at such a high financial cost.

For over three years, I rotated between Missouri and Santo Domingo. I used all our frequent flyer miles quickly and then earned them back while buying my own ticket to/from the beautiful island.

The quality time that I was able to spend with the folks is simply irreplaceable. Dad and I spent hours hunting Indian artifacts together. I helped Mom with countless things around the house. Liz and I did some painting and wallpapering for them. Twice I took

Mom to Montana to visit her sister Anna Lou for her ninety-ninth and one-hundredth birthdays. I took them to Arizona, so they could say farewell to Dad's sister Edith who was terminally ill. I drove them to Oklahoma for my cousin Jane and Parker Hightower's fiftieth wedding anniversary. We attended a number of other family events during that time. Priceless memories.

My Sixtieth Birthday in Hawaii

Joe generously sent me to Hawaii for my sixtieth birthday. He was working and not interested in going at that time. Consequently, I celebrated a three-generational trip with Juliana, Gretchen, and her daughter Jennifer in September 2003. It was a blast once we all got there. Gretchen and Jennifer beat us by a day because Juliana and I missed a connecting flight in Memphis and had to spend the night in Los Angeles. Meanwhile Gretchen had rented a car in Honolulu and bought leis to welcome us to the airport.

Juliana and I had a scary, but later humorous, situation on the plane as we taxied down the runway in Springfield. It was an aircraft unlike any other design we had flown. It appeared that the luggage door was open. Juliana started screaming. The man behind us said we were going to die. Turns out it was the wheel cover. The stewardess said we weren't the first to make that mistake, but we were the first ones to cause total panic.

We spent a week touring Hawaii. We went snorkeling and saw gorgeous fish. We swam with seven large sea turtles. We walked through botanical gardens to a beautiful waterfall. Juliana and I visited Pearl Harbor and took a city tour. My nephew Kristopher Gander was stationed at the US Marine base there, so we picked him up a couple times. We enjoyed a fantastic luau and enjoyed the food and dancing. All of us loved shopping at the World Market. We took walks on the beach and saw helicopters circling sharks. Juliana and Jennifer took surfing lessons, which was not easy. They rode float-able tractors into the surf. A shark warning brought them peddling back to shore as fast as their legs would carry them. It turned out to be a weekly siren test. We visited the Dole Pineapple factory and drove to the north coast of the island. Most of all, it was a fun time together.

Jennifer's Graduation Cruise to Mexico

With a blink of the eye, our granddaughter Jennifer was grown up and graduating from high school in California in June 2004. I was able to attend the graduation along with her other grandmother, Carol Merrill. It was a memorable time as a streaker ran across the stage right before Jennifer got her diploma.

Joe and Juliana flew out to join the Merrill family and I on a cruise to Mexico. We boarded Carnival Pride in Los Angeles and made the first stop at Cabo San Lucas. We hired a boat and enjoyed it. Next port of call was Puerto Vallarta, where Joe and I took a tour to a rum factory. Of course, we bought some and still haven't drunk it thirteen years later. Meanwhile the rest of our family hired a taxi and they had a fun time touring the city. Last port was Mazatlan and I cannot even remember what we did there. However, we did have a great time on the cruise.

Jennifer Married Michael Black

We happily attended our daughter Jennifer's marriage to Michael Black in Las Vegas on September 6, 2004. An added blessing was that this union also provided our second grandson, Joseph Black.

Dad Died February 15, 2005

I returned to the Dominican Republic for Valentine's Day after calling my dad to wish him a happy eighty-ninth birthday. He and mom were going to their favorite restaurant in Hannibal for a special celebration.

The next day Joe came home from work in the middle of the afternoon. He was crying. Mom had called. Dad had died peacefully from an aneurysm while watching his favorite soap opera after having graded the road that morning. Dad passed on his own terms. When his doctor had told him on Christmas Eve that he had developed another aneurysm, this time in the brain, Dad responded that was the best news he ever heard. He wanted to go quickly and not be a burden to his family. He got his wish. Dad's visitation and funeral drew huge crowds. He was well-known and well-respected in the community. Mom was very brave although it was tough to lose someone she had loved so dearly for seventy-two years. He had been a faithful husband and had loved us four kids even though he was sometimes awkward about showing it or telling us.

Iberostar and Other Resorts

An advantage of living in the Dominican Republic was the fantastic restaurants and the all-inclusive resorts. Our personal favorite was the Iberostar Bavaro in La Romana. We took my mother there. We took Joe II, Gretchen, Jenny, and Juliana there. We took cousins Floyd and Judy and Molly there. It was only a couple hours' drive from Santo Domingo, so we would spend an occasional weekend just to get outside the busy city.

Joe's Work and Friends

I have only described my life while Joe was working away on the country's electricity problems. I acutely felt the lack of electricity at the apartment complex where we stayed on the fourth floor. The power would go off for hours and hours at a time and the landlord would only crank up the generator when it was time for the men to come back from work. We were the only American citizens living in that building. The other ladies, their kids, and I didn't have a voice in using the generator. Anyway, I could attest to the problems which Joe was dealing with. Regarding Joe's work, I have been asked "What exactly does an economist do?" It varies by country and circumstance. But in the case of the Dominican Republic, as the deputy leader of the Economic Opportunities Strategic Objective Team, Joe provided technical leadership in economics, education, and environment. According to his employee evaluation report, he accomplished the following tasks:

- Provided senior-level expert analysis on economic and development policy and guidance on strategies, programs, and activities for the USAID General Development Office.
- Provided a full range of consultative, advisory, information-gathering, analytical, and evaluative technical services of broad scope and complexity.
- Worked with energy sector to resolve energy crisis and recommended reduction in energy sector subsidies.
- Provided leadership on economic policies that sustain growth and impact the poor, including competitiveness, trade, fiscal, public investment, environment and education policies.
- Had broad latitude to deal with senior government officials, members of the National Assembly, local government officials, as well as senior leaders in the nongovernmental arena. Implemented a program of monthly economic reporting and analysis on the Dominican economy.
- Authored a 240-page in-depth analysis, "Non-Apparel Export Industry in the Dominican Republic: Opportunities and Challenges" which was widely used by both public and private sector in the Dominican Republic for sector development.
- Engaged in policy dialogue debates on needed fiscal reforms. Collaboratively developed a draft competitiveness policy law.

Perhaps this helps to understand the scope of what an economist does.

The best outcome from our life in Santo Domingo was the close friends we made both Dominicans and Americans. We stay in touch with David Delgado, Judith Timyan, Andy and Tracy Herscowitz, Donnie and Naida Harrington, Elena Brineman, Charlie and Nancy

Crane, Dave and Lorraine Noble and others. Friendships are very dear in the foreign service community and last far beyond our tours.

Guyana Encore

When Joe finished in the DR, he went to Georgetown, Guyana, for two months of work while I stayed in the condo at the lake and visited my mother often.

Return to Cusco and Machu Picchu, Peru

During our tour in the Dominican Republic, Joe had a business trip to Lima, Peru, in October 2005. We paid for me to accompany him. Since our previous visit to Machu Picchu in 1977 had been such a misadventure, I was keen to return without the children to absorb the Inca culture. I researched history books prior to our trip, so I had a greater appreciation of the marvelous sights in Peru. We booked the luxury Orient Express train to Machu Picchu and that was lovely.

We flew from Lima inland to Cuzco, the ancient capital of the Inca empire. We spent an extra day getting used to the altitude of eleven thousand two hundred feet above sea level in the Andes mountains and visited ruins located nearby. One of the most spectacular sites was the fortress of Saqsayhuaman outside of Cuzco. It took twenty thousand laborers, thirty years to quarry, shape, and position the rock walls of the fortress with some rocks weighing more than one hundred tons. The workmanship is incredible as these huge rocks fit so tightly that you could not slide a knife blade between the stones.

Joe is our family historian, so I learned from him that the Inca empire was established in 1438 and expanded about two thousand five hundred miles from Ecuador in the north down below what is now Santiago, Chile, in the western side of South America.

The empire included coastal deserts, much of the Andean mountain range with peaks over twenty-two thousand feet, and the Amazon jungle on the eastern side of the Andes. The empire only lasted a little over a hundred years before Spanish soldiers led by Francisco Pizarro captured the Incan king and claimed the whole empire for Spain in 1532. The resulting war of conquest lasted for forty years before the subjugation of the people.

In the resulting war, the Inca were driven into the jungle. The war and the policy of the Spaniards to impose their culture on the Incas led to the destruction of most of the Inca cities and fortresses. With the death of the last Inca leader, the location of the last Incan capital was lost. In 1911, Yale professor Hiram Bingham led an expedition into the Peruvian jungle northeast of Cuzco to find the last capital of the Inca empire. He did not find the capital, but he did find Machu Picchu on the top of a jungle peak. It is a spectacular place to visit.

CHAPTER 31

Marvelous Morocco

In March 2006, along with our daughter Joan, cousin Molly Lamb, and friend Kris Fleming, we flew out of New York for an adventure in Morocco. We had spent many years living in Africa but had only had one overnight layover in Casablanca. Through Gate 1 Travel, we found a trip so cheap that we could not pass it up.

Upon an early morning landing in Casablanca, we were met by Nouradin, who turned out to be one of the best professional tour guides we have encountered around the world. He offered to show us more of the city that very afternoon even though it was not on our itinerary. We went to the Hassan II Mosque, which has the tallest minaret in the world. We saw the Koutoubia Minaret and drove around the historical and beautiful city. That evening Joan could not resist making a trip to Rick's American Bar, named after the bar in the movie *Casablanca*.

From Casablanca, we took a bus with thirty other passengers around the country. We stopped in Rabat and then on to Fez where we enjoyed a home hosted meal. In Fez, we visited a tannery and watched leather being made but the smell of the raw hides overwhelmed me until I vomited in a flower pot. We thoroughly enjoyed a traditional Moroccan meal under a tent, complete with belly dancing.

We saw snow on the Atlas Mountains. We were surprised at the ever-changing climate and beautiful scenery throughout our bus trip in Morocco.

The third-century ancient Roman ruins of Volubilis were truly amazing.

Joan mentioned to our guide that she would like to ride a camel. We stopped in the middle of nowhere, and she got her wish, though riding bareback might not have been what she had in mind. Kris was also brave enough to experience a camel ride in the desert.

It was only when we stopped for the camel ride that we realized we were being escorted by undercover security because the same man we had noticed at other stops pulled up behind our bus. Our guide admitted that we indeed did have an escort as a security precaution. We weren't sure whether to feel more relaxed or afraid about that revelation. Moroccans were nothing but friendly to us.

Naturally, we were taken to a carpet dealership. And naturally, most of us bought one. Joe and I bargained before Joan, and she got a tremendous deal. She was wearing a University of Missouri sweatshirt and they assumed she was a student so gave her a much better price. The wool carpet we purchased is beautiful and will last for many generations.

Of course, there was plenty of souvenir shopping around the country. Besides the carpets, we brought back beautiful pottery and silver decorated ornaments. Again, Joan was the best shopper and scored some gorgeous pieces.

We arrived in the beautiful pink city of Marrakesh, where we spent another two days touring. The markets were fascinating, and Joe enjoyed the snake charmers although they were a bit sluggish as it was a chilly day. Joan and Kris got their hands decorated with henna. Molly and Kris hired a "pusher" to help translate in the market. We weren't quite sure what he was saying but he was insistent.

I hate to fly and have to take a pill for nausea. Leaving Marrakesh early that morning, I grabbed a water bottle and took a big swig to swallow my pill. I about chocked to death for it was pure vodka in the water bottle that Molly had left in our room the prior evening. Molly had smuggled the vodka because she thought that it would not be available in an Arab country. Michelle was very concerned about her mother doing that and getting caught. But Molly happily enjoyed her nightly screwdriver.

Actually, we found nice wine at most hotels and restaurants. One of our fellow passengers attached herself to our group for most of the trip. She was a real moocher. She never contributed to food or drink even though we took turns. Always had an excuse or would say "next time." Finally, Kris had the courage to tell her that her time had come. After that, she left us alone.

Roman ruins of Volubilis in Morocco with daughter
Joan, cousin Molly Lamb, and Kris Fleming in 2006.

Road Trip to California with Mom

In the summer of 2006, we took my mother on a three-week road trip to California. She was a wonderful travel companion. She sat in the middle of the back seat so that she could see everything. Often she would remark that "if Cliff had known about this place, we would have visited here." Dad did take her on many trips and they had always enjoyed their adventures. She was sad without him, so we wanted to share new experiences with Mom.

We visited my cousin Jane in Oklahoma. Then on to New Mexico to tour the Carlsbad Caverns. We spent a couple days in Tucson, Arizona, to attend the fiftieth wedding anniversary of my cousin Carol and Dave Groetken where Alice joined us. It was so much fun to spend time with our relatives there.

Naturally, we went to the Grand Canyon. Dad and Mom had already been there, so we decided to do something different and took her on the train tour from Williams to the Grand Canyon which she enjoyed.

Next destination was Sequoia National Park, where we were blown away by the enormous and gorgeous old trees. It was thrilling to walk among them, and Mom did a good job of keeping up with us in her ninetieth year.

We then headed down to Oceanside, California, to visit Gretchen, Scott, and Jennifer. It was nice to show Mom their beautiful home and for all of us to have a chance to share time with all of them. We had the champagne brunch at El Coronado Hotel, saw seals at La Jolla, and simply had a really good visit.

When we drove through Las Vegas without stopping, I think Mom was a bit disappointed. Mom recalled the fun trip she and dad had taken there on an anniversary trip.

Joe and I love national parks, so we were not disappointed in the beauty of Zion National Park and Bryce Canyon and Arches National Park.

I had read about a scenic highway and was tired of interstate driving so suggested we take the shortcut through Route 12. Well, it was scenic for certain but also petrifying at times. One stretch connecting two mountains had no shoulder and no guardrail and was at least five thousand feet straight down. We went really slow and were grateful not to meet another car on that pass because Joe was also scared and driving down the middle of the road. From there it was a very crooked road down the mountain.

We stopped in Denver and were so happy to have Christi Harter join us for an evening of catching up. She was a PCV in Ghana and like a daughter to us.

Onward to Nebraska to visit my dad's nephew George and Jan Phelps. They entertained us royally and it was also so nice to spend the night in their beautiful home. Jan had sat a gorgeous table with an exquisite Belgium lace tablecloth. Poor Joe bumped the table leg when he sat down, and the wine splashed over the white lace. Instinctively, he began to shake salt all over the wine to absorb it. He looked up to apologize and saw Jan's horrified face. He asked what she usually used for wine spills. Her sweet reply was "I have never had anyone spill wine on my tablecloth before." We felt terrible about it and offered to pay for the dry cleaning, but they refused. Nevertheless, we were glad that we got to visit them as George is no longer with us.

The following day we drove all the way to Monroe City to take Mom back home. We are both so grateful to have had that precious time with my mother.

China, Tibet, and Hong Kong

Knowledge comes from learning.
Wisdom comes from living.
—Anthony Douglas Williams

This twenty-three-day adventure was the second major trip that we shared with Floyd and Judy in 2007 along with twelve other people in our tour group. We got along beautifully and loved the experience that was organized by Overseas Adventure Travel. Here is an abbreviated version of our itinerary as advertised in OAT's brochure interspersed with our personal experiences.

Day 1 and Day 2

Flew from the USA to Beijing, where we were met by our guide, a young woman who was with us for the entire visit in China, Tibet, and Hong Kong.

Day 3: Tiananmen Square and the Forbidden City

Visited Beijing, the modern political and administrative center of China, full of monuments and treasures from the imperial era. We visited the largest square in the world, Tiananmen Square, known for the student demonstrations in 1989. A giant portrait of Chairman Mao hangs above the Gate of Heavenly Peace. Mao is entombed in the Memorial Hall in a crystal sarcophagus, his body draped in the red flag of the People's Republic that he founded in 1949.

We visited the Forbidden City, a nine-thousand-room maze of courtyards, palaces, and ceremonial halls, where twenty-four emperors and two dynasties ruled the Middle Kingdom. Protected by thirty-foot-high walls and a one-hundred-sixty-foot-wide moat, the Forbidden City was indeed a forbidden place; commoners were kept out for nearly five hundred years. The greatest achievement of the visionary Emperor Yongle, this architectural triumph was completed in a mere fourteen years by two hundred thousand workers.

We visited the Temple of Heaven, built between 1406 and 1420 by the same Yongle emperor who was responsible for building the Forbidden City. It is a UNESCO world heritage site due to its architectural and landscape design.

Day 4: The Great Wall

We visited a factory specializing in cloisonné, the beautiful enamel artwork that predates the Ming dynasty and is known for its colorful glazes and patterns. I bought a beautiful blue vase that adorns my kitchen.

Next, we toured the Great Wall, the most authentic sections of the Great Wall. China's Great Wall may be the world's greatest civil engineering feat. The massive ramparts were begun in separate strategic sections between 403 and 221 BC. During the reign of China's first Qin emperor, three hundred thousand men were put to work connecting the segments into one huge, snaking fortification. Archaeologists estimate that the wall once ran for 6,200 miles through an expanse that now covers sixteen provinces. Today, the wall is still impressive at 3,750 miles in length, stretching from the Bohai Sea to the Gobi Desert. And it can be seen from outer space.

The Great Wall was more than just a barrier. It served as an elevated highway linking the defensive forces along China's rugged northern frontier. The roadway atop the wall provided a means of rapid communication and deployment of troops, arms, and food.

After our visit to the Great Wall, we went to a theater for a Chinese opera performance where we promptly fell asleep from jet lag.

Day 5: Carpets and Summer Palace

A visit to a Beijing carpet factory where the silk carpets are still hand-made was on our agenda. We learned about the production process and how to distinguish real silk from artificial. Then we continued our cultural discoveries at the Beijing Municipal Opera School, where we interacted with students learning traditional Chinese operas, including singing and dancing.

We headed for the Summer Palace, which has the largest and best-preserved royal garden in China. Early in the Jin dynasty, an imperial palace named Golden Hill Palace was built on the present site of the Summer Palace. Through the centuries, portions of the grounds and buildings were destroyed during warfare, then restored or redesigned. The Summer Palace of today is more or less the same as the palace rebuilt in 1903. After the last Qing emperor, Puyi, was thrown out of the Summer Palace in 1924, the garden was turned into a park. Surrounded by lovely Kunming Lake and classic Chinese gardens, the palace halls and pavilions are filled with ornate furnishings and fine artwork.

Day 6: Lunch with Chinese Family and Board Train

A glimpse of everyday Chinese life on a guided walking tour of a Beijing hutong was followed by lunch in the home of a local Chinese family.

We departed for the train station in Beijing to board a high-speed train to Xian. The station is so crowded that entrance is regulated according to departure schedules. There are no signs in English, so we were grateful for our guide. We had a sleeper car, but it was difficult to sleep with the speed at which we were traveling and meeting other trains on the eleven-hour journey.

Xian was the largest city in the world during the Tang dynasty (AD 618–907), the capital of eleven dynasties, a major trading hub along the Silk Route, and a center of Chinese civilization. Though its glory days are long over, it is still a cultural and intellectual capital, boasting some eleven universities, a thriving artists' community, and a burgeoning film industry.

Day 7: Tours of Xian

Judy and I participated in a tai chi demonstration in a local park while Joe and Floyd imitated us. Then we went to the seventh-century small Wild Goose Pagoda.

After visiting the pagoda, we explore Xian's City Wall, one of the most complete structures of its kind in all of China. Constructed during the Ming dynasty, the City Wall is one of the largest ancient military defensive systems in the world.

We opted to visit a lacquerware factory, where raw tree sap is used to create beautiful furniture. I bought a few souvenir lacquerware trays there.

That evening we crowded around a table for a Mongolian hot pot dinner. This traditional group meal originated in the Mongolian city of Hothot and is prepared with a variety of ingredients, including beef, chicken, tofu, and vegetables.

Day 8: Terra Cotta Warriors

Finally, the day arrived that would be a highlight of our trip. We longed to visit Xian's terra cotta army. Life-sized soldiers, generals, charioteers, and horses of Xian's terra cotta army are considered one of the foremost archaeological discoveries of the twentieth century. The two-thousand-year-old terra cotta army was discovered by accident in 1974 by local farmers digging a well. The six-thousand-plus life-sized figures are arranged in vaults at the entrance to the tomb of Qin Shi Huangdi, the first Qin emperor, a major architect of the Great Wall and unifier of China. The soldiers are ranked in military order, hold actual spears and swords and, incredibly, have unique facial expressions. There is also an exhibit of a remarkable miniature model of a Qin dynasty bronze chariot, complete with horses and coachmen.

Next we went for a Chinese noodle-making demonstration at a restaurant. Later we visited a jade factory to learn about the history and importance of jade carving, one of China's cultural legacies. Of course, I bought a jade necklace there.

Day 9: Visit the Countryside

We travel into the countryside to Donghan, a village where the color-ful "peasant" painting style originated in the 1950s. I bought a paint-ing of a panda. We visited the community-founded Guang Ming Primary School, which is supported in part by donations from Grand Circle Foundation—part of the World Classroom initiative. We met students and teachers and gave them some school supplies.

Day 10: Fly to Chengdu

We flew to Chengdu the site of the panda research center and walked around the city before going to an opera. This time we didn't fall asleep. The performers get dressed in the hallway.

Day 11: Visit to Panda Sanctuary

Joe and I loved the visit to the Panda Sanctuary, located just outside of Chengdu. We gave a donation, which allowed us to be able to enter the area and take a picture with a giant panda who was eating bamboo. To our surprise, his fur was bristly. Because of its location in Sichuan Province, native habitat of the giant panda, this facility has live pandas, the largest number you can see anywhere in the world. There are only one thousand pandas still living in the wild in all of China, mostly in northern Sichuan and in Gansu and Shaanxi prov-inces, in elevations between four thousand and ten thousand feet.

First appearing in the fossil record some three million years ago, the giant panda is under siege in this century—from habitat eradica-tion, cyclical starvation, and poachers who get as much as $10,000 for a giant panda hide in Hong Kong and Japan. China's ambitious ten-year conservation plan aims to preserve existing habitats, expand existing reserves, and create new reserves in an international effort to stave off the extinction of this elegant, almost mystical, animal.

Given the scale of the battle being fought for the panda's sur-vival, places like the Giant Panda Sanctuary just outside Chengdu are essential. The sanctuary is not a zoo but a simulated habitat, with acres of space for its inhabitants to roam and thrive as nature intended.

Day 12: Fly to Lhasa, Tibet

Early in the morning, we transferred to the airport for our flight to Lhasa, Tibet. When we arrived in Lhasa, we were told to relax at the hotel and not walk around due to the high altitude of twelve feet. It hit Judy hard, and after lunch, she went to lay down. Joe and I could not wait to get closer to the Potala Palace, so we snuck out and walked around until we found the palace and took photos.

For 350 years, Lhasa, the City of the Sun, has been at the political and economic center of Tibet. The country itself has existed since the seventh century as a remote mountain theocracy based on the mystical tenets of Lamaism, a form of Tantric Indian Buddhism coupled with Tibetan shamanism. Here, feudal Lamas whose spiritual authority was matched by their complete control of internal affairs ruled the rural population. Some reigns were benevolent, while others were ruthless.

The autonomy of the Lamas waxed and waned during various Chinese dynasties, with almost complete independence enjoyed during the republican period (1912–1949). But things changed during China's Cultural Revolution. In 1951, through military action and pressured negotiation, China reestablished its sovereignty. After years of steadily increasing oppression, a revolt broke out in 1959, and the Dalai Lama was forced to flee to India.

Widespread persecution of the Tibetan people continued, reaching a peak during the Cultural Revolution. Thousands of monks and nuns were sent to labor camps. Hundreds of ancient monasteries were destroyed wholesale. Arbitrary agricultural reforms, such as imposed planting of unfamiliar crops and the collectivization of yak and goat herds, undermined traditional Tibetan life. The population was further destabilized when the Chinese government encouraged non-Tibetan Han Chinese people to settle in Tibet, thereby weakening the cultural foundations of the region.

In spite of these hardships, Tibetan culture has continued to thrive under the stewardship of the exiled Dalai Lama, who received the Nobel Peace Prize in 1989. A charismatic figure, he has been able to force the Chinese government into seeking normalized relations, restoring temples, allowing some religious freedoms, and permitting some degree of free enterprise. Attempts by the government to bring the Dalai Lama back to China have been unsuccessful so far. The Dalai Lama, along with international celebrities and activists, continues in the struggle to safeguard Tibetan human rights.

Day 13: Climb to Potala Palace

One of the grandest monuments in all of Asia: the extraordinary Potala Palace. Built in the seventeenth century (atop the original seventh-century site), it boasts more than one thousand rooms, including the Red Palace (where the Dalai Lama once lived), ten thousand chapels, and a labyrinth of mysterious dungeons. It took seven thousand workers and one thousand five hundred artists and craftsmen more than fifty years to build the adjoining White and Red palaces. This Eastern architectural triumph was the world's tallest building before the creation of twentieth-century skyscrapers.

There are 425 steps, so we took our time but were proud of everyone for making it to the top as we viewed an array of Buddhist treasures along the way. Of particular note are the rich gold and jewel-encrusted tombs of eight Dalai Lamas. Perched on Red Mountain, the palace offers sweeping views of the city and the surrounding immense peaks that are as extraordinary as its interior.

Then we visited the Tibet Museum, where extensive exhibits on Tibet's history and culture are housed in a building built in traditional Tibetan style. Thousands of years of Tibetan history, politics, religion, and customs are revealed in displays of books, sculpture, art, and daily items like clothing.

Day 14: Barkhor Bazaar

We walked to the Barkhor Bazaar, a section of the oldest part of Lhasa that bustles with marketplace activity and religious devotion.

We entered the 1,300-year-old Jokhang Temple, where we saw Buddhist pilgrims making clockwise circuits on their hands and knees in reverence to one of Tibet's most sacred sites. Thousands of yak-butter candles flicker inside beneath the enlightened gaze of the golden Jowo Sakyamuni, the seventh-century Buddha statue that the temple was built to house.

Day 15: Fly to Chongqing to Board Ship

Another flight this time from Lhasa to Chongqing where we had dinner at a local restaurant in Chongqing before embarking on our Yangtze River cruise ship and spent our first night onboard

Day 16: Cruising Up the Yangtze River

We visited Shi Bao Zhai (or "Precious Stone Fortress"), a rocky buttress that is best known for the historic twelve-story wooden pagoda that grips the side of its cliff.

Day 17: The Three Gorges

The Yangtze River cruise took us through Qutang Gorge, the farthest upstream of the Three Gorges. Although the shortest of the three, the Qutang is by far the most dramatic, with sheer cliffs and such remarkable features as the Meng Liang staircase, painstakingly carved by a loyal bodyguard attempting to recover his master's body from the cliff face. We passed Daxi Village, the site of western China's earliest known civilization. The seventy-four tombs here contain archaeological finds up to six thousand years old. Overlooking the west end of the gorge is Baidicheng, or White Emperor City. Baidicheng dates to AD 25 and has long been a refuge for would-be kings and poets. We explored Lesser Three Gorges. We enter the Wu Gorge, renowned for the quiet beauty of its forested mountains. The Twelve Peaks are ranked alongside the gorge.

At Wushan, we boarded smaller river craft for an excursion up the Daning River or the Shennong Stream, both tributaries of the Yangtze. Here we drifted through the exquisite Lesser Three Gorges: Dragon-Gate Gorge, Misty Gorge, and Emerald Gorge where the water is actually an emerald green color. We passed between sheer precipices and saw burial tombs on the high walls.

Day 18: Tour of the Three Gorges Dam

We disembarked for an interesting tour of the Three Gorges Dam, the world's largest dam, measuring 606 feet high and 6,500 feet long.

Although a dam was proposed as long ago as 1919 by Sun Yat-Sen, the present site was selected by an American team of engineers in the early 1940s. The project gained momentum in the 1980s and began in earnest in 1990. In 1997, the cofferdam was completed, and the main structure begun. The dam has two five-stage locks to raise and lower ships to the different river levels. Each lock in the five stages is 65 feet high and 910 feet long.

This massive project has pitted China's economic interests against the concerns of historic preservationists and environmentalists worldwide. In addition to flooding some of the world's most spectacular scenic areas and rich ecosystems to a depth of 325 feet, the waters submerged some thirty-five notable historic sites (some of which were relocated). The 632 square miles of terrain being inundated as the reservoir fills include 13 cities, 140 towns, 1,352 villages, 657 factories, and 66,000 acres of cultivated land. Approximately 1.3 million people are being relocated to new towns above the high-water mark.

The Chinese government points to the benefits of the Three Gorges Dam, including its ability to control the area's severe flooding, the huge and much-needed hydroelectric potential, the opening of the upper Yangtze to ten-thousand-ton ships, and the irrigation value of the water.

We reboarded the ship and cruised to Yichang, where we disembarked and had lunch before boarding a bus for a six-hour ride to Wuhan where we spent a night.

Day 19: Fly to Hong Kong

After flying to Hong Kong, we took an orientation walk to learn how to use the public transportation and had the rest of the day at leisure.

Day 20: City Tour of Hong Kong

We started out by bus on a city tour. We explored the city's traditional Chinatown district, including bustling Ladder Street. We took the Midlevel's Escalator, the world's longest covered outdoor escalator, which takes about twenty minutes to travel from end to end. It was raining, and my spirits were dampened. I was simply homesick. I get that way after about ten days of travel and I was so ready to go home to sleep in our own bed by that point.

Day 21: Hong Kong at Leisure

Hong Kong on our own time but all I recall is packing to go home and a farewell dinner that evening. Of course, Joe did some shopping for T-shirts.

Day 22 and 23: Homeward Bound

The flights back to St. Louis were long but without a hitch. We were happy to have made this trip together but also very happy to get back home safely.

Forbidden City
Beijing, China 2007

Potala Palace
Lhasa, Tibet

CHAPTER 34

Three-Generation Safari 2007

Three generations of our family shared a wonderful three-week trip to Tanzania and Zanzibar. Joe and I visited Joe's former St. Stephens classmate Bede Smith and wife, Doreen, in London, England on our way to East Africa and shared dinner with Bede again on the return trip.

We spent two days on the Island of Zanzibar with our friends, Charlie and Nancy Crane where we toured the historical area of Stone Town and tasted local delicacies on the beach as the sun set over the Indian Ocean. Zanzibar is famous for its carved and highly decorated wooden doors as well as carved chests. We visited a rain forest with a large colony of red colobus monkeys, a species found only on Zanzibar. A tour of the spice area from which so many rich spices are grown and exported was interesting.

Family members who joined us in Tanzania on a photographic wildlife safari were Mike, Jill, Taylor, and Trevor Sorensen of Springfield, Missouri, and Scott and Gretchen Merrill of Oceanside, California. In Mwanza, our son Joe who was working at the GEITA Goldmine in Tanzania met and joined his family for a week of vacation.

A charter flight took our group to Rubondo Island in Lake Victoria, which is the second largest lake in the world. Everyone caught and released large Nile Perch. The biggest fish caught by Scott weighed more than eighty pounds. At night hippopotamus grazed on the grass in front of the tented camp, and during the day, large crocodiles were spotted in the area. After three days on Rubondo Island, we flew back to the mainland and began a safari journey through the Serengeti Plains where we had the rare good fortune to encounter two leopards in a tree in addition to other game.

The highlight was spending a full day in Ngorongoro Crater, which was recently named the Eighth Wonder of the World, a classification that we felt it deserves. The floor of the beautiful extinct volcanic crater is twenty-four miles wide and contains a large variety of African wildlife. We witnessed a rhinoceros chasing six lions out of his territory. We saw hundreds of Cape buffalo and elephants, plus thousands of zebras, wildebeests, antelopes, and gazelles. In total, our group found over thirty lions, five rhinos, and countless giraffes during the safari. It was the season for migratory birds, so we spotted a large variety of birds ranging from the tiny red bishops to the huge ostriches and saddle-billed Storks.

Our family had lived in Dar es Salaam, Tanzania from 1980 to 1983 on assignment with the USAID, so visiting the capitol again was nostalgic. Gretchen and Jill had the opportunity to show their husbands and kids where they had lived, gone to school, and played in their youth. It was a fun three generational experience.

Family leaving Rubondo Island, Tanzania 2007

CHAPTER 35

Life at the Lake of the Ozarks

No Place Like Home

Not having a home back in USA that we could call our own had always bothered me while living abroad. I wanted a place where our kids could establish roots, at least temporarily, during our home leaves. My parents were always fantastic about accommodating our large family. But it was stressful for everyone to invade their home for long periods with lots of luggage.

Over the years, we had bought a couple homes that we had rented out, but we never had much luck with those properties. We always lost money on them and those places were never available for our use.

So after the embassy bombings in Kenya and Tanzania in 1998, we began to seriously look for a place to buy at the Lake of the Ozarks region where we often vacationed with the family. We found a four-bedroom condo and Joan and Jill checked it out for us since we were in Ghana. They approved so we purchased a place at the Ledges. It served our purposes well for the next thirteen years.

The condo was located right on the water. It had two levels and an enormous patio overlooking the Lake of the Ozarks at the mile 20 marker. Joan beautified the adjacent hillside by planting flowers and a Japanese maple tree.

We bought an entire house full of furniture and then rented it out during the summers for the next four years while we were still abroad. We blocked out weeks when we or family or friends wanted to use the condo.

Our family spent many holidays together enjoying each other and the lake view. It became a tradition to host New Year's Eve parties with twenty-five to thirty family members enjoying the gourmet meals prepared by our cousins Judy and Floyd Mahon. We loved to BBQ on the patio and watch the boat races. We screened in the upper deck and added windows so that area became a three-season room.

The condo became our home away from home. We would stay there together for prolonged periods between assignments. Juliana used it while freelancing. I spent three years of going back and forth between the condo, visiting my parents and being with Joe while he was working in the Dominican Republic. Then when he went off to Pakistan to work for eight months in 2008, I was there alone.

Home Invasions

It was not so much fun to be at the condo by myself. We had security grills installed on the patio door, kitchen door, and windows. This was a result of having had a break-in soon after we bought the condo and had it furnished, even before we had put it on the market for rental. My dad always worried about how we would get out in case of fire. Actually, Dad mentioned this concern to me again on the phone when I called to wish him a happy eighty-ninth birthday the night before he died.

I was more concerned about how easily someone could get inside without being seen since our condo was one level below the parking lot and hidden on two sides. One cold January day while Joe was out of the country and I was staying there alone, I returned from shopping in the middle of the day and realized the kitchen door had been pried open with a crowbar. I opened the door and yelled "Who is in my house?" My dumb question and stupid reaction was met with silence. I ran back to the car and called the police. Meanwhile the thief or thieves ran away without my seeing anyone. It was obvious to the police and me when we did enter that they had been inside when I came home and shouted. They had piled up stereo equipment and other valuables and had left in a hurry. One thing that they did get away with was irreplaceable for us. We had a beautiful leather case that held our home videos taken when the kids were little. We checked the trash bins all around to no avail just hoping that they might have tossed our videos.

We were relieved to finally sell the condo in 2011 after two years on the market during a housing bust. We bought our retirement home in Springfield, Missouri.

Winter Park, Colorado
December 2007

CHAPTER 36

Bali and Singapore

With Juliana, Molly, and Kris in 2007

Shortly after returning from our family safari in Tanzania, Joe and I had another opportunity to extend our travel adventures. Escapes Unlimited advertised a ten-day trip to Bali and Singapore for under twelve hundred dollars including airfare from Los Angeles, hotels with breakfast, and tours. That was too great a bargain to turn down. Joe and I, our daughter Juliana, cousin Molly, and friend Kris flew on Singapore Airlines, consistently rated as one of the best airlines in the world.

Our first stop was Singapore. This small island state has been a twentieth century success story. From a per capita GDP of five hundred US dollars at independence in 1965, it has risen to fifty-six thousand dollars in 2015, a period of fifty years. The infant mortality rate declined from twenty-six per thousand births in 1965 to only two per thousand in 2015. There has been a dramatic change in home ownership from 4 percent in 1965 to 85 percent in 2015. This has been achieved by adopting an export led policy of economic growth, welcoming direct foreign investment and putting a large emphasis on educating the population (in 2015 35 percent of the labor force had tertiary education level versus 2 percent in 1965).

This impressive performance was achieved as a result of the leadership of Lee Kwan Yew who incorporated what some call soft authoritarianism. This latter is reflected in the number of laws that have jokingly resulted in Singapore being called a "fine city." Some of these include: chewing gum $500 fine; not flushing a public toilet $500 fine; urinating in an elevator $500 fine. We purchased a coffee cup in Singapore with these and other fines that illustrate what we would consider the heavy hand of government. Without a doubt, the Singapore of today is a beautiful modern city. In our two days there, we enjoyed wonderful Indian and Chinese cuisine. While riding the beautiful new modern subway with our guide book in our hand, we were approached by a gentleman who offered to show us around. He was smartly dressed and spoke good English, so we decided to trust him. He took us to a number of highlights, so we invited him to join us for lunch. We asked him to select the restaurant. He took us to an Indian restaurant where the plates were banana leaves. He ordered the food and it was delicious, except for one dish that included fish heads. Since neither Joe nor I like fish, we passed on the dish. We rode the subway from down town to the Singapore zoo to see the orangutan section where the orangutans are allowed free roaming privileges. Joe had his movie camera and wanted to record the orang-utan swinging through the trees. As he was filming, an orangutan overhead had a bathroom emergency and dumped his feces on Joe's head and shoulders. He was a mess, but Juliana helped wash his shirt and cap. We purchased new ones at the zoo gift shop. We went to the world's famous Raffles Hotel for a Singapore sling cocktail created in the hotel bar in the 1920s.

After two delightful days in Singapore, we flew to Bali. One of more than seventeen hundred islands that make up the republic of Indonesia. While Indonesia is predominantly Muslim, the popula-tion of Bali is 95 percent Hindu. Balinese are known as gracious and friendly, and the island beaches are lovely. We spent our first two days in Bali close to the beach at Sanur, then spent two days in the interior at Ubud, the cultural capital of Bali.

Our wonderful guide and driver took us around the island. We were able to see and photograph the rice terraces for which the island is known. In Ubud, one of our favorite sites was the monkey temples in the Sacred Monkey Forest Sanctuary. However, we were warned the monkeys are always looking for food and could snatch it. We were able to ride elephants through the forest, visit Hindu tem-ples, and learn of current and past cultural practices. One custom we found interesting was the tradition of enclosing newlyweds together in a house for thirty days as a "honeymoon" period. Weddings were arranged so the newly married couple knew little about each other, so this was a "get acquainted" period. They could only leave the building temporarily to go to the toilet.

The Bali and Singapore trip was truly one of our favorite trips and great value for money.

CHAPTER 37

Australia and New Zealand

We had been friends with my cousin Judy Mahon and her husband, Floyd, for a number of years. We had discussed traveling together overseas but had never finalized anything. Finally in 2006, we agreed to take a joint trip to Australia and New Zealand. We held several planning meetings and narrowed the trip focus to the South Island of New Zealand, and the southeastern part of Australia, including South Australia, Victoria, and New South Wales. We restricted ourselves to these areas so as to meet our budget and time restraints.

We decided to plan the trip ourselves rather than use a travel agent. This meant agreeing where we would stay and when, as well as making all of the reservations. We researched travel guidebooks in the internet and made a few calls to Australia. It took us several weeks to arrange everything, but it was worth the cost savings.

For years, Joe and I had wanted to visit California wine country but because of our overseas assignments had never been able to work it into our schedule. We reasoned it would be cost-effective to visit California on the way to Australia.

San Francisco and Napa Valley

In September 2006 Juliana, Joe, and I flew to San Francisco and we were picked up by Gretchen and Scott who had driven up from Oceanside and they had enjoyed scenic Highway 1. We spent a couple days touring San Francisco. We stayed in a hotel downtown and visited Pier 39 to see and smell the seals. We ate crab soup served in sourdough bowls. We walked and walked up and down hills and went to a Chinese restaurant for dim sum. When we arrived at the dim sum restaurant, we found we had a misunderstanding about lunch. Joe and our daughter, Gretchen, had assumed that we were going to a nice comfortable Chinese restaurant where we would have a nice a La Carte Chinese meal. In fact, a dim sum experience is somewhat the opposite of their concept. Dim sum is where small portions of individual foods are placed on tiny plates and pushed on carts around the restaurant. As you can image, it is not quiet and in that Chinatown restaurant in San Francisco, the carts were being pushed by people who had very little command of the English language. While both, Juliana and I, knew what to expect and like the dim sum restaurant concept for the others in our group, the judgment was less favorable, and I have never been able to get them back into a dim sum restaurant.

We drove down the crooked Lombard Street. We took the trolley. We enjoyed a tour of Alcatraz. Then Scott drove us out to Napa Valley to soak up wine country. Scott was such a good sport about being our designated driver. We stayed one night at Yountville in a refurnished train. Joe and Juliana went to The French Laundry where they had an amazing but very expensive eleven-course meal. We celebrated Gretchen and Scott's twentieth anniversary with a wonderful gourmet meal at the Chandon Vineyard. We sampled wine at as many vineyards in Napa Valley as time would permit before returning to the airport in San Francisco.

New Zealand, Here We Come

Floyd and Judy met us at the San Francisco airport after we had already checked into Qantas Air, where we had been surprised with an upgrade to first class. Floyd was able to charm the gal into upgrading them also. It was a fourteen-hour flight to Auckland so that was pure luxury to be able to stretch out and sleep. From Auckland, we caught a connecting flight to Christchurch on the South Island of New Zealand. We took a taxi to our rather drab hotel and decided we needed to go for a walk rather than spend time in that room.

New Zealand consists of two large islands: the North Island and the South Island. In planning our trip, we had decided to focus on the South Island because we believed it had greater natural beauty.

The South Island has what are called the Southern Alps which run the length of the island and provide beautiful alpine vistas. In addition to the alpine beauty of South Island, the sounds (fiords) on the western coast of the island are tourist attractions. South Island is also more rural, having only about 20 percent of the total population (1.2 million people) while having more than 50 percent of the land area. Sheep and dairy production are the largest economic activity, with the sheep population outnumbering the humans by more than twenty to one. The largest city on South Island is Christchurch, named after Christ Church College, Oxford.

We proceeded to take a three-hour walking tour around Christchurch with a wonderful former school principal as our delightful guide. It was an educational tour. He asked if we were going to Australia. When we answered in affirmative, his response was to remind us that "Australia was settled by convicts while New Zealand was settled by English gentlemen." I am so glad that we had enough energy to do that tour after our long trip, but first class made the difference. It was springtime in New Zealand and the flowers were gorgeous. Since then, Christchurch has been devastated by two major earthquakes which destroyed some of the beautiful old buildings that we had toured and admired.

The next day we caught a train across the South Island from Christchurch to Greymouth through the snow-capped mountains. There we rented a vehicle and began the drive on the left side of the road to Queenstown. New Zealand has many one-lane bridges and we did not understand the yield signs on the bridges so got a few angry fists when we crossed out of turn. Joe was driving when we crossed a joint railway and road bridge and hit something sharp. Within seconds, we had a flat tire. It was raining. The guys had to remove all our luggage in order to reach the spare tire. Judy and I held umbrellas over their heads while they changed the tire the tire change. On we drove toward Fox Glacier, but the car began making a strange noise. We would stop and look and not see anything wrong. It was a Sunday so there was no place open to get the tire repaired.

We enjoyed our hike to Fox Glacier which is the only remaining glacier located in the tropics. Joe went off alone to explore more and the rest of us fretted when it was getting dark and he had not returned. Just when we were about to seek a search party, here came smiling Joe. We had rented a nice cabin in the woods.

Next day we continued to drive toward Queenstown, and the noise grew ever louder. We were going around a curve in the mountains when a car suddenly passed us and flagged us down. We stopped and were shocked to learn that the tire was about to come off. A charming New Zealander with bulging muscles wanted to know who in the world had changed that tire. Judy and I giggled and pointed to our husbands. Obviously, they had not tightened the tire lugs enough. If we had lost that tire on that particular mountain road, we may never have been found and our families would not have known what happened to us. New Zealand reminded us of the United States in the 1950s when you could get two-bedroom cabins with cooking facilities cheaply.

When we reached Queenstown, we managed to call the car rental company. The flat tire was beyond repair and driving on the loose tire had damaged it too. So they offered us to trade vehicles. Well, the second one didn't have as much space in the trunk, so Judy and I had to hold luggage on our laps the rest of the way.

Floyd never liked heights, but he was willing to go up the cable car to the top of the mountain overlooking Queenstown so that we could have dinner at a nice restaurant and watch the sunset. It was less frightening for him to come down in the dark when we could not see the height. We stayed in a lovely condo there.

The next day we started our drive back across South Island for an overnight cruise on Milford Sound. The South Island of New Zealand reminds me of parts of Switzerland. Milford Sound is not really a sound but a fiord. Early settlers named it incorrectly. A sound is formed when a river valley is flooded by the sea, whereas Milford Sound was formed by the erosion impact of glaciers. Milford Sound is one of New Zealand's top tourist attractions. The ten-mile long Sound is a sheer narrow valley opening to the sea. The steep walls of the Sound include several mountain peaks, the most famous being Mitre Peak, so named because of its resemblance to a bishops mitre.

Because of the high amount of rainfall (over 270 inches a year) the Sound has a number of waterfalls.

To go from Queenstown to Milford Sound we had to cross the mountains. This meant taking the 3,490 foot Homer Tunnel through the mountains. Imagine our surprise when after departing sunny eastern South Island we exited the tunnel in a snowstorm on the western side of the mountains. Joe and I were delighted to see snow as we had been living in the tropics so long but for Floyd and Judy it was no big deal. After a couple miles, we stopped the car and got out to enjoy the snow. When we walked away from the car, green parrots arrived and began to attack the rubber seals around the car windows. We later found out that those parrots did like the taste of rubber. When we arrived at Milford Sound, we discovered that shortly after our exit the tunnel was closed for the day because of a concern for avalanches. Consequently, our overnight cruise only had fourteen passengers instead of the sixty-two who had booked passage. I am sure there were many frustrated and angry people on the other side of the tunnel. The service on our cruise was great with only fourteen passengers and the food was plentiful and good.

We spotted a tiny species of penguins while cruising the Milford Sound. Our boat backed into a waterfall on purpose so we all got splashed. We stopped at a research center where we went down into an observatory where we could see all the beautiful fish underwater.

On our return to Queenstown, we took a Lord of the Rings tour in the area where the movie had been filmed. Unfortunately, it was a bitter cold and windy day, so we didn't get to do everything listed for the tour, but it was interesting.

Before boarding our plane for Australia, we made an attempt to visit the Kawarau Gorge Suspension Bridge the place where bungee jumping started but nearly ran out of gas, so we decided to return to the airport for our flight to Adelaide. It wasn't exactly smooth sailing as Joe had a visa problem, and it took some arguing for them to allow us to board the plane. He had paid for the Australian visa online but somehow it was not recorded in the system.

Australia

For this trip, we had booked all the hotels, tours, and car rentals ourselves. It had taken some time, but we had saved a lot of money. The hotel in Adelaide was substandard and our room was on the second floor without an elevator. Joe always over packs and had a huge and heavy suitcase to lug upstairs.

Judy and Floyd were interested in taking the market and culinary tour, so we tagged along. It was delightful, but I had a toothache. We had eaten at a pub and I had cracked my tooth on a tough steak the prior evening. Our nice guide on the food tour kindly called her own dentist and got me in immediately. She walked us all there and he worked on my aching tooth. Later back home I had a root canal and crown put on that tooth, but I appreciated the temporary fix.

We spent one day on a bus trip to Kangaroo Island, where we found many seals on the beach, wonderful rock formations, and our first glimpse of wallabies and kangaroos and koalas

Next we rented a car and headed for Sydney, a distance of six hundred miles across the Outback. Joe did most of the driving. The first stop we made was in the Barossa Valley at the vineyards. In Australia, the wine tastings are free and plentiful. My favorite memory is of having lunch under a gum tree at a vineyard. We purchased a bottle of wine and their sampler snack plate. The tray only cost $11 and we could not eat all the unique goodies. It was a magical moment of making memories together.

We stayed in Mildura for a week at a timeshare condo that Judy and Floyd had managed to trade. I wondered what we would do in Mildura, a town of about forty thousand, for a week but we had a ball. Sunday morning, we attended Mass. After the sermon, the priest asked his parishioners to fill out a form. We were sitting up front, and while the others worked on the form, the priest came over to speak to us. He then invited us to his house for breakfast after Mass. We were delighted to meet an Australian couple, Laurie and Cath Fry, at Father Murphy's home and had easy conversation with them. Laurie asked what we would like to see, and naturally, we replied kangaroos. Laurie said that he was a beekeeper and would drive us to the countryside where we might find some kangaroos. He collected us from the condo and off we went. Sure enough, we located kangaroos. Then we picked up Cath and went for lunch at a vineyard outside of Mildura. Much to Cath's horror, Joe ordered a kangaroo steak. We then went back to their home, which was surrounded by citrus trees and rosebushes and had tea and coffee and got to know the Frys a little better. Laurie was a retired school superintendent, and Cath was a retired schoolteacher. They were around our ages and we found them to be so open and hospitable.

The next morning there was a knock on the condo door. There stood Laurie with a full basket of fruit and eggs and honey from his hives. He took us to the grocery store so that we could get supplies for our week in Mildura. He suggested that we might want to visit the Gem Shop outside of town. Well, yes, that sounded like a good place to go. Joe bought me an opal ring there. Judy bought some pink quartz for my mom.

Laurie also took us to his club, the Workman's Bar historically a men's club, but Judy and I were allowed to enter. We had wondered how the St. Louis Cardinals were doing in the playoffs and Laurie said that was the only place we might get reception. It was a beautiful club and we actually did get to see the Cardinals win a crucial game and visited local vineyards.

We took turns cooking in the condo and played lots of cards and games. It was a relaxing week that passed too quickly.

From Mildura we continued driving across the Outback to the Blue Mountains. There we had booked an old cottage that was full of antiques. They had provided sufficient food for us to make our breakfasts. We went for high tea at a shop that displayed over three thousand tea sets from around the world and a store full of old wedding dresses and other relics. Floyd fell in love with the scones that were covered in a fresh strawberry jam and clotted cream. He bought a jar to take back to our cottage. It really was delicious. We viewed the famous sandstone pillars that are called the Three Sisters.

Continuing on the drive to Sydney, we stopped at a reserve that cares for koalas and kangaroos. Judy fed the kangaroos and they got a little aggressive with her. We all got to hold the cute koalas. We had seen a few in the wild but it was nice to be up so close to them. We also rode the Katoomba Scenic Railway, an open-sided cog-rail that descends at a fifty-two degree angle.

Arriving in Sydney itself was a bit scary. We had a map but were unsure of which road to take when we came to a fork. Joe pulled into the middle of the road and people honked at us. Judy and Floyd had a reservation at the Marriott and Joe and I had reserved a different hotel. We did manage to find our way to our hotel and Floyd and Judy then got rid of the rental car. It was a relief to be free of that responsibility, but it had served us well.

We spent the next several days in Sydney. We walked across the Sydney Bridge but made no attempt nor had any desire to climb it as many people were doing. We strolled over to the Sydney Opera House and took a tour of that magnificent building with its rich history. The tour was fascinating and informative. The Sydney Opera House is today recognized as one of the twentieth century's most distinctive buildings. The design of the opera house was selected via international competition launched in 1955. The winner was Jorn Utzan, a Danish architect. While the design presented by Utzan was indeed beautiful as construction started on the building, it was discovered that the technology at that time did not exist for the construction to be completed. Consequently, the project started in 1963 was not completed until 1973 after resolving a number of the technical problems associated with the design. The original cost and schedule estimate was seven million dollars, with an estimated completion date of 1963. The actual final cost was one hundred two million and the completion time was sixteen years. In spite of the problems in turning a vision into a reality, the final product was a great success. We learned that *The Pirates of Penzance* was playing but were told it was sold out, but there may be seats available early next morning. Judy and Floyd went to the box office the next morning and scored four incredible seats in the center only seven rows from the stage. We dressed up for the performance as best we could with clothes that had been traveling for a few weeks. We marvel at the acoustics in the opera house. It was an awesome experience.

The Sydney Aquarium was most spectacular. It is probably the best we ever visited in the world. We had a fantastic lunch buffet at a rotating restaurant in Sydney. Judy and Joe devoured the fresh oysters.

Twenty-three days of traveling with our cousins without a cross word being said. We parted company in Sydney with the promise to travel together again. Joe and I flew back home while Floyd and Judy flew up to Hamilton Island, so they could enjoy the beaches. They missed their connection on the return trip so were delayed a day in getting home. All in all, it was a memorable trip for all of us.

CHAPTER 38

Pakistan

In December 2007, Joe received a request from a former USAID colleague to consider applying for a position at the USAID/Pakistan mission for six months. Under terms offered in critical country posts, he could use accrued leave after three months. USAID/Pakistan had received a large supplemental funding level subject to the condition that the mission could develop projects on an urgent basis and be able to impact both the economy and welfare of the poor. Joe's role was to help jump-start the design of projects in the private sector, agriculture, health, education, and infrastructure sectors of the economy. After discussing the situation, we agreed that Joe should go to assist the mission.

On February 4, 2008, Joe left for Islamabad for a six-month consultancy. No spouses were allowed in country unless they had an assigned position either with USAID or the embassy. We endured a painful separation that extended to eight months with only two reunions during his tenure there. He came home in May to take me to the Kentucky Derby, and again in September to celebrate our forty-fifth wedding anniversary on Easter Island.

It was a tense and worrisome time apart as the security situation deteriorated during his stay. Shortly after his arrival, Joe had a close encounter with terrorism. Joe and several colleagues were eating at an Islamabad restaurant when a restaurant, a block away, was bombed. Immediately, Joe called to assure me he was okay although I had not yet heard or seen the report. Several months later, the Marriot Hotel was bombed and shattered the windows in the guest house where Joe was staying. Fortunately, he was in Missouri at the time of the bombing but his broken bedroom windows were boarded for a couple months after he returned to Pakistan.

Given the work load and the security situation, Joe and the other USAID staff worked seven days a week for ten to twelve hours a day. During Joe's absence, I spent precious time with my widowed mother, and I cherish those memories. Whenever I needed a retreat, I would return to our condo at the Lake of the Ozarks and work on making a memory quilt for Joe. Our condo was a central gathering place for our Missouri kids, and I always enjoyed their visits.

We both hated the forced separation. We decided to search for another country to work after the Pakistan assignment where we could be together. He applied for an assignment in Indonesia and was accepted to begin work in early 2009. I was happy when he returned safely from Pakistan. Unfortunately, another close friend and colleague, Warren Weinstein, was not so lucky. Joe and Warren were in Pakistan at the same time, and occasionally he and Warren would have dinner. After Joe's departure, Warren was kidnapped from his home, held captive for a number of years and was accidentally killed by a "friendly fire" drone during a rescue attempt.

Diplomatic assignments overseas are dangerous especially today, but they are an important component of our foreign policy, and my husband and I are proud to have represented our country abroad.

CHAPTER 39

Kentucky Derby

My mom instilled in me a love for the Kentucky Derby at a young age. So when Joe surprised me with a four-day package to attend the derby in 2008, I felt a bit guilty not to take her with us. But Joe had been away for months working in Pakistan and we were anxious to have some alone time.

We drove from our condo in Missouri to Lexington, Kentucky where the tour group was staying. We talked nonstop and never once turned on the radio. It was so good to be together again, and I was over the moon to be fulfilling a dream. We visited a stud farm and a thoroughbred farm where our guide was the son of my favorite jockey, Gary Stevens. I asked to take a picture with him and he kindly consented, remarking that all the ladies loved his dad.

At the Woodford Reserve, we learned all about making Kentucky whiskey and had a tasting at the end of the tour. Naturally, we bought a bottle.

Our tour took us to the Kentucky Horse Museum where we visited the gravesite of Secretariat. We spent two hours going through the International section and didn't have time to tour the national part. One day I want to return and finish the tour as it was so well done and interesting.

I had three lovely hats decorated by cousin Barbara Lafond Carlson and thought I looked spiffy in my new linen suits. But it rained. It poured on the day of the Oaks races. Joe had paid extra to get a box in the upper level, so we were mostly protected from the rain, but we got soaked to/from the bus. The suits still wilted.

He had also bought the package for all-inclusive food and drinks and was under the false impression that the special area was near our seats. Instead, the tent was beside the red-carpet area about a fifteen-minute walk away. That was a waste of money because it meant missing some of the races. Seating was also crowded. Some people never left that area and simply watched the races on the small TV.

A record crowd of 163,000 people attended that year. I loved the hats of both men and women and all the fancy clothes.

One complaint we had was the center of the racetrack has been built up with concession stands to the point that one can't see the horses when rounding the opposite side of the field. In fact, one can watch the races better from the comfort of home rather than being there in person. We will not likely go to the derby again, but it was a thrill to do it one time. Instead, we started a new tradition on derby day. We break out the Woodford Reserve that we bought on the tour and make some delicious mint juleps.

Joe and I aren't big gamblers, but we did wage two bucks on each race to keep it interesting. In the end, we broke even. For the big and final derby race, we splurged and bet $5 each. Our money was on Big Brown and on Eight Bells, the filly who ran her heart out and broke her leg during the race. We were so excited that she came in second but were totally unaware of the tragedy on the track as the goal line was on the other side of the track and they didn't broadcast what was happening. Eight Bells was put down after the race. I cried and cried when I learned this. Big Brown had an impressive victory and went on to win the Preakness but stumbled coming out of the gate at the Belmont, so he didn't win the Triple Crown.

You can bet that Joe and I and our little mascot Bella was cheering loudly in 2015 when American Pharaoh won the Triple Crown. It was a longtime coming since Affirmed won it in 1978.

CHAPTER 40

Easter Island
(Rapa Nui) Moai

Since Joe was busy working in Pakistan for eight months in 2008, he left the planning for our forty-fifth anniversary trip up to me to decide where we should go and work out the details. Usually Joe acts as travel agent so I felt a big responsibility on my shoulders. When I decided that we should make the trip to Easter Island and Chile, then Juliana asked to join us. We always enjoy traveling with her so of course we urged Juliana to come along. I researched many avenues.

After a long flight to Santiago, we walked around the city center and booked tours to visit vineyards in Chile. Joe and I had enjoyed a tour of *Concha y Toro* vineyard in 1979, so we wanted to share that experience with Juliana. It was so delightful that we went again after Easter Island. We also toured and tasted wine at a boutique vineyard on the outskirts of Santiago, where we were introduced to a delicious Carmenere reserve. The Carmenere grape was a well-known wine in the Medoc region of France until it was effectively wiped out by a Phyllorera plague in France in 1867. As a result, the grape was considered to have been lost forever. In 1994, a French researcher in Chile discovered that a Chilean grape thought to be a merlot was in fact a Bordeaux Carmenere. Apparently, cuttings of Carmenere had been taken to Chile from France before the plague. The growers in Chile thought that the Carmenere was a merlot and processed the two wines as one. After 1994, the Chilean Department of Agriculture officially recognized Carmenere as a distinct variety. We fell in love with that inexpensive wine, so we bought six bottles to take home. That ended up being an expensive deal because they were so heavy that my brand-new luggage got busted beyond repair.

Easter Island had long been a top priority on our bucket list. The *moai* sculptures and mysterious history of the tiny island located two thousand miles off the coast of Chile are fascinating. It was a nearly six-hour flight on LAN Chile to one of the most isolated islands in the world. Not easy to get to and not easy to land there. Due to the winds, planes come in fast and we made a turbulent and hard landing which kept Juliana and I white knuckled.

This tiny speck of volcanic rock in the ocean is one-thousand-two-hundred-forty miles east from the nearest Polynesian island neighbor. Mysteriously between AD 500–900 groups of Polynesian settlers arrived on the island.

The history of Easter Island should be a lesson learned. Over the time, the population reached an estimated 15,000 before the numbers crashed due to environmental degradation and overpopulation. By the arrival of the first Europeans in 1722, it had fallen to under three thousand people. Around AD 900–1100, the islanders began carving large basalt statues from the volcanic rock and transported them up to six miles from the quarry where they were carved. The statues called moai, on average were thirteen-foot tall and weighed about ten tons. The tallest erected statue was thirty-two-feet tall and weighed seventy-five tons. Most of the statues were carved from one volcanic site with work continuing until 1600. The moai are believed to be statues of gods and/or deceased chiefs. The moai were, with one exception, always facing inland at the coast. There is no positive proof how the moai were moved from the volcano where they were carved to the coast where they were placed. There is general agreement that trees were cut, and the moai were rolled on them. The use of trees for the moai and the need to clear forests for cropland led to deforestation and erosion. Likewise, the destruction of the forests meant no wood for boats which severely restricted the diet as they could not catch fish. It is possible that the declining food production led to war and cannibalism, and the declining population.

In 1722, when a Dutch trading ship "discovered" the island on Easter Sunday, the population had declined precipitously. Like many encounters between native inhabitants and European explorers, the history of Easter Island encountered disease and slavery. In

1888, Chile annexed the island which it still claims. Easter Island is a Chilean owned Polynesian island in the southeastern Pacific Ocean. It is famous for its extraordinary collection of archaeological sites, including 887 monumental statues, called *moai*, which were created by the early Rapa Nui people. The population has dwindled to around five thousand now.

The official name of the eight-mile-wide by fifteen-mile-long island is Rapa Nui although it is more popularly known as Easter Island. It is like visiting an open-air museum. Rapa Nui is simply spellbinding, fascinating, and intriguing.

Isolation has helped preserve the 1,500-year-old mysterious congregation of huge volcanic rock sculptures. The landscape is unique. We didn't spend any time on the uncrowded beach but understood that the snorkeling is superb in clear water.

The first guided tour we took was less than satisfying. The teenage guide was more interested in talking on her cell phone or to the bus driver. In fact, we were more knowledgeable about the history of the island than the young lady who lived there.

Fortunately, I had booked a full-day tour on our anniversary with an American archeologist, Paul Pownall, who had worked and lived there since 1968. I was fortunate to have seen Paul's name recommended on Trip Advisor and had contacted him. What a difference a day makes. Paul's knowledge and warm personality made our tour educational and worthwhile and it was one of the most pleasant days we have ever spent with a tour guide.

I had come down with a stomach virus the night before our special day and almost missed this great tour. We went to a French restaurant that night and shared a delicious *paella* which was amazing. Joe also got sick the next day, but thank goodness, Juliana remained healthy. Usually she is the one with the bad luck on trips.

My favorite site was an amazing collection of fifteen moai facing inward on the beach at Ahu Tongariki. These were once knocked over by a *tsunami*.

I still ponder one of the most mysterious places on Earth. I am so grateful to have had the opportunity to witness its mystique in person with Joe and Juliana.

Joe, Juliana and Hope with *moai* sculptures on Rapa Nui in 2008.

CHAPTER 41

Indonesia

Jakarta, Indonesia, January–August 2009

Our friend Donnie Harrington informed Joe about a vacant position with USAID in Jakarta, Indonesia. Joe was selected and there we met his boss, John Pennell, who would have a big influence on our lives and vice versa ever since. It was meant to be a two-year assignment, so we packed out again.

We were housed in an apartment on the fifth floor of the Shangri La Hotel complex. It was spacious enough and the view was lovely. I met Mei Lee Bullington while reading the newspaper in the lobby, and we became fast friends. Mei Lee introduced me to other women staying there and we had a fun group. We also clung together when there was a terrorist attack on another hotel. We hugged and chatted when a strong earthquake rattled our nerves too. These lovely women were my salvation as I could not work and would have been bored.

But the traffic in Jakarta . . . oh my, the traffic was horrible. They drove on the left side of the road, which made me more nervous. So we purchased a used Toyota and hired a driver. He took us to church, the market, the mall, the bead lady, and the airport and any place we wanted to go. I was so intimidated by the traffic that I preferred staying at the Shangri La with my friends, so our sweet driver had an easy job as he only took Joe to/from work.

We felt totally pampered whenever we partook of the brunch at the Shangri La and it was very inexpensive, relatively speaking. Joe enjoyed the champagne and the fresh seafood while I normally selected the Thai food. There were ice sculptures and an entire room full of desserts. It was always a feast to remember.

Indonesia turned out to be one of our favorite postings. Joe enjoyed his work in the USAID Agriculture and Economic Growth Office. The Indonesian government was committed to the development of the country, and our cooperation with them in the areas of agricultural development and economic policy was conducted in a productive and collaborative manner. Whenever we had the opportunity, we also traveled around Indonesia to see its many attractions. Traveling was not always easy and inexpensive as Indonesia is a country of over seventeen thousand islands scattered over a distance of thirty-two hundred miles from east to west. This meant having to fly to most locations which at times was challenging because of the maintenance problems of some of its airlines. Nonetheless, we were committed to see as much of the country as possible.

Borobudur

Standing long before Angkor Wat in Cambodia and the great cathedrals in Europe, Borobudur Temple has stood gallantly in the land of Java, Indonesia, since the mid–ninth century. The building is a UNESCO world heritage site and named as the most magnificent and the largest monument and stupa complex in the world. Buddhist people seek enlightenment there. Borobudur Temple wall panels are filled with 2,672 sculptured reliefs. Tourists seek and find beauty. Borobudur, originally constructed as a Buddhist Temple, was abandoned in the fourteenth century after the island's conversion to Islam. It consists of nine platforms, one on top of the other, six large square terraces with three circular ones and a stupa on top. It is ninety-five-feet tall and contains over five hundred statues of Buddha and covers an area of around four acres. Over centuries, the abandoned temple became covered by a combination of vegetative growth and volcanic ash from volcanoes situated close by. The temple was rediscovered by Thomas Raffles in 1814 who organized the clearing of the temple.

I was fortunate enough to visit the temple twice while living in Jakarta. My first time was with Juliana and we took a sunrise tour. It was magnificent to sit on a stupa and watch the sun rising over the nearby twin volcanoes of Sindoro-Sumbing and Merbabu-Merapi, one of which was belching gas and ashes. It has since exploded. The same volcano had erupted many times over the centuries covering Borobudur with ash which accounts for the dark color of the stones.

The second visit was with Joe, Jenny, and Mike in 2009, but that day there was a haze that completely shrouded the volcano. Nonetheless, we had a good tour of the temple before Mike and Jenny took an elephant ride around the grounds.

Borneo to Seek Orangutans

Joe and I along with Mike and Jenny flew from Jakarta to Kalimantan, where we boarded a boat, for a four-hour ride to an eco-lodge in the jungle. The next day the four of us were the only passengers on a small boat. It reminded us of scenes from *The African Queen* as the river became more and more narrow until we were pushing through reeds on both sides. We saw a baby crocodile in the water and imagined that there were lychees and large snakes down there too. There was a cool breeze and that trip is high in my memory bank for pleasurable adventures.

Our quest was to find orangutans. The first attempt was not successful after a long trek through dense trees. But the second try was amazing. We encountered a large family of orangutans deep in the forest. It was interesting to watch their interactions. They played, fought, scratched themselves, beat their chests, hooted, ate leaves, and gracefully swung from the trees. They almost seemed oblivious to our presence. On the return boat ride, we saw more orangutans as well as a large colony of big-nosed proboscis monkeys in the trees.

We sat on the floor of the small boat which had shade covering us in order to eat lunch. It was delicious, and we were hungry from our long walks. After lunch, we saw them washing our dishes in the dirty river. Nobody got sick, but we would not have had such a hearty appetite if we had seen that happen before our meal. Just goes to show that sometimes ignorance is bliss.

Komodo Dragons

High on our "bucket list" of things to do while living in Indonesia was to fulfill Joe's childhood dream of seeing a komodo dragon in the wild. The komodo dragon is the largest living monitor lizard in the world. It typically reaches a length of ten feet and a weight of one hundred fifty pounds although it has been known to reach a weight of over three hundred pounds. It is only found on five islands in the eastern part of Indonesia. It only became known to the outside world in 1910. Because it was first identified on Komodo island, that became the name by which it is known. The two principle islands on which the dragons are located are Komodo and Rinca. Juliana had a choice of going to see the orangutans or the Komodo dragons and she chose the latter. We first flew down to Denpasar, Bali, to spend the night. We took a glass-bottom boat out over the coral reef and saw lots of fish and a rare sea snake. We walked on a beautiful beach area.

Then we boarded a plane for Labuan Bajo on Flores Island where we spent a night and took a city tour although there was little to see but poverty everywhere. The following day Joe, Juliana, and I were the only passengers (plus a crew of five) on the small MV *Keti* slow boat to Rinca Island, inhabited by a large number of Komodo dragons. The boat we hired for a day was built similar to a Chinese junk. It had sleeping and cooking accommodations. The top of the boat had a flat shaded area where we could sit and observe beautiful islands as we floated along. It was a gorgeous three-hour ride past a number of the seventeen-thousand-plus islands that comprise Indonesia. The water was the deepest turquoise color and was calm and pristine. We were served delicious fruit smoothies for a snack and delicious fried chicken on the return trip.

After taking a tender to the tiny Loh Buaya port, we were accompanied to the ranger station where our guide presented the Komodo National Park entrance certificates. A delicate teenage girl approached us with a forked stick and proclaimed that she was our appointed guide. Around the station there were eight Komodos lying in the shade and several smaller ones roaming about. At one stage, a very large Komodo came out of the bush and chased a smaller one straight in our direction. It didn't take Juliana and I long to find refuge behind a tree while Joe captured the pursuit on video.

We trekked three kilometers through the forest in search of Komodos to no avail. It was sweltering hot and too late in the morning for the reptiles to be moving around but we saw much evidence of their recent passing on the trail. We encountered two wild buffalos standing in mud, many monkeys, and a snake. The guide had warned us of spitting cobras in the area, so we didn't get close to it. In all, we saw a total of fifteen Komodo dragons on Rinca Island, all of them not too far from the port. Other people we met at the airport had gone to the larger Komodo Island without finding a single dragon, so we felt very fortunate.

When we got back to the boat dock, there were dragons in the area. One was a seventy-year-old Komodo and I managed to get a good photo of him. We went up on a platform to have tea and watched a number of younger dragons jostling and running below us. It was impossible to get a picture with them in the background without looking like a giant. But we were thrilled and satisfied with what we were able to witness even though we suspected that they were feeding them to attract them to that area for the sake of tourists like us.

Leaving Flores Island was rather frightening. Every passenger had to be weighed because we were departing on a small plane. There were some Asian fishermen with chests full of fish. We wanted to make certain that those got weighed so we watched intently. What we didn't realize was how short the runway is until our plane moaned and groaned and only lifted off seconds before we reached the ocean. Again, we dodged a bullet as another flight landed in the sea while trying to take off from there last year. Oh, the joys of third-world travel. Our son has lived about thirty years in Africa and has traveled the continent extensively. He has some hilarious and some hair-raising stories to tell, some of which I will share if space allows in this book.

Western Australia Vineyards

JetBlue offered a cheap trip to Perth from Jakarta so Joe, Juliana, and I hopped on the four-hour flight and found ourselves "down under" for a fabulous four-day weekend. We rented a car and Joe drove us to Margaret River where we explored wine country. Then from Perth, we joined a wine train to Snowy River wine country. Both experiences were extraordinary. The Aussies are some of the most hospitable people in the world. And we have grown fond of Australia wines over the years of experimenting. They are a bargain and offer good quality.

Ending the Good Life

Alas, all good things must come to an end. We had settled well into our routines in Indonesia when Joe's boss, John Pennell, got reassigned to Afghanistan. We fade farewell to John and Alia and their son Fuad and knew we would miss them but intended to finish Joe's contract in Jakarta.

Shortly after John arrived in Kabul, we received a phone call from him asking Joe to consider joining the agricultural team there. He had a huge budget and needed to get projects designed quickly and felt he could rely on Joe. Joe responded that he would not go without me. Spouses had to be working in order to be in Afghanistan. John asked for my CV and said he would follow up on job vacancies. He did indeed, and I landed a job at the US Embassy in Kabul. Since Afghanistan was designated a critical threat country, it received priority over other missions. Specifically, we did not have to repay our shipment costs to Indonesia though we had only spent nine months there. It was always waived in favor of finding people to fill the needs in Afghanistan.

Buying Our Retirement Home

Another complication is that while Juliana was visiting us that summer in Jakarta Joe had seen an advertisement for a home in

Springfield, Missouri, with a turret that he wanted her to check out when she returned home. She and Jill toured the house, took lots of pictures, and each wrote us their opinions. Both said we would hate the small master bedroom downstairs. Both said there were other features that we would love. So sight unseen, we bought the house. I left a couple weeks before Joe in order to close on the home which I didn't get to see until the walk through. But I did like it and hoped that Joe wouldn't regret the decision. He had merely admired the turret entrance online and there was much more to it than that feature.

Visiting Borobudur Temple in Java, Indonesia with
Michael Black and Jennifer Goodwin in July 2009.

CHAPTER 42

Retirement Home

In August 2009, we purchased our retirement home in Springfield, Missouri, in order to live closer to grandchildren. We had bought it without seeing it in person, so it was a risky purchase.

Our new home was four years old and had been lovingly and well built by a family whose business was not doing well. We purchased it for about $50K below cost so instantly had equity in the home. Later we refinanced and used some of that equity to extend the master bedroom and built a couple fireplaces. I used my savings from working in Afghanistan to focus on the backyard as the front yard was already nicely arranged. I had a deck built and then a gazebo built by the Amish installed next to the deck. We had a fence built to enclose the backyard. Jill and Mike built a brick patio area for the BBQ grill.

Landscaping was the next priority for me and I sought the help and guidance of daughters Joan and Jill. Joan brought me a number of flowers, and she built raised garden beds for me. I am now reaping the benefits of the day lilies, knockout roses, butterfly bushes, irises, clematis, Oriental lilies, etc. Joan also planted a beautiful maple tree and crepe myrtles and a weigela bush. I am enjoying all the seasons and love all the blossoms. The screened-in gazebo is the perfect spot to admire my flowers, read, meditate, and pray or to entertain. I love it.

It has taken a long time to get settled and we still have a number of boxes in the garage as we ran out of storage space. It is true that we have too much stuff and I am ready to divide it with our children, but Joe is reluctant to let things go yet. The truth is that our kids are well settled in their own homes and really don't want to inherit a lot of our eclectic junk collected from all over the world.

Besides the proximity to some grandchildren, we love living in Springfield and enjoy our parish priests and friends we have made there. The opportunity to attend daily Mass is such a privilege and pleasure. No better way to start the day.

CHAPTER 43

Afghanistan

In September 2009, Joe departed for a year stint in Afghanistan. After taking the antiterrorism courses, I joined him in November. We lived in a little apartment on the grounds of the US Embassy, which was much larger than most of the staff who occupied shared furniture crates. Our abode was directly under that of the main ambassador. It was an unusual embassy hierarchy in that there were six different ambassadors, a situation we had never encountered in previous posts.

Joe worked at USAID in designing projects for the Agricultural Office and I was assigned to the US Embassy Project Support Unit. My job was to facilitate the civilians who were chosen in Washington to work throughout Afghanistan. We provided all their equipment from armor protection to computers. The civilians were always met and welcomed to the embassy grounds where they would spend one week doing orientation with our team before being sent to the countryside.

We worked virtually seven days a week for 10-12 hours daily. It was stressful, and it was rewarding. We relied on one another. Rarely did we leave the confines of the embassy grounds. Occasionally we got to visit one of the military bases where there was a Thai restaurant that provided a lovely change of pace from the everyday food we were served in the dining halls. Military and diplomats and civilians all ate together. The food was plentiful, and they celebrated special holidays in style.

Security was always a concern, even on the embassy compound. One morning around 5:30 a.m., there was a loud explosion outside our building. A rocket had landed about seventy-five feet away. Another time we were under lockdown due to attacks nearby and had to spend most of the day hidden in our bathroom. When given lemons make lemonade. I crawled out to the living room and retrieved a guidebook on India and we spent the day planning the next R&R between prayers and waiting for the all-call clearance radio signal.

Going to and from the airport was always nerve-racking. One time we got stuck in a traffic jam right at the circle and were unable to move for about ten minutes. People surrounded the Embassy vehicle and we tried to be as inconspicuous as possible. Even once we reached the airport, we did not feel safe as it was frequently attacked. However, those of us working in the capital Kabul felt very privileged and more protected than our colleagues in Kandahar and all the outposts.

In addition to earning danger pay, we were encouraged to leave the country every two or three months to keep our sanity. Our trip was to go back to Missouri in early January 2010. We celebrated a late Christmas with the family. I am so grateful to have made that trip. When we parted, my brother Paul had hugged me tighter than he had ever done before and told me to be careful and that he would pray for me. It would be the last time that I would see Paul.

Just after returning to Kabul, we received the sad news that my sister's husband, Joel Dobson, had lost his nine-year difficult battle with Alzheimer's disease in South Carolina on January 23. We were very sad but had been expecting this news. Alice held a memorial service for Joel which was attended by my brothers Don and Paul and Anne and Mom, who remained behind with Alice.

On February 1, 2010, we got more horrible news from home. My brother Paul was working on restoring our dad's old tractor when the strap that was holding the engine block broke and crushed his head. It was such a shock. Joe got me a ticket and I returned alone for the funeral. We held visitation on Paul's sixty-ninth birthday and buried him the next day. I stayed nearly a week before going back to Kabul.

In March, Joe and I took the second R&R and went to India for ten days of pure luxury. He had always wanted to go there but I had been hesitant. Joe booked everything first-class so that we didn't have to worry so much about disease and poverty. It was an enchanting trip and exactly what I needed as I was still in deep shock and mourning for my brother. We had a private car and driver for the whole trip from New Delhi to Agra to Jaipur to Ranthambhore National Park to Udaipur and then flew back to New Delhi from there. The Taj Mahal was magical. We had booked a room at the Oberoi Amarvilas, hotel where every room has a view of the Taj. The next morning, we were the first in line before dawn to enter the gate. Sunrise was majestic. Our photos turned out so beautifully. In Jaipur, we stayed at the Rambagh Palace and were treated like royalty. The high tea there was sumptuous, and the waiter was pompous. We then stayed at the Lake Palace Hotel in Udaipur, which was featured in the James Bond movie *Octopussy*, which we watched in the suite with complimentary popcorn and cokes.

We spent three days of nearly futile safari, looking for Bengal tigers to no avail. We did manage to see the largest leopard just hanging over a cliff and he was gorgeous. He posed for a while before disappearing. We saw bear tracks and chital deer. Otherwise, that was the most disappointing part of our time there.

One image, one missed opportunity that I have never forgotten from that trip was the lovely vision of five Indian women beautifully dressed in their colorful saris, bending down, cutting wheat by hand. Our car whizzed past that field so quickly and I wish we had returned to take a photograph. The way the sun stuck the wheat and the beauty of their dresses has never left my mind.

We were surprised to see hundreds of working camels in India. Their hides were of many different colors. One would see herds of camels walking on the highways which slowed our journey at times. We also observed ox carts and skinny horses.

One of my favorite cuisines happens to be Indian so I was ecstatic to eat such delicious food properly cooked. In New Delhi, we experienced a fabulous lunch at the Sheraton's Bukhara restaurant.

Upon arrival back in Kabul I twisted my back while trying to get my luggage off the carrier. The pain plagued me for more than two months and caused a great deal of inconvenience at work. It was the beginning of many episodes with my back and sciatic nerve pain which became chronic.

By May, it was time for R&R again. We chose to meet our daughters Jennifer and Juliana in Jordan for a ten-day visit. We also invited Juliana's college friend Emmanuel who was living in Dubai to join us while in Amman. It was meant to be a surprise for Juliana. Emma came on time, but Juliana was delayed by a day due to missing a connection in Chicago after a tornado. So their time together was very limited, but it was a happy reunion. I was still down in my back and walking with a cane. Our luggage never came so we had no fresh clothes. I borrowed shirts from my daughters, and we bought T-shirts for Joe and a few other things. It was an imposition. We got the luggage back in Kabul a month later, but it was missing half of the contents.

Anyway, Jordan was still a wonderful vacation. Petra was astonishingly beautiful. Joe hired a fellow with a horse and cart to take Juliana and me to the entrance of Petra so I could view the Treasury. We would have been better off walking with them as it was excruciatingly painful on the bumpy rocky road. We walked several miles and that actually helped my back.

We were entitled to another R&R and Joe was pushing to return to India to pursue the tigers in another area. But that year was so hot that people were dying. Besides, I was still limping around in pain, so we canceled those plans.

Instead we went back to Missouri in August to meet up with our kids for a family reunion. However, health issues popped up while we were on leave. After discovering that he had atrial fibrillation, Joe's medical clearance was pulled by the State Department and we didn't get to return to Kabul. Our friend Mei Lee Bullington oversaw the pack out of our effects. The issue was the blood thinner medication could cause bleeding. Kabul was not conducive for transfusions. Sadly, we didn't have a chance to say farewell to our colleagues there.

Riding an elephant up to the Amber Fort in India in 2010.

Jennifer, Hope, Juliana and Joe in front of The
Treasury in Petra, Jordon in 2010.

An early dawn visit to the incredible Taj Mahal
in India was magically romantic.

CHAPTER 44

Reunion and Proposal

In August 2010, we returned to Missouri on leave from Afghanistan for a holiday where we planned to host a family reunion at the Rusty Moose in West Branson, Missouri. We were missing Jennifer, Mike, and Joey, but otherwise it was a full house.

A few days after arriving home, however, Joe woke up with extreme pain in his shoulder and arm. Juliana called her doctor who agreed to see him immediately. After an EKG which diagnosed atrial fibrillation (irregular heartbeat), I rushed him to the hospital where we spent five days with a blood clot in his heart in danger of moving to his brain. Clot busters seemed to do the trick after five days.

The kids were soon to be arriving, so we talked the doctor into discharging him with the promise that Gretchen would give him shots in the stomach. There was a disconnect that nearly cost his life. He was discharged with blood thinner pills and also told to take the shots. Then the hospital made a mistake and called our home phone instead of the numbers we had given them and left a message to stop taking the shots. Of course, we didn't receive that message and his blood became so thin that he nearly hemorrhaged to death.

Meanwhile we rented a boat and hired a driver and had lots of fun on Table Rock Lake that week. The kids enjoyed water skiing, tubing, jumping off a cliff from a rope into the lake, fishing, swimming, and zip-lining. We also attended a Chinese acrobat show in Branson. Lots of food and drink was shared around the big table.

One night, Adam Via told us to get our cameras ready because he was going to propose to our granddaughter Jennifer Merrill. Gretchen asked if he was kidding because they had been dating about five years and she had about given up hope. All our family were thrilled to share this very special moment with them and felt bad for the Via family who weren't there but were called as soon as Jennifer accepted.

Joe busted open the champagne and drank some that evening which was the worst thing he could have done with his thin blood. He didn't want to spoil the family's celebration, so he went to bed and didn't even call me when he started to hemorrhage. It was a horrifying scene when I went to our bedroom. Nothing that I want to describe here. Our son and I rushed him back to the Springfield hospital at midnight with his pulse down to 60/30. It was touch and go for a few days while he was in intensive care. It was so difficult for the kids to leave for their homes and especially difficult for Jenny who wasn't able to be at the reunion.

Joe wasn't ready to give up working and he spent much of the fall of 2010 at home fighting to get the State Department medical clearance reinstated, albeit class 2 clearance. That just means that he is not eligible to serve everywhere in the world. Rather he has to get approval from each post's medical unit before being assigned. That didn't prove to be very easy.

Family Reunion in California

Two years after Jennifer and Adam's engagement, we went to Fallbrook, California, for their gorgeous wedding and had a wonderful family reunion. This time Juliana and John were unable to join us because their daughter was due that week. Isabella Caroline Cazort was born on August 17, 2012. What blessings!

Family enjoyed the wedding of Jennifer Merrill and
Adam Via on August 18, 2012 in California.

Chapter 45

Antarctica:
Our Seventh Continent

Among our most memorable travels ever was when Joe and I and our daughter, Juliana, fulfilled our mutual dream of visiting all seven continents.

We reached this goal during a truly adventurous expedition to Antarctica from December 1–19, 2010. At the end, we all agreed that it was not a vacation but rather a true badge-earning, certified expedition.

We endured a long overnight flight from Springfield to Dallas to Argentina with the worst seat assignments on any plane by being in the back row, which does not recline. Meanwhile the folks in the row in front of us were laying back into our faces. That was a bad omen for beginning such a long journey.

Our spirits were revived in Buenos Aires where we indulged in wonderful wines and fantastic meals of steaks and seafood.

The next day we flew to Ushuaia, the most southerly city in the world. Before boarding the ship, we had a quick walk around Ushuaia for a little souvenir shopping. We stumbled across a little restaurant with a tank full of live crabs in the window. Naturally, we went inside to inquire about the crabs. We were told to choose the one we wanted to eat, and we would be charged by weight. Juliana pointed to a five and a half pound crab. Within fifteen minutes, it was brought to our table, beautifully prepared along with a bottle of champagne to wash it down. The waiter assisted with getting the claws open for us. He showed us what parts we should avoid. It was the most delicious and freshest crab any of us had ever eaten. What a marvelous memory we created together. We didn't leave a single morsel.

Completely stuffed with crab, we boarded the 113-foot MV *Fram*, a Norwegian expedition research vessel. To reduce the cost, we had agreed to share a triple room with Juliana. We located the assigned room which was the first one on the lower deck with only a tiny porthole window. We had two sets of bunk beds crammed together. It was an extremely tiny space, and since I tend to be claustrophobic, I decided to spend as little time as possible in that cubicle. We later discovered that only a thin wall separated us from the anchor and its mechanism. Loud!

The first four days were spent cruising through the Beagle Channel and the Straits of Magellan, making ports of call in Chile at Punta Arenas, Puerto Williams, and Cape Horn. We were treated to beautiful views of giant glaciers in the Chilean fjords. That was all very pleasant and lulled us into thinking that cruise wasn't going to be too bad. We were unprepared for what was yet to come.

However, while cruising in the normally calm Gabriel Channel, hurricane-force winds of one hundred miles per hour made the seven-story vessel lean precariously, causing concern among two hundred passengers. From the comfort of the panorama lounge, we watched in awe as water tornadoes passed close to the ship. Joel Dobson, my brother-in-law, had told me about seeing water tornadoes when he was in the Navy. Joel had wanted to go to Antarctica with us. Sadly, Joel had died that year and I was carrying a tiny vessel with his ashes so that he could make the journey.

Juliana was also carrying ashes of her friend Nicole Dial who had been murdered by the Taliban in Afghanistan where she was building schools for girls in 2008. Nicole and Juliana had planned to go to Antarctica together someday. Juliana is a journalist for the Springfield News-Leader and had written an article about Nicole and her intentions to scatter her ashes on the continent of Antarctica.

Big Brother is watching. There was a letter waiting for Juliana in our room, which stated that she needed to see the cruise director immediately to discuss the ashes. We asked ourselves how anyone would have known about the tiny amount of Nicole's remains that Juliana possessed. Somehow, someway, someone in Virginia had read the article in the Springfield, Missouri newspaper and had contacted several countries without our knowledge. Apparently, it was not legal to drop an ash on Antarctica. Juliana was told that she could scatter the ashes at sea after we were sixty miles away from the continent. When we reached that point, we ordered a bottle of red wine, said some prayers, and raised our glasses with the salute "to world peace" like Juliana and Nicole had always done together.

We made wonderful new forever friends in Jim and Suz Vinson from Conway, South Carolina. Meeting and sharing the adventure with the Vinsons made all the bad moments worthwhile. They are such a lovely and fun couple and we bonded over Pisco Sours in the lounge.

When we reached Cape Horn, the *Fram* crew was very excited that the waters were calm enough for the ship to anchor for the first time during the past eight years. This famous point, where hundreds of ships have sunk, is where the Pacific Ocean meets the Atlantic. Shore excursions were executed via Polar Cirkel boats.

From Cape Horn, the ship began the six-hundred-mile stretch of crossing the treacherous Drake Passage between South America and the tip of the Antarctica Peninsula. It began with sunshine, light breezes, and smooth seas. But on the second day, the winds kicked up to fifty knots creating high waves. Conditions improved as the South Shetland Islands were reached.

Meanwhile Juliana and I were often seasick. We made Joe sleep on the top bunk so that we could get to our shared bathroom quickly since he has no problem with motion sickness. The first time he heard me wretch into a bag in the bunk beneath him, he inquired why I didn't go to the bathroom, and then he realized the reason was because Juliana had already claimed that tiny space for her own sickness. She and I were exhausted the next morning while Joe woke up fresh and bragging about how well he slept. We felt like choking him.

One night the ship tossed so violently that everything in the room ended up on the floor. I reached down to the floor in the night and touched my eyeglasses that had been on the dresser at the far end of the cabin. The ladder from Joe's bunk bed came tumbling down. Still he did not wake up. Juliana and I were sick all night. We felt jealous of his ability to sleep and snore thru it all. In the morning, he wondered why we had made such a mess in the room. Go figure.

Many educational and interesting lectures and slide shows were presented throughout the two-week cruise of the fascinating icebergs and pristine continent and we took advantage of all the opportunities to go ashore. We were fortunate to see about 250,000 penguins and five types of seals up close plus some whales and seabirds. Actually, we saw five of the seventeen species of penguins that exist.

We explored Deception Island, Livingston Island, Paulet Island, Brown Bluff, Cuverville Island, Neko Harbor, Port Lockroy, Half Moon Island, and Yankee Harbor during the five days actually spent in Antarctica. It was all so gorgeous.

At Deception Island, which was created by a volcano that was still active under the water, some folks were courageous enough to do the Polar Plunge. We opted to take photos of the Vinsons. That locality had been used as a whaling station and all kinds of debris littered the island. When we sailed out of the narrow opening, I saw the first floating iceberg and knew we were getting close.

Crossing the Drake Passage on the return trip to Argentina was a major challenge with full gale and waves reaching fifty feet at times. Breakfast went flying off the table. Glasses and dishes were broken. Another ship that crossed the Drake Passage the day before us had major damage from the waves and had to be towed back to Ushuaia. Unfortunately, that was on the news channels back home and our family did not know the name of our ship, so they feared it was us and worried about us. Now we never leave home without providing details to all.

Despite the seasickness, everyone agreed that it was worth it to be left with such beautiful memories and a unique experience of a lifetime. I am so grateful that I had the opportunity to go to Antarctica but would never want to repeat that trip.

Reaching Antarctica in December 2010 meant that
Juliana, Hope and Joe had visited all seven continents.

CHAPTER 46

Uzbekistan and Nicaragua

Uzbekistan Consultancy

Joe left January 3, 2011, for a two-month assignment in Tashkent, Uzbekistan, where he designed a project for USAID. In coordination with the country office team, Joe led the design, development and finalization of a new Uzbekistan $13.1 million-dollar agricultural project (Agriculture Linkages Plus) to expand horticulture production and exports, building upon successes and lessons learned from current agriculture program. Meanwhile, Hope spent precious time with her mother fearing the end was near as she was becoming more fragile.

Nicaragua Contract

Immediately after working two months in Uzbekistan, Joe accepted a six-month personal services contract to work in USAID/Nicaragua from March to September 2011 as the mission's senior economic growth advisor. He was home in Springfield for just one week between the assignments and we were busy preparing for the change in climate and repacking his suitcases for the long haul.

Nicaragua is the second poorest country (after Haiti) in Central America. It has volcanoes and lakes perhaps without all the natural beauty of some Central American or Caribbean countries. The beaches are polluted. There is no good place for snorkeling. The charm and saving grace are the gentle people.

Housing was in short supply, so we were put in the InterContinental Hotel for six months. That hotel had an amazing Sunday champagne brunch that was not very expensive. Every evening we enjoyed their happy hour which included drinks and snacks and desserts. That would usually be our meal. I had no facility for cooking, so we were grateful for their service. The pool provided a relaxing place for me to read and swim while Joe slaved away at the office. Days were long and boring.

We were happy to welcome our daughter, Jennifer, for a visit. Shortly afterward our daughter Juliana and her friend/colleague Didi Tang also came to visit us.

Managua does not have a lot to offer in terms of tourism, but we spent about three hours hitting the highlights of museums and monuments. Managua was destroyed by an earthquake in 1972 and the downtown was never rebuilt. There are very few tall buildings either. There were four shopping centers in 2011.

We all loved our trips to Granada which is a colonial city less than an hour's drive from Managua and where we had spent two months in 2002 studying at the Nicaragua Spanish School. So we hired a horse carriage ride to visit several churches, a fort, a museum, and a park. Afterward we took a boat out on Lake Nicaragua for a floating tour past some of the 365 islands created about a thousand years ago by the Mombacho Volcano. We consumed a nice lunch in Granada at El Zaquan. We walked around the town square and did a little shopping before checking into the Alhambra Hotel. Afterward we went up to the Volcan Mombacho for the view of Granada and a drink to watch sunset.

Next on our tourist itinerary was San Juan del Sur about two hours from Granada. We always took a walk around the little market area before having a seafood lunch at El Timon, which is the best restaurant in the crescent-shaped beach area.

After checking into a beach side hotel, we proceeded up to Pelican Eyes for drinks and to watch the sunset.

On the way back to Managua, we stopped at the Masaya Volcano, which is active and spewing stinking sulfur. That was very interesting. Also, we visited the Masaya Market, which has the largest selection of handicrafts in Nicaragua.

This was standard fare for all tourists visiting Nicaragua. When Jennifer visited, she and I also toured the city of Leon but the only place that we found really interesting there was the Basilica Catedral de Asuncion. We even climbed up the narrow stairs to the bell tower from which we had a magnificent view of Leon.

Joe had very nice colleagues at USAID/Nicaragua and he was enjoying his work, but I had begun to be concerned about his health. He had fainted a couple times and he was very fatigued and plagued by acid reflux. On Mother's Day, we were sharing brunch with Norma Parker, the USAID director, and Dan Cruz de Paula and his beautiful wife, Rosa Jimenez, who was due to deliver their son David that week. Suddenly Joe excused himself and said he was going back to our room to get some Tums. But when he didn't return right away, I grew anxious. Finally, a hotel staff came and told me that Joe was unconscious in the lobby and they had called an ambulance. We all rushed off to the Nosso Senhora Hospital with him. The doctor in ER determined that he was having atrial fibrillation and decided to keep him overnight for observation. I was allowed to stay in his room all night. He stayed in the hospital about thirty-six hours and then we went home, and he rested one more day without any reoccurrence of problems. So he went back to work but made an appointment with his cardiologist in Springfield. She did an angiogram and determined that he had some blockage but not sufficient to warrant a stent. He returned to Nicaragua and finished his contract.

Along with a staff of seven, Joe provided strategic vision and direction for a portfolio of activities that promote trade and investment, food security including the Feed the Future Presidential Initiative, more equitable and sustainable economic growth, enterprise development, natural resource management, tourism, and disaster relief. He frequently engaged in policy dialogue with USAID/Washington and other donors and international organizations.

Almost Albania

After we returned from Nicaragua, Joe applied and was selected for a senior economic growth advisor position in USAID/Albania. We were both excited as we had never lived in or ever visited that part of the world.

We set about the big task of preparing to go abroad again. I spent hours and hours in our hot garage sorting and packing. We bought consumables and other things we would need. Our shipments were packed, crated, and taken away.

For our forty-eighth wedding anniversary we made a quick trip to Eureka Springs, Arkansas, to visit a winery and an amazing glass church in the woods.

Once again, we said goodbye to family and friends. Our suitcases were packed, and our tickets were issued. It was only two days until we were scheduled to fly away on a new adventure and felt we were up to the challenges ahead.

Then a bombshell fell on us. Dr. Scott Turner our family practitioner called with worrisome news. We had done lab work to check on our liver functions since we both take medication for high cholesterol. Dr. Turner said Joe's hemoglobin count was extremely low and advised him to go for a colonoscopy immediately. We countered that was impossible as we were leaving for a year two days later. Besides, Joe had just had a colonoscopy one year earlier, and it was clean. But Dr. Turner insisted that we postpone the trip and job until he got tested again. Very reluctantly, we agreed to listen to his advice. It turns out that the doctor likely saved Joe's life for which we are eternally grateful.

CHAPTER 47

God Called Josephine

The Angels Came

My plans to join Joe within a week of his departure to Nicaragua were delayed for three weeks by the death of my beautiful mother, Alice Josephine Jarboe Gander, early on the morning of March 18, 2011.

Two days before I was due to leave for Managua, I had an urgent call from my sister-in-law Liz relating that Mom was in the hospital. Mom had been in a nursing home for only six weeks and was suffering from COPD. She had been very fortunate to remain in her own home, but we were all so worried about her fragility that winter. Don and I had to take her to the nursing home and she was not happy with us. But the family all agreed it was the best solution at the time.

I spent the next five days at her bedside, along with many family members. My sister Alice was in Morocco at the time on her retirement trip. I had always figured it would be me who was in Africa at such a time.

After a valiant fight, my ninety-four-year-old mother expired peacefully, surrounded by love. Although it was a terribly sad loss for all of us, I was so grateful to have had the opportunity to hold her hand and pray with her.

Her funeral was postponed for eight days to allow Alice and Joe and many relatives to arrive to pay their tributes to a great lady. We were so touched by the effort of those who came from great distances from as far away as Honolulu and Key West, Florida. We were all humbled by the outpouring of love.

Condolences came from many sources. Mother was the youngest of nine lovely Jarboe sisters. Her nephew Marc Montgomery wrote these beautiful words about her and the Jarboe sisters on the day of her passing, which I want to share.

The Death of Josephine, March 18, 2011
By Marc Montgomery

Today all nine Jarboe sisters are finally together. Alice Josephine Jarboe Gander, the last of the Jarboe Sisters, died this morning. Her aging body could no longer contain the energy of her beautiful soul that became one with her sisters . . . that became one with her God. There is no sadness today. It is a day of rejoicing because today Bernadette Cecelia, Lucille Bell, Francis Genevieve, Anna Louise, Mary Rosalie, Della Gertrude, Lillian Magdaline, Mildred Kathleen, and Alice Josephine are all together for the first time.

I believe that the rejoicing is real, and the celebration is grander than all the February birthday parties put together. Wouldn't it be simply incredible to be present at this initial gathering of these sweet, sweet spirits?

Aunt Jo died today and a generation of Jarboes has come to an end. This has been an incredible journey for a group of beautiful sisters. To think that Grandma and Grandpa Jarboe were married in March 1897, it is only fitting that their generation of children should end in March.

They were of hearty stock, raised on a farm, nurtured by the rain, and the sun and the soil. They all grew roots and stood tall as trees. They were as solid as rocks, and as beautiful and unique as the flowers growing in the fields. They loved God and were part of God. They were gentle, loving, and kind. To be with them was a blessing. The loss of this generation is profound and too much for words.

I recently read this poem by Clarence Heller, and this morning I could hear my Aunt Jo and my mom in unison with their sisters saying,

Oh, to be aware that my flesh
is but soil fleetingly transformed,
and that my blood is water borrowed

292

from the rivers and the seas.
Oh, that I may be as faithful as a tree,
as holy as a rock,
as selfless as a flower.
I gladly return the life
you have given me, Mother Earth . . .
that life may carry on,
that others may live,
that we may be reunited.

And when all memory of me has passed away,
still I will know,
still I will know,
that I always was,
and I always will be,
a part of God.

Josephine was gentle, loving, and kind. To be with her was a blessing and a privilege. The loss of this sweet, sweet person is profound and too much for words.

CHAPTER 48

Kicking Colon Cancer's Butt

Instead of flying to Albania as scheduled on September 15, 2011, we found ourselves at St. John's Hospital in Springfield, Missouri, with Joe having a colonoscopy. Afterward Doctor Nelson, the surgeon, looked grave. He told us that Joe had a growth in his colon. He was careful not to call it a tumor or cancer. But I knew.

He showed us the comparison film from the same test he had done one year earlier. The doctor noted that our health insurance was not good at St. John's Hospital. He said that the best surgeon in Cox Hospital was his friend and he called him and explained the situation. Normally it takes a long time to get an appointment, but Dr. Dominguez was willing to see us during his lunch hour.

So with the ugly pictures in hand, I drove Joe to the Ferrell Duncan Clinic to meet with the surgeon. Dr. Dominguez was very kind and immediately called the Martin Center for a complete CAT scan that afternoon. He also scheduled Joe for colon surgery four days later.

Joe was still groggy from the colonoscopy when we arrived home. Neither of us truly comprehended the gravity of his problem. We both assumed that if it was cancer that it would just be stage one since he had been clean a year earlier. We thought he would have surgery, recover for six weeks, and then off to Albania we would go. We notified Joe Williams, the USAID director in Tirana of our delay and he understood and was willing to wait for Joe.

The following afternoon Joe was in his library. We had just eaten lunch about ten minutes earlier when I went into the library to pick up something. Joe was in his desk chair with his back to me, leaning sideways and appeared to be looking at his books. Then I noticed that his brand-new glasses were on the floor. I called his name and touched his shoulder but got no response. I swirled his chair around and realized that he was unconscious. The right side of his face had dropped at least one inch and I recognized the sign of stroke. Immediately I dialed 911.

I shook Joe frantically and smacked his cheeks. It took some time before he opened his eyes and there was only a distant stare. I asked if he knew me, and he shook his head negatively.

The fire department arrived with four guys before the ambulance came. By the time he was being wheeled out the door, Joe was beginning to comprehend their commands. He even asked me to bring the book he was reading earlier. I was relieved that he knew the title of the book.

Just then, the phone rang. It was Juliana who was at work at the News-Leader. She had overheard the police scanner saying a sixty-nine-year-old man on Knob Hill had possibly suffered a stroke. Juliana instinctively knew it must be her dad. I told her not to panic but asked if she could meet us at the Cox South Hospital. She called Jill and both of them arrived at almost the same time as the ambulance.

Joe was kept in the emergency room for five hours under observation during which time his speech was very slurred. Our friend Casey Klein also came to keep us company. One memory that Jill found comforting was when the ER nurse asked if he needed anything, and he said he was curious when the wine and cheese cart would be making the rounds. Jill later said, "This was when I knew he was feeling better, and the real Dad was coming back around and was such a relief to see the dad we know and love so much coming back out."

Finally, Joe made a remarkable recovery and started to talk normal. The doctor then transferred him to the stroke unit. That room was in a shabby condition. There was a big hole in the bathroom door. The toilet broke twice while we were there. Juliana and Jill were saying how ridiculous it was that they would expect him to prep for the surgery with no privacy and Juliana got out her phone and started to take pictures for a possible story for the paper. They were making it known that this was not acceptable for their dad to be treated this way by talking plenty loud. Five minutes later maintenance came in to fix the door and toilet.

Late that afternoon the hospital received the results of his CAT scan. They agreed to let Joe spend the evening of his sixty-ninth birthday at home. As Jill told me recently, "Maybe the hospital just wanted to get rid of us. We were so excited to be able to take him home before surgery. Little did we know what a long road ahead there would be."

Kevin Klein made us the most beautiful birthday steak dinner that evening, which Mike and Jill brought to our house. It was appreciated so much.

Sunday dawned, and after attending mass, Joe began the surgery prep for the second time in four days.

Early Monday morning we were headed back to Cox Hospital. I was so grateful that both Jill and Juliana were able to spend that long day of waiting with me. When they took Joe away, they neglected to tell us that he was going to get two transfusions before the surgery. That took a couple extra hours while we were anxiously awaiting word. Four hours later we got to see the surgeon. He said that Joe had come through it well and explained exactly where the tumor was located. He had removed a foot of his colon. He then recommended an oncologist.

The next four days were nerve-racking while Joe was in the intensive care surgical unit. His a-fib (irregular heartbeat) kicked in for prolonged periods, lasting about seventeen hours each time. He was kept in a comatose state and has no memory of that time. Jill and Juliana came to visit often. Mike and John came as well as our dear friends Ken and Marilyn Quinn. I was relieved and comforted.

On the fifth day, we were able to move him to a regular room. After that, we met Dr. Ellis, the oncologist, who brought us the bad news that Joe did indeed have colon cancer and that it was at stage three. That was a shock to us as we all had expected it to be stage one. But it had spread to the tissue. However, out of forty-one biopsies, only one had cancer. We were still expecting a good outcome. I was glad that Juliana was there when Dr. Ellis explained all our treatment options.

On the eighth day, we were told that I could take him home after Dr. Dominguez saw him. Well, the doctor took one look at the wound and decided it had to be reopened because it was full of blood clots. He removed the stitches and cleaned it out. He said the nurse would show me how to care for the wound three times a day and told us to check out. We were in disbelief. The incision was so long and so deep. We were sure Joe would have to stay in the hospital longer but guess the doctor thought our home would provide a more sterile environment.

The first time that I had to clean and dress the gaping hole, I feared that I might faint into the abyss. It was truly unbelievable. A hospice nurse came twice a week to measure it and check that it wasn't getting infected during the first month and then she made weekly visits for the next two months. I took Joe to the surgeon's office frequently for checkups on the healing progress. When Dr. Dominquez started cutting some of the dead skin, Joe reminded the doctor that he was awake. The good doctor joked that he would have to remember not to say "Whoops." It took twelve long weeks for the open wound to heal.

Joe finally began a seven-month regiment of chemotherapy on November 7. The medicine we chose was Xeloda. It caused him to lose five toenails, which never grew back. His hands blistered, and he lost feeling in them for months. At one point, he had to take a two-week break from the chemo in order for his blisters to heal. Otherwise, he tolerated it pretty well and took medication for the nausea.

We are grateful for the combined skills, knowledge, patience, and understanding shown to us by all the medical teams in both hospitals and clinics. We are also gratified by the prayers, cards, flowers, calls, and visits of family and friends while we hibernated all winter while fighting the cancer. Joe slept in his recliner for several months as it was more comfortable for him. He watched television, read, and slept many extra hours until he regained his strength that the chemo zapped.

By the time spring arrived, we were plotting our next adventure. Miracles do happen, and life continues.

CHAPTER 49

Atlantic Coast Cruise

To reward ourselves for finishing chemotherapy and surviving Joe's colon cancer, we decided to take a fifteen-day cruise from Ft. Lauderdale, Florida, to Montreal, Canada, in late April to mid-May 2012 on the Holland America.

We were joined by our beloved cousins, Floyd and Judy Mahon, Molly Lamb, and their friend Elaine Snyder. Floyd had also been diagnosed with colon cancer a few months before Joe and had been valiantly fighting it for about a year at that time. Unfortunately, his was at stage 4. But he was doing really well and loved to take cruises and we loved to spend time with them. Floyd and Joe had been best buds for over fifty years. We had enjoyed trips together to New Zealand, Australia, and China, so we knew that we would be a compatible group. We had a marvelous trip and made more beautiful memories. So often Joe remarks that is what life is all about.

Ports of call were Ft. Lauderdale, Florida; Charleston, South Carolina; Newport, Rhode Island; Bar Harbor, Maine; Halifax, Nova Scotia; Sydney; Canada; Charlottetown, Prince Edward Island; Gaspe, Quebec; Sept-Iles, Quebec; Saguenay, Canada; and Quebec City, Canada. The ship went on to Montreal, but we disembarked in Quebec so that we could fly back to Missouri for a fun family weekend at the Gander farm.

It was early spring, so the weather was still a bit chilly and often rainy, but our spirits were never dampened.

The ocean was too rough when we were docked offshore in Newport, Rhode Island and the little boats were bobbing so much that we decided to stay onboard that day.

Otherwise, we took full advantage of all the interesting stops along our journey. We all still talk about the lunch of lobster rolls, crab cakes, and seafood soup in Bar Harbor, Maine. It was amazing and was just a small café off the main street.

Halifax, Nova Scotia, was very interesting. We visited one of the graveyards where many victims of the Titanic from 1912 are buried. Ships from Halifax had been part of the recovery effort.

Thousands of other lives lost in the horrible explosion in December 1917 were also buried there. A French cargo ship the SS *Mont-Blanc* was fully loaded with wartime explosives and it was involved in a collision with the Norwegian vessel SS *Imo*. Although both ships were going slow at the point of impact, a fire set off the explosives about twenty minutes later. Approximately two thousand people were killed by debris, fires, and collapsed buildings, and about nine thousand others were injured. Whole communities were destroyed. The blast was the largest manmade explosion before nuclear weapons. I was unaware of this tragedy before our tour and was very touched by the city's history and its inhabitants.

The hospitality of the Canadians simply amazed us. When we arrived in Saguenay, we were met by citizens decked out in costumes handing out slices of blueberry pie. Joe and I opted to attend their play about the history of Canada which was one of the most impressive productions we have ever witnessed. And every member of the cast was a volunteer. Sadly, they only receive a couple cruise ships a year so don't get to raise much money for the little town.

We did encounter some health problems with the norovirus on the cruise ship. Both Judy and Joe succumbed to it at different times. Judy missed out on going to visit the Alexander Graham Bell museum, which I was keen to see as he is our distant relative on our grandmother Bell's side of the family.

One reason we chose Holland America is because they provide a priest to say daily Mass. A ninety-year-old priest, Father Winschman, was assigned to our cruise. He was most interesting because he has been a missionary at Medjigory in Bosnia Herzegovina for thirty years. Last fall we met Father Winschman again at a Marion Conference in Springfield. We had bought his beautiful rosary video.

CHAPTER 50

Miracle Grandbabies
Born in 2012

How can we be so blessed? In the midst of Joe's chemotherapy treatment, we learned that we were going to have two new grandbabies. Both were unexpected and absolute miracles. We were old enough to be great-grandparents, but we were so happy with the news.

First, Chloe Lakisha Goodwin was born in Kampala, Uganda, on March 14, 2012, to our son Joe II and Myriam Musrinange. Joe always wanted a daughter named Chloe and he was delighted. We didn't get to actually meet that beautiful little girl until she was twenty-one months old, but she stole our hearts from the first picture Joe sent to us. It is sad to live so far away from them and not get a chance to really know Chloe, but it helps when we Skype. She was five before we met her again.

Five months later, we were blessed with the birth of Isabella Caroline Cazort in Springfield, Missouri, on August 17, 2012. She is the adored daughter of Juliana Goodwin and husband John Cazort. Juliana had medical problems as a teenager and was told she couldn't have children, so this was such a joyful surprise.

We were unable to be at her birth because we were in California participating in our granddaughter Jennifer Linn Merrill's wedding to Adam Via which took place the day after Bella's birth. The wedding provided an excuse for a wonderful family gathering in a beautiful home we rented in Fallbrook, California.

When Bella was two months old Juliana returned to work at the Springfield News-Leader and John would drop Bella at our home on his way to teach high school art classes in Ozark. During the following five months, we truly bonded with that sweet baby. She was always healthy and happy, and we loved having the chance to get to spend time with our grandchild. When there was a vacancy at Tiger Paws Day Care, they registered Bella. We cried. She had been protected from germs at our house, so she got sick immediately. We continue to take care of Bella whenever she gets sick. Sometimes I think Bella pretends to be sick just so she can come and play at Papa and Mimi's house.

Hope holding eleven-month-old granddaughter
Isabella Caroline Cazort.

Joe Goodwin II with his daughter Chloe Lakisha
Goodwin at safari camp in Kenya.

CHAPTER 51

Mediterranean Cruise

Sometimes the best vacations are those which are unplanned. Thanks to a last-minute cheap deal offered by Holland America in September and October 2012, we shared a beautiful two-week Mediterranean cruise with dear friends Ken and Marilyn Quinn.

Although we had been lifetime friends, we had never travelled together for an extended period. It worked out beautifully as we explored so many places in Italy, Spain, Monaco, and France. Due to security concerns, I was disappointed that the port call at Tunisia was canceled. Cagliari, Sardinia, was substituted.

In Italy, we hired a driver/guide for a private tour. He was very knowledgeable and took us to the leaning tower of Pisa, the Tuscany area, and the amazing city of Florence. We managed to get up close to the marvelous Statue of David. The paintings on the inside of the dome at the Basilica di Sant Maria del Fiore in Florence have lasted for centuries.

To be honest, when we reached Monte Carlo, Marilyn and I stayed on the ship and had a terrific visit on deck while Ken and Joe toured the town.

We loved the architecture found everywhere along the Mediterranean and enjoyed the French Riviera and the beaches in Nice.

Barcelona, Spain found us taking a thrilling bus ride up to the Montserrat Monastery. We loved the Familia Sagrada Catedral in Barcelona, but unfortunately, it was raining really hard during our tour. We made a port call at Palma de Mallorca, Spain, and visited another beautiful church and a bullring.

We had arranged for a driver/guide to meet us in Naples for a private tour. My favorite memory was the Amalfi Coast gorgeous winding drive above the blue Mediterranean. It was some of the most beautiful scenery that we have seen in the world. Then we savored the lunch at the top of Positano. Our Italian food was served by a fun family and the view was breathtaking. We bought Limón cello at Sorrento and viewed Pompeii and Mount Vesuvius.

Great memories are made of this.

CHAPTER 52

Eastern Europe 2013

Macedonia

We had never lived in Eastern Europe until 2013 when Joe spent a month there as supervisory program officer for USAID/Macedonia.

I stayed busy at our home in Missouri during his TDY and also had the privilege of attending our grandson-in-law's graduation in North Carolina as an aviation survival technician. Adam Via was number 847 to survive this very difficult coast guard search and rescue swimmer program over the last thirty years. He was one of two out of eighteen who began to actually make it. We are very proud of Adam and of Jennifer for her encouragement and support.

Mozambique

This job was followed closely by a five-week assignment in Mozambique working in Maputo at USAID in the agriculture, trade, and business office. The price of a ticket was too high and his time there too short for me to consider going. Besides there was a lot of yard work requiring my attention at home.

Macedonia Again

In July 2013, Joe was called back into the foreign service to be the acting USAID director in Macedonia. He wanted me to join him and raved about the friendly population. In fact, Macedonia had been named the most friendly country in the world. They certainly earned that award. My flowers were in full bloom, so it was hard to leave at that time, but I also missed my husband, so I pulled out my luggage again.

We lived in the Holiday Inn Skopje beside the Vardar River, which was lined with marvelous restaurants on one side and elegant buildings on the other riverbank. Every evening we tried a different cuisine. There were so many choices and we tried and liked all of them. Our favorite salad was called Skopje, which was named after the city in which we were living. It was similar to Greek salad but the cheese on top was like the fresh farmer's cheese that we bought in Brazil. Sweet and salty at the same time, that cheese was the main ingredient of the salad of cucumbers and tomatoes.

Skopje had the most beautiful and unique fountains that I have seen outside of Italy. Sculptures of Alexander the Great were prominent on the town square. I enjoyed a city tour that included a home where Mother Teresa had lived.

Meteora, Greece

We took advantage of a long weekend to go down to Greece to visit the Eastern Orthodox monasteries on the mountaintops that were built in the fourteenth century. We hired a car and driver who was a very good guide.

He drove us into northern Greece to visit Meteora near the town of Kalambaka. The area of Meteora is noted for the number of rocky pinnacles. Many had been used for building Greek orthodox monasteries. In the ninth century AD, a number of hermit monks began to occupy some of the pinnacles. Over time, twenty-four monasteries were established on top of various pinnacles of which six are still functioning. Access to the monasteries on top of the pinnacles was difficult requiring long ladders or winches. In the James Bond film, *For Your Eyes Only*, Bond climbs one of the pinnacles to capture the "bad guys." Today, the monasteries are accessible by staircases and pathways cut into the rock formations. Even the monastery that James Bond is shown climbing has a rock-cut stairway which Joe and I climbed. We visited all of the functioning monasteries and had a wonderful time touring and enjoying Greek food and wine.

After the new country director arrived, we took advantage of being in the region to visit Romania and Bulgaria. Our daughter Jennifer had planned to join us, but when she became seriously ill she had to cancel her visit.

Romania and Bulgaria Tour

From Macedonia we flew to Bucharest—the capital of Romania. We were still praying for our daughter Jennifer who was supposed to share this adventure with us but was fighting for her life in the hospital in North Carolina. So we felt very sad and worried at this time. We had a fantastic driver/guide throughout the nine days of this tour.

Bucharest—Bucovina

We drove north to Bucovina passing through the vineyards of Vrancea to see the Moldavian countryside with its village architecture.

Bucovina Painted Monasteries Excursion (UNESCO Sites)—Piatra Neamt

One of our priorities while in Romania was to visit the Bucovina painted monasteries/churches. The churches were built in the fifteenth and sixteenth centuries. Besides, the quality of the paintings, the unique feature of these churches is that they are covered in Bible scenes on both the exterior and interior walls. Because the population was mostly illiterate, the painting of the Old and New testament allows people to see the Bible that they could not read. The paintings were done with natural vegetable dyes and minerals from the region. The quality of the painting after five hundred years is exceptional, especially those in the interior of the church. The Bucovina churches are truly artistic masterpieces. Bucovina monasteries are gems of medieval Moldavian architecture and artistry. Began our day with Voronet, the most famous out of all, known as the Sistine Chapel of the East and featuring one the best-preserved Last Judgment fresco in this part of the world. Next was Moldovita Monastery where the

UNESCO Golden Apple Award given to the painted churches in 1975 is kept. Enjoyed an egg-painting demonstration by a local artist in her home. Then she served us a beautiful lunch. We ended that day with the Monastery of Humor, the only one without a belfry tower.

Piatra Neamt—Bicaz Gorges—Sighisoara

Reach Bicaz Gorges where the surroundings are dramatic. Next up was the Red Lake, formed by a mountain sliding in the 1830s. Sighisoara world heritage site and the only still inhabited medieval citadel in Europe. It was developed by the German settlers as of late twelfth century. It stands on a network of tunnels and catacombs and, according to one version of the myth, this is where the Pied Piper brought the children of Hamelin after their ungrateful parents refused to pay him his due. The walking tour included the two squares of the Citadel (Upper Town), the Scholars' Staircase, the House with Antler, the Tower with Clock, the Torture Chamber, and the Weapon Museum. Sighisoara is the place where the Vlad the Impaler (Dracula) was born in 1431. The birthplace is one of the main tourist attractions.

Sighisoara—Jidvei Winery—Sibiu Tour—Sighisoara

The village of Jidvei—Transylvania's most famous winery was delightful. Then we had lunch with wine tasting, with three different sorts—white wine, champagne, and red wine. Afternoon arrival to Sibiu, the chief city of the Transylvanian Saxons still surrounded by defense walls and guild towers. Took a walking tour of Sibiu, the chief city of the Transylvanian Germans. One of the landmarks of Sibiu is the Bruckenthal Museum assembled by Baron Bruckenthal, governor of Transylvania at the beginning of the nineteenth century and the second art museum to open to the public. The Evangelical Cathedral was completed in its actual shape in 1520.

Morning drive to Brasov included the famous fourteenth-century Black Church with its four-thousand-pipe organ and over one hundred Anatolian prayer rugs, the Council Square. Visited the old

Romanian quarter known as Schei for a tour of St. Nicholas Church then saw the narrowest street in South–Central Europe.

The highlight was touring the famous Bran Castle, also known as Dracula Castle. It was built in 1377 to safeguard the trading route between Transylvania and Wallachia, then enlarged and restored in the 1920 by Queen Marie of Romania. To be honest, we were a little disappointed in its location and the number of tourists there made it impossible to get good photographs.

We took a scenic drive to Sinaia mountain resort. Named after St. Catherine Monastery on Mount Sinai, Sinaia became the unofficial capital of the Kingdom of Romania toward the end of the nineteenth century. The orientation tour of the resort included a visit to Sinaia Monastery and a view of the casino building, inspired by the one in Monte Carlo.

Our favorite guided tour was of one of the most important tourist attractions of the country: Peles Castle and Gardens, the royal residence of King Charles I of Romania, and known as one of the most beautiful summer royal residences in Europe.

Bucharest—Ruse—Roman Ruins at Nicopolis—Veliko Tarnovo

Left Bucharest and crossed the border into Bulgaria. Toured the town of Ruse with its classical architecture, Bulgaria's largest port on the Danube. Drove south through the Bulgarian countryside to Veliko Tarnovo with a stop to the Roman ruins at Nicopolis and Istrum, built in the second century AD under Emperor Trajan.

Veliko Tarnovo, the former capital of the First Bulgarian Kingdom, was next on the itinerary. The Tsarevets Fortress is one of the largest and most well preserved of the Northern Balkans.

Veliko Tarnovo—Village of Arbanassi— Ivanovo Rock Hewn Churches—Bucharest

We visited the village of Arbanassi, known for its typical architecture. The main points of interest are the Konstantalieva merchant house dating from the eighteenth century, looking more like a fortress than a dwelling. Next stop was the superb Church of the Nativity, adorned with frescoes and proof of the Bulgarian Christian faith all throughout the Turkish rule. On the way back to Bucharest made a detour to the Ivanovo Rock-Hewn Churches, a UNESCO world heritage site, with its thirteenth- and fourteenth-century frescoes. Those were fascinating to both of us.

Beautiful Peles Castle in Romania was the summer
royal residence of Romanian Kings.

CHAPTER 53

African Safaris and Adventures

Safari in Zimbabwe and Botswana in 1999

We took our two oldest granddaughters Angie and Jennifer on a safari in Zimbabwe and Botswana in 1999. We were joined by Juliana, Gretchen, and Joan and Karen Kassen, a former colleague of Joan's who was so much fun.

We had a very close lion charge which caused me to have nightmares for years afterward. My heart still beats faster when I recall that frightening episode. We had come upon a pair of amorous lions and the driver had followed them. Then another safari vehicle which contained a crying child pulled up beside us. The big black mane lion lost interest in his lady immediately and his ears perked up as his eyes became slanted as he looked in our direction. The offending group were smart enough to back away and turn around. I could tell that the male lion was very angry, and Juliana and I begged the driver to leave. But Joe was standing up in the open top Land Rover filming the lions and since he did not give the word to depart, the driver ignored us. The rest of our family were in a second safari vehicle right behind us, so they witnessed the whole scene.

In a flash, the lion roared and charged our vehicle. He only stopped a couple feet from the hood when Joe finally realized the seriousness of the situation and sat down. Joe captured part of the charge on tape and it is still scary to watch.

The safari had been successful. The granddaughters had loved sleeping in a tree house. We saw so many elephants that we started to ignore them. At one watering hole our, vehicle had been surrounded by seventy-five elephants which was a little unnerving, but none charged us. In Chobe National Park, we must have encountered about five hundred elephants. On the last evening of our safari, we were watching a mother and her baby drink from the river when suddenly she decided to chase us away. Gretchen and Jennifer and I were riding in the rumble seat. The driver took off throwing dust so thick that it was difficult to see them, but you could hear both the mother and her young baby trumpeting at us. They gave chase for at least a quarter mile. Elephants can be unpredictable.

Bus Trip to Cote d'Ivoire

The Community Liaison Officer in Ghana organized a bus trip to neighboring Cote d'Ivoire over an Easter weekend, which Joe and I happily joined. Our destination was the beautiful Our Lady of Peace Basilica in Yamoussoukro, which was built between 1986 and 1989 in the middle of nowhere and was meant to rival and imitate St. Peter's in Rome. The African choir was marvelous and brought me to tears at the impressive Easter Mass. For once, I didn't complain about the lengthy service.

On the return trip to Accra, our friend and neighbor Gina Lapp had an allergic reaction to the mosquito spray that the guide used on the bus. Gina couldn't breathe. I have the same reaction to perfume and many chemical sprays but had covered my nose when she had sprayed the bus. We quickly returned to Abidjan and got Gina to a hospital. The rest of us spent the night in a hotel. Fortunately, Gina survived, and we made it back home.

Three-Generation Safari 2007

Three generations of our family shared a wonderful three-week trip to Tanzania and Zanzibar. Joe and I visited Joe's former St. Stephens classmate Bede Smith and his wife, Doreen, in London, England on our way to East Africa and shared dinner with Bede again on the return trip.

We spent two days on the Island of Zanzibar with friends, Charlie and Nancy Crane where we toured the historical area of Stone Town and tasted local delicacies on the beach as the sun set over the Indian Ocean. Zanzibar is famous for its carved and highly decorated wooden doors as well as carved chests. We visited a rain forest with a large colony of red colobus monkeys, a species found only on Zanzibar. A tour of the spice area from which so many rich spices are grown and exported was interesting.

Family members who joined us in Tanzania on a photographic wildlife safari were Mike, Jill, Taylor and Trevor Sorensen of Springfield, Missouri, and Scott and Gretchen Merrill of Oceanside, California. In Mwanza, our son Joe who was working at the Geita Gold Mine in Tanzania met and joined his family for a week of vacation.

A charter flight took our group to Rubondo Island in Lake Victoria, which is the second largest lake in the world. Everyone caught and released large Nile Perch. The biggest fish caught by Scott weighed more than eighty pounds. At night hippopotamus grazed on the grass in front of the tented camp, and during the day, large crocodiles were spotted in the area. After three days on Rubondo Island, we flew back to the mainland and began a safari journey through the Serengeti Plains where we had the rare good fortune to encounter two leopards in a tree in addition to other game.

The highlight was spending a full day in Ngorongoro Crater, which was recently named the Eighth Wonder of the World, a classification that we felt it deserves. The floor of the beautiful extinct volcanic crater is twenty-four miles wide and contains a large variety of African wildlife. We witnessed a rhinoceros chasing six lions out of his territory. We saw hundreds of Cape buffalo and elephants, plus thousands of zebras, wildebeests, antelopes, and gazelles. In total, our group found over thirty lions, five rhinos, and countless giraffes during the safari. It was the season for migratory birds, so we spotted a large variety of birds ranging from the tiny red bishops to the huge ostriches and saddle-billed storks.

Our family had lived in Dar es Salaam, Tanzania from 1980 to 1983 on assignment with the USAID, so visiting the capitol again was nostalgic. Gretchen and Jill had the opportunity to show their husbands and kids where they had lived, gone to school, and played in their youth. It was a fun three generational experience.

South African Safari in 2016

By far the most luxurious safari we have ever experienced was in South Africa and shared with our daughter and son-in-law Gretchen and Scott Merrill and our granddaughter Jennifer and her husband Adam Via. We took charter flights from Johannesburg to Ulusaba (owned by Sir Richard Branson) where we had close encounters with leopards, crossed roaring rivers, and found the big five easily. Then we flew to Camp Jabulani where we rode elephants, had gourmet food, beautiful air-conditioned cottages, and absolutely amazing luck in finding wildlife.

Adam and Jennifer Via, Joe and Hope, Scott and
Gretchen Merrill enjoying sunset at Camp Jabulani
in South Africa while on safari in March 2016.

CHAPTER 54

Fiftieth Anniversary in Australia

Being happily married for fifty years is no small feat. Our five daughters and their families and some of our friends joined us for renewal of our wedding vows and Bella's baptism. Our son arrived from Uganda a few days later. We had a family reunion at a rented house in Branson. The weather was not nice as it rained a lot, but our spirits were not dampened as we always love being with our family.

Joe told me to choose where we would spend our actual fiftieth anniversary day since it was also my seventieth birthday. Without hesitation, I decided on Australia even though we had been there twice previously. Aspire Down Under did a custom trip focused on areas, which were new to us. It was the time of our lives.

First stop was historic Darwin, which we explored mostly on foot. It was really good to walk so much after the long flights from the United States. We took a tour of Kakadu National Park but just saw a few kangaroos.

Next we boarded the luxury legendary Ghan Train, which Joe had talked about for many years. It took twenty-four hours to reach Alice Springs. We were the only Americans and had nice chats with the friendly Aussies.

A half-day tour of Alice Springs took us to the School of Art where the students are educated by live ham radio instructors. We toured the Royal Flying Doctor Service, which cares for people in the Outback without medical services. We went to the first Telegraph Station where the first Europeans settled. The tour ended at Anzac Hill with a beautiful view of Alice Springs at sunset.

From Alice Springs, we took a bus to Ayers Rock where we spent two nights. That monolith did not disappoint. The first night we had cocktails at sunset and watched the rock change colors. Early the next morning, we were taken to a point to watch sunrise over thirty-six domes of the Olgas, but there were too many busloads of people there who had claimed the best viewing points. Being a short person, I was unable to take good photos. Then we hiked around Kata Tjuta. That night we enjoyed the Sounds of Silence dinner at the foot of Uluru. It was a spectacular sight at sunset. A didgeridoo player entertained us during the dinner of bush meats. An astronomer was so helpful with a stargazing lesson.

When given a choice of a bus ride or hiring a charter plane to take us back to Alice Springs, Joe and I sprung for the flight. It was disappointing waste of money. They seated us according to weight and Joe got assigned the copilot seat. He fell asleep while I was crammed between people and could not see out the window.

We flew to Cairns and went down to Port Douglas so that we could experience the Great Barrier Reef. It is as magnificent as all the photos we had seen. We went by catamaran out about twenty miles to Agincourt Reef. A submarine awaited us there and we took it twice. Each time we saw different fish, turtles, and beautiful coral reef in so many shapes and sizes. Joe has wanted to do the dive wearing a bubble suit but once they learned he has a-fib he wasn't permitted to do it. Joe was disappointed, but I was secretly relieved. I was content to watch the fish from the platform.

We toured an Aborigine center where they tried to teach us how to throw a boomerang. Afterward we took the Kuranda Skyrail, which provided a gorgeous view of the tropics, rivers, and mountains.

Our return trip home was long. We had plane trouble and nearly landed on top of another plane as we approached Sydney. I actually witnessed the plane landing below us. The pilot took off again and we flew out over the ocean for another twenty minutes before making another approach. He never explained what had happened nor did he come out of the cockpit, but I knew exactly the cause. After forty-two hours we were finally back in Springfield exhausted but happy.

Joe and Hope celebrating their 50th wedding
anniversary at Ayers Rock in Australia in 2013.

CHAPTER 55

Kenya, Rwanda, and Uganda

PSC Contract October 2013–April 2014

USAID's East Africa Regional Office persuaded Joe to take a six-month contract to assist in writing a five-year strategy to include seven African countries. It was the third attempt to develop an updated strategy. Joe worked extremely hard and his team's version was approved by Washington. However, shortly afterward the ambassador in Kenya decided to draw down the staff and consolidate positions. Result was that the new director wanted to go in a different direction and the strategy, as Joe and his team had written it, has not been implemented.

Living Next to US Embassy

We were assigned an apartment next door to the US Embassy, which allowed Joe to walk to work. Across the street was the United Nations compound which had a beautiful nature walking trail complete with monkeys and beautiful birds. My time in Nairobi was greatly enhanced by two wonderful Brazilian American women, Julia Goughnor and Sueli Burkhart. I cannot even imagine how boring life would have been for me were it not for their generosity in including me in fun excursions, game viewing, restaurants, and simple trips to the grocery store. We also were happy whenever we got to share time with John and Alia Pennell and Andy and Tracy Herscowitz and their three darling children, friends from our time in the Dominican Republic.

Thanksgiving in Maasai Mara

Over the Thanksgiving holiday we flew out to Maasai Mara and stayed at Governors Camp for three days of game viewing. It was a marvelous time and we found all the big five plentiful. Perhaps the highlight was seeing a leopard with its kill hanging from the tree. We counted thirty-six lions and everything else we hoped to see. The big surprise was to watch the migration of wildebeests and zebras crossing the river while crocodiles tried to grab them. It was mesmerizing.

Christmas in Uganda

On Christmas Eve, we flew to Kampala, Uganda, where our son, Joe II, lives. It was wonderful to finally meet our granddaughter, Chloe, was who twenty-one months old. She won our hearts instantly. Joe hosted a gathering, so we could meet his friends. We spent Christmas Day with them around the pool at the home of one of his colleagues. After a short but a sweet visit, we flew back to Nairobi the next day.

Visit from Joan and Gretchen

In mid-January 2014, our daughters Joan and Gretchen joined us in Nairobi. They also visited old friends in Tanzania and went to Zanzibar for a few days. The main focus in Kenya was to go on safaris. First we flew out to the Maasai Mara where we viewed more animals than one could ever dream of seeing. It was a success. Then we flew up to Lewa Safari Camp to search for rhinos. To our utter amazement, we saw sixty white rhinos and nine black rhinos. We had one too close encounter with a young male elephant who was in musk and very angry. He chased us and got too close for comfort. We saw three leopards. It was such fun to share these experiences and make memories with these two daughters.

Gorilla Trekking in Rwanda

Gretchen accompanied us to Rwanda to trek mountain gorillas while Joan flew to Dar es Salaam to visit friends. Gretchen's friend/colleague, Kameri Larson, joined the party. We stayed at the bottom of the Virunga Mountain range close to the national park where the gorillas roam freely. After a restful though chilly night, we got an early start. Among the tourists was an eighty-two-year-old Italian lady with her grandson who had hired porters to carry her on a litter. I admired her spunk to fill her bucket list. It had rained so it wasn't easy walking through the brush. For me the hardest part was getting over the high wall into the park. I shall never forget the moment that I heard the dominant male silverback snort the first time. Agasha was warning us that we were getting close to his family of twenty-two gorillas. We were only allowed to spend one hour among the gorillas and suppose to stay at least ten feet from them, but one youngster came rushing past me and touched my leg. It happened too fast for a photo but was a thrill. Gretchen and Kameri took a lot of great photos whereas I made a huge mistake in trying to take shots on a good camera, my iPad, and the movie camera. I wish I had just focused on being there and let the others take the pictures. Next day we visited a colony of golden monkeys, but they were rather illusive and hung in the tops of the dense forest.

TDY in Djibouti

Joe was sent on TDY to Djibouti for eleven days, so I went with him. We stayed at a nice hotel but were surrounded by drab desert. The mosquitoes were horrible even in the dining room. One night we ate at the seafood restaurant on the ocean, but my legs were covered in bites, so it was hard to enjoy the food. We took a city tour one Saturday but there wasn't a lot to see. I was really happy when it was time to fly back to Kenya.

Reconnecting with Franco

The nicest surprise about living six months in Nairobi was the opportunity to reconnect with Franco Brescia who had lived with us for a full school year in Dar es Salaam in 1980–1981. Joan, Joe II, and Gretchen all got to spend some time with Franco in Nairobi and we loved seeing our "second son" as a successful adult. He is a musician on the side and gives concerts and records CD albums. It seemed as though the thirty-two years since we had last seen Franco never existed. We picked up where we left off. Joe II was able to visit us twice from Kampala while we lived in Nairobi. Joan also reunited with a former friend Kiran Ahluwalia from Tanzania days. Kiran and her husband were very kind to us.

Ambulance and Nairobi Hospital

Joe gave me a scare one Saturday morning while eating breakfast in our apartment. He appeared to be having a heart attack. There was a clinic on our compound, so I walked him there. We had no car. After an EKG, they called an ambulance and sent us to the big Nairobi Hospital. More tests. They kept him overnight. Finally they released him with a diagnosis of acute angina. We scheduled a cardiologist visit upon our return home.

Gretchen, Joe and Hope with mountain gorillas they trekked
on the Virunga Mountains in Rwanda in January 2014.

CHAPTER 56

Effects of Terrorism

One only needs to read my chapter on our forced evacuation from the Sudan in 1986 to realize the effects that experience had on me personally. It still weighs heavily on my mind three decades later. There have been other acts of terrorism that have deeply affected me.

Domestic Terrorism

At the time of the Oklahoma City federal building bombing on April 19, 1995, Joe was at work at the State Department in Washington, DC. Our seven-year-old granddaughter Jennifer Merrill was visiting us in Virginia at the time. She sensed my distress even if she didn't comprehend the ramifications. As we sat together on the sofa watching the news coverage, Jennifer patted me on my knee and in her sweet little voice said, "It's OK, Grandma. Sometimes bad things happen." I shall never forget that moment with Jennifer trying to reassure me.

Learning that the OKC bombing had been carried out by domestic terrorists was a shock to me. Somehow it shattered my comfort zone while back on USA soil. We had had our share of frightening situations while living abroad and I had always felt secure when we would return to our homeland. But the killing of 168 innocents simply rocked my world even though I did not know any of the victims.

Terrorism Abroad

When devastating truck bombs were simultaneously detonated by an al-Qaeda terrorist group on August 7, 1998, at the US embassies in Dar es Salaam, Tanzania, and in Nairobi, Kenya, there were 258 beautiful and innocent souls lost with over 5,000 people injured in the two cities.

These terrorist acts deeply affected so many people. Joe and I were living and working in Accra, Ghana, at the time. There were rumors of imminent attacks coming to our work places and our travel was restricted. Always there is talk of evacuation plans and reactivation of the warden systems when these things happen. We personally wondered where we would go if we had to leave suddenly. We owned a house in Virginia and one in North Carolina, but both were rented at the time. On the very day of the embassy bombings, we received an unsolicited offer to purchase the Durham house from our renters. Feeling vulnerable at that time and wishing to live closer to family one day, we agreed to sell the house. Later that year we bought a condominium at the Lake of the Ozarks so that we would have a temporary place to call home.

September 11, 2001—Terrorism on US Soil

Where were you when the world stopped spinning? Every American alive on September 11, 2001, can likely tell you exactly the moment they learned about the unimaginable terrorist attacks on US soil that day.

That date has gone down in history as a game changer, creating a new and more violent world order. Four hijacked planes carrying nineteen foreign terrorists wreaked havoc on the World Trade Center Twin Towers in New York, the Pentagon, and the fourth one that was crashed in Shanksville, Pennsylvania.

Joe and I happened to be enjoying a quiet sunny day at our condo in Osage Beach, Missouri, when we saw the news flash about a plane crashing into one of the towers at the World Trade Center. We watched in horror as the second plane deliberately smashed into the second tower. Uncertainty and fear gripped us as more rumors and confirmations of terrorist acts were broadcast. It is an indescribable feeling to watch live coverage of the towers collapsing.

As a country, we pulled together after this unimaginable tragedy. Our allies were fully supportive. We took off our rose-colored glasses, and for the first time in ages, we began to assess our position in the world. We lost our innocence. How it affected me personally was in countless ways. It is much more difficult to get on an airplane and move to a foreign land where I am now more apprehensive. I now look at fellow passengers with suspicion. I don't like the fear that replaced the pride I had always felt to represent my great country abroad.

We had remote connections to three of the 2,996 innocent people killed that day. One was an Ethiopian doctor on the plane that hit the Pentagon, who had been a classmate of our son in the Abbey boarding school. Another was a colleague of our son-in-law who happened to be at a meeting in the Pentagon that morning. Scott was on TDY working close by and could easily have gone to that meeting. The third person was a cousin of a friend who worked in the World Trade Center. Our hearts bled for every person affected on that horrible day, including and especially the firefighters trying to rescue people.

Lost Lawsuit on Virginia Home Same Day

A few hours after the Twin Towers fell, we received a devastating call from the lawyer who had defended us in a lawsuit brought by an unscrupulous tenant in our Virginia home. His news that we had lost the court case seemed irrelevant compared to the innocent people who had lost their lives the same day. Nevertheless, we felt the financial sting of this frivolous lawsuit, which cost us to lose the dream home in Virginia. It had been a year-long nightmare battle of him not paying rent for eight months, evicting him, spending forty thousand to repair damages, renting the house to someone else who offered to buy it, them moving in, then the lawsuit and prospective buyers moving out. Adding up lawyer fees, repairs, court fees, and difference on amount we were forced to sell the home to the tenant, it cost us about $220,000 in losses. Our lifetime of hard work went down the drain needlessly. The stress created a huge strain on our marriage.

Attacks in Nairobi

As I wrote this chapter from Nairobi, the psychological scars on those survivors at the embassy bombings in 1998 were still evident. I spoke with a Kenyan lady who survived the bombing and yet continued to faithfully work at the US Embassy despite feeling apprehensive every morning when she reports to work. I also pray for Joe as he enters the compound even though it is more fortified and appears safer now in a new building in a new location.

The senseless attack on the Westgate Mall in Nairobi in September 2013 that killed at least sixty-eight people has been extremely hard to comprehend and endure for most citizens living and working in Nairobi. For those US Embassy survivors, in particular, it brought back horrible memories of their own experience in 1998. One of the victims in that most recent attack was the wife of a USAID employee who was expecting their first child. She was a well-known television personality and is missed by the Kenya nation and mourned daily by her husband and family and friends.

I also notice the effect that mall attack has had on friends who were there at the time too. Some reached almost to the paranoia stage and suffer constant tension that caused nightmares and headaches like I experienced after the evacuation from the Sudan in 1986. We arrived in Nairobi one month after the Westgate attack but listening to their fears made me reluctant to go to the mall to shop. We never lingered long in the grocery store and skipped other shops unless absolutely necessary. There has been a huge economic impact on the country post-Westgate. Nairobi has the highest security rating of critical threat. Home invasions and carjacking's are becoming the norm again.

Nairobi newspapers reported that a truckload of sophisticated explosives was confiscated in the port city of Mombasa. Some Somalians were arrested and confessed to additional vehicles with explosives that escaped. My own level of fear was raised with their target and intentions unknown. We lived next door to the US Embassy and across the street from the United Nations compounds. Suffice it to say that I was relieved when we departed Kenya and even more so when our plane touched down safely in Europe.

CHAPTER 57

Terrific Train Travels

Train travel has fascinated me since I was a child and took the Wabash train from Monroe City to Shelbina to visit Aunt Frances Buckman. This covered a distance of only seventeen miles but to me it was very exciting.

As an adult, I have experienced much more luxurious train accommodations and more diverse scenery. When Joe and I took the best train in Africa, we reminisced about our previous train travels, summarized here.

Belo Horizonte, Brazil, to Rio de Janeiro in 1977

The first train trip we made as a family while living in Brazil was a four-hundred-mile journey from Belo Horizonte to Rio de Janeiro when Juliana was a baby. Since I often suffer from motion sickness, we invited the nanny to accompany us. It was a twisted and grueling track and poor Dalva was sick for most of the trip, so I had two babies to care for instead of one. However, she enjoyed the time in Rio so much that it was worth seeing her discover her own country.

Cusco, Peru, to Machu Picchu in 1977

When we left Brazil in December 1977, we thought we should tour more of the surrounding countries, thinking that we would never have another chance. So we set off with six kids and sixteen pieces of luggage to visit Bolivia and Peru. Our next assignment ended up being Bolivia so that was kind of a waste of money and energy, but one cannot see the future. The train that we took was rickety from Cusco to Machu Picchu. Note the chapter about that misadventure.

Cairo to Luxor, Egypt, in 1983

Along with our six children, my aunts Lillian Hagan and Kathleen Montgomery, Joe and I set off from Cairo for an overnight train trip to Luxor in 1983. We went there to take a Nile cruise all the way to the Aswan Dam, which was another memorable adventure. We had bunk bed sleeper cars which were very nice compared to most trains in Egypt. Tragically, this same train caught fire and many people burned to death in later years as the windows had bars which prevented escape. But our family enjoyed the ride and the Nile cruise.

Fairbanks to Anchorage, Alaska, in 2004

Following a fantastic cruise on the Inside Passage in Alaska (along with Juliana, my parents, and our foreign service friend Billie Stewart), we took my parents on the Princess Midnight Sun train from Fairbanks to Anchorage. We stopped in Denali National Park for two nights and a tour of the wildlife in the park where we saw bears at a distance and only one sickly moose. From the doomed lounge, we saw beautiful scenery along the tundra and even saw the top of Mount McKinley for a few minutes as it is normally cloud covered.

Unfortunately, my mother was feeling quite sick and we had to summons an ambulance to meet us outside of Anchorage. After a hospital stay, we were able to get her safely back to Missouri where she later had stomach surgery and fixed the problem, but it was a big concern at the time.

Orient Express from Cusco to Machu Picchu in 2005

While living in the Dominican Republic, Joe had to attend a conference in Peru. I accompanied him, and when he finished working, we flew to Cusco and then took a luxury return trip to Machu Picchu on the Orient Express. That was a treat. We had a champagne brunch on the way to the famous ruins. Then after our three-hour tour of Machu Picchu, which I thoroughly enjoyed, we had high tea. Boarded the train and had a gourmet dinner on the way back to Cusco. That is when we decided that we like luxury trains.

Grand Canyon Railway from Williams, Arizona, in 2006

The year after my father died, we took Mom on a road trip to California. At Williams, Arizona, we boarded the 1901 Grand Canyon Railway for a 130-mile RT to the south rim of the Grand Canyon. The train slowed down enough that a gang of robbers on horseback could jump on the train. One of the so-called robbers sat down by Mom and asked where she was from. When she replied Missouri, he said, "Oh, I'm sorry." It was a fun ride.

St. Louis to Glacier National Park in 2012

Amtrak provided a relaxing means for us to share a wonderful vacation train trip with my cousins Judy and Floyd Mahon. Floyd loved train travel and he was battling colon cancer, so we decided that would be an easy way to travel. We caught the train outside of St. Louis to Chicago where we spent a lovely overnight and toured some of the Windy City. Next day we boarded Amtrak. Due to price, we opted not to get a sleeper, but the reclining seats were comfortable enough to rest although I wished for a blanket as the train was really chilly. It was a smooth and pleasurable ride as we passed many hours in the doom of the lounge car playing cards and the game of Rumicubes. The journey took us through the northern heartland including the booming oil fields in North Dakota. We finally reached Glacier National Park, where we spent a couple days before returning back to Missouri on the train again.

The Ghan from Darwin to Alice Springs, Australia, in 2013

The Ghan is a legendary Australian rail service that has been operating since 1878. Originally known as the Afghan Express, the Ghan takes its name from the nineteenth-century Afghan camel drivers who arrived in Australia and helped to explore the country's remote interior.

For years, Joe had talked of taking the Ghan. For our fifteenth-wedding anniversary in September 2013, we made our third visit to Australia and fulfilled his dream while totally charming me. The trip from Darwin to Alice Springs took twenty-six hours and was so enjoyable to spend all that time with Aussie fellow passengers as we were the only Americans aboard. The food was delicious and the sleeping car efficient.

The Rovos Rail from Cape Town to Pretoria, South Africa, in 2016

Pure luxury and impeccable service awaited us on the Rovos Rail, which is considered the best in the Southern Hemisphere. The authentic locomotives and the 1920s era coaches are lovingly restored wood paneled cars refurbished in pristine condition. We booked last minute, so were forced to get a suite which was more expensive but more spacious quarters. The food was the finest cuisine we have ever experienced and not what one normally expects in Africa. Our train ran on electricity most of the 960 miles and took fifty hours to reach Pretoria from gorgeous Cape Town. The landscape was ever changing from ocean to mountains, to vineyards, to desert in the Karoo, to flamingo-filled lakes, to ostrich farms, and back to greenery again. We enjoyed the three-hour stop at the Kimberley Diamond Mine where we were given a fascinating tour. The diamond ring Joe purchased for me in Cape Town in 1989 came from that mine, so it was extra special to tour the area. We met interesting fellow passengers and it went so quickly that we hated to disembark and return to Joe's consultancy job and reality.

Second visit to the magnificent ruins of Machu Picchu
in Peru was made via Orient Express train.

CHAPTER 58

Tulip Time in Michigan

Road Trip to Michigan in May 2015

I had long wished to visit Holland, Michigan, during the Tulip Festival. So when our granddaughter Jennifer and her husband, Adam, moved to Michigan I began to plan a trip there.

Joe and I drove to visit Alice at the farm the first night. We had a pretty long drive from there to Holland the next day, but we skirted around the edge of Chicago which was the worst part of the trip. After that, the drive was beautiful.

Immediately we set out to explore Holland and take in the beauty of seeing over seven million tulips in bloom at the same time. We went to the oldest working windmill that had been imported from Holland. Rows and rows of vibrant tulips graced the city. It was truly gorgeous. We watched a parade. Joe seemed to be enjoying himself, which I didn't expect as he doesn't have the same appreciation for flowers that I have. It was a really fun two days for me and I got to cross off another bucket list item.

We drove across the state and through Detroit at rush hour traffic, which was not so fun. Gretchen had flown into Detroit earlier. When we reached Adam and Jennifer's beautiful new home, we had a great reunion and Gretchen grilled lobsters for us. It was Mother's day and Jennifer had bought a bouquet of flowers for me. I was so touched.

Jennifer drove us down to Detroit to show us the good and the bad parts of the city whose economy is still struggling. We went to Adam's base and he gave us a tour of the helicopter on which he rides whenever there is an emergency. Adam is a US Coast Guard aviation survival technician (also known as search-and-rescue swimmer). We are very proud of Adam and the career he has chosen.

Joe always wanted to stay at the Grand Hotel on Machinac Island. The five of us drove to the Upper Peninsula and took a ferry across to the island. There are no cars allowed on the island. It was a bitter cold and rainy day. The rest of them stayed at a hotel near the dock while Joe and I grabbed a horse drawn carriage and nearly froze on the slow trip up the hill to the Grand. When Gretchen called to see if we wanted to join them for a tour of the island the next morning, we declined. We had paid a fortune so wanted to savor every moment in that old Victorian hotel. We were assigned to the Ford presidential suite and it was lovely but too cold to spend any time on the balcony with a view of the lake. Our family loved their tour of the city. They joined us for the beautiful buffet lunch at the Grand. We all stuffed ourselves before taking the ferry and driving back to the Via's home.

We enjoyed our visit so much. It was hard to leave Jennifer and Adam, but Gretchen rode back to Missouri and stayed a week with us so that was a bonus. We left early morning as it was an eleven-hour drive to Alice's home where we spent a night on the way home to Springfield. We took Gretchen to Branson for a night and took in restaurants on the Landing and shopped at the outlet mall. She got to visit some of her sisters and nieces and a nephew. We didn't do anything special, but the week passed very quickly.

CHAPTER 59

Road Trip to
California in 2015

On August 18, 2015, Joe and I and my cousins Molly Lamb and Judy Mahon departed from Springfield for a road trip headed west. Our first stop was in Kingfisher, Oklahoma, to visit our cousin Jane Hightower. We had a lovely evening and got to see some of her family too. She is such a fun and wonderful person.

As we left the next day after breakfast, Jane said we must take time to stop in Texas to see the Stations of the Cross just off the highway. It had rained, and we ended up on a slick road, which threw mud up into the wheels which caused us grief for the next three hundred miles until we reached Santa Fe, New Mexico, even though we stopped to have the underbelly washed.

We were all impressed with Santa Fe where we had a delicious dinner at the Vanessie with dueling piano music that Juliana had recommended. The main reason we visited Santa Fe was to see the miraculous staircase at the Loretto Chapel. It is believed that it was built by St. Joseph the Carpenter himself. Knowing my grandmother's devotion to St. Joseph, I got goose bumps when I saw the gorgeous winding staircase that has no support and no nails. It truly is a construction miracle and the mysterious man who built it disappeared without payment. I personally believe in the legend of the miracle.

Molly and Judy and I took a city tour while Joe took the car to the Mercedes dealer to dig out the mud. We stopped at the end of the Santa Fe Trail. We had an authentic Mexican lunch that was excellent.

Next stop was Durango, Colorado, where we took a bus to Silverton and then caught the old train back to Durango after a lovely lunch in the Diamond Bell Saloon as a young pianist played so beautifully that Joe bought her CDs. We walked around the unique shops in Silverton, but it was misting rain and rather chilly, so we couldn't take advantage of all it had to offer.

Visiting the cliff dwellings in Mesa Verde was the next challenge. It was a hard descent and climb back up ladders but all four of us managed to not fall off the cliff and enjoyed the history lesson at the same time. We were not impressed with the Far View where we stayed in the park or the food offered there.

Just outside the entrance to Monument Valley in Utah, we stopped for lunch and had delicious Navajo tacos and toured a museum about the westerns.

We stayed in the View at Monument Valley and had an amazing view of the monuments. Sunset and sunrise over the monuments was an incredible experience. Joe drove us on a self-guided tour of the area and it was surreal. Joe had wanted to visit Monument Valley since his childhood as he recalled that a lot of John Wayne western films were made there. We watched the first movie John Wayne made from the patio as it was shown on the hotel wall. There was a cool breeze, and in the moonlit night, we could see some of the monuments close by which were in the movie background.

It was worth a quick stop at Four Corners where four states come together. After taking photos on the spot, we shopped at the Navajo trinket stands.

We moved on to Paige, Arizona, where we had arranged to visit Horseshoe Bend and also Antelope Canyon. We checked into a nice Holiday Inn Express where Judy talked them into an upgrade. We needed the space and were tired of cramped quarters. It was really hot outside, but Joe wanted to go to Horseshoe Bend, which was another memory from the old western movies. As we started up the hill without hats or water, we were stopped by two young men who warned us how dangerous it was to make the trek without water. We must have looked very old to them. But we should have listened to them. The sun was unbearable. Once we reached the bottom of the hill overlooking the river, I felt a bit faint while trying to take pictures. I gave Joe the camera and Molly and I started back to the top of the hill. Fortunately, Judy stayed behind and began walking with Joe. He became extremely dehydrated. I saw them sitting on a bench resting but didn't realize how serious the situation was with Joe. Judy asked for help and someone poured their precious water over Joe's head, which helped a little. He told her he just wanted to lie down on the bench. Judy knew she had to get him out of the sun. I ran back down to help Judy help him up, and he put all his weight on our shoulders. His eyes were scary, and I could tell it was affecting his heart. Another Good Samaritan stopped to share their electrolytes with Joe which gave him enough strength to keep going. Judy and I sang to keep him alert as we literally dragged him up the hill. We never told our kids about this incident, so they are learning about it for the first time when they read this book. We returned to the hotel and Joe stayed in bed drinking lots of water all evening while we women prayed.

The next day Joe seemed to have recovered sufficiently to go ahead with the tour run by the Navajos of Antelope Canyon. It was just as gorgeous as our friend Jerry LaBenz had described and all the pictures we had seen of it. The tour only lasted an hour and we felt like we were being herded like cattle. We would like to have lingered longer to take more photos as the sun struck the narrow canyon walls at different angles. It was truly beautiful. The ride on the back of a pickup truck while seated on benches and bouncing through the sand was not so pleasant. We were grateful to be in the lead truck, so we didn't have to eat the dust from other trucks moving way too fast for the condition.

Las Vegas, here we come. Gretchen flew in from San Diego and checked into the Venetian. Rob Lamb was kind enough to pick her up from the hotel and take her to their apartment in Henderson where we had a wonderful supper. Molly and Judy then stayed with Rob and Nancy for a few days. We got a little lost finding our way back to the Venetian that night. Gretchen showed us all around Las Vegas the next day. Then we went back for breakfast at Rob's and followed them to Hoover Dam. We drove further and took a boat down the Colorado River all the way back to the dam. We were thrilled to see seven Rocky Mountain goats clinging to the cliffs. Rob drove the boat and we just had a wonderful time. We returned to Henderson and visited a cute wine shop and then devoured barbecue that evening at Lucille's BBQ.

It was sad to say goodbye to Gretchen as we don't get to see her often, but we were so glad that she had made that effort to visit with us in Vegas.

Now came the part that I had been dreading most on our road trip. Joe wanted to cross Death Valley. I was dead set against it and looked as the maps over and over to find an alternative, albeit longer, route. Joe won, and he drove until we reached Death Valley. I wanted to take over and be able to control the speed and let Joe look around. In the first fifty miles, we did not meet another vehicle, but I was beginning to relax. We stopped at the lowest place in the United States and the car registered 115°F. I drove on to Furnace Creek where we had lunch and the thermometer registered 121°F. Joe took over for the rest of the way through Death Valley and on to Mammoth Lake, California.

Arriving at the hotel in Mammoth Lake the proprietor informed us to remove everything from the car because bears were breaking into the cars at night. No elevator and we were on second floor, but we did listen to the advice and drug everything upstairs. We were tired by the long drive so walked across the road to the Loco Frijole restaurant, which was run by a Mexican family and certainly served wonderful food and margaritas. I felt like we had earned those drinks.

Our ultimate goal had been to visit Yosemite National Park, so we sat off the next day and entered through the east gate. It took several hours to reach the Ahwahnee Lodge, which was another hotel on Joe's bucket list. We are glad that we did drive all the way across Yosemite as it is as beautiful as we dreamed it would be. There were large areas that had been burned from lightning strikes but mostly we gawked at mountains and valleys and lakes and pristine rivers. We took a tour around the hotel area to visit Half Dome and other famous peaks. That evening we celebrated with an awesome prime rib dinner at the Ahwahnee.

We had the champagne brunch the next morning, but I was not feeling very well so it was kind of a waste for me, but Joe made up for it by drinking my portion of champagne. That meant that I had to drive on our journey to Carmichael, California, to visit a dear friend Patty Frank that we had not seen in twenty-nine years since after we were evacuated from the Sudan. We had a lovely evening with Patty and Dale and then left after breakfast the next day. It was wonderful to catch up with Patty and to meet Dale who we were pleased to see makes her happy.

Our original travel plans were to visit the Redwoods and go as far north as Portland, Oregon. But we had received an email that lead us to believe that we needed to go home and do some paperwork and that the work in South Africa was imminent. We drove like crazy, averaging 650 miles a day for the next three days, until we reached home on our fifty-second wedding anniversary. We went to Outback for dinner. Then we sat and awaited security clearance for the next four months. Frustrating!

Nevertheless, we got to spend Thanksgiving and Christmas at home and see Bella's excitement at age three of opening presents.

CHAPTER 60

Family and Class Reunions

As we get older, we tend to appreciate life more each day. The memories that we make with our family and friends are priceless.

Since leaving South Africa eighteen months ago, we have been fortunate to spend quality time with many of those we hold dear.

It goes without saying that our church family at St. Elizabeth Ann Seton are extra special as we share breakfast nearly every weekday after the privilege of receiving the Eucharist at daily mass. Our parish is blessed with phenomenal priests. Monsignor Thomas Reidy is the most dedicated pastor we have ever had the pleasure of knowing.

Despite our offspring being spread from coast to coast and living as far away as Uganda, we have managed to have two family reunions which were fun. Our family always enjoy vacations at the Lake of the Ozarks and at Table Rock Lake. We try to rent a large place to accommodate our growing family and share the cooking and cleanup duties, which work out very well.

Joe's four close-knit classmates from St. Stephens High School, along with their spouses, held three reunions. The first one was a ten-day tour of Ireland in April 2016, which enabled us to visit Bede and Doreen Smith. It was a fabulous trip with memories to last a lifetime. Then we reunited at the Lake of the Ozarks this spring. Last month we all got together in Monroe City and had a blast when the Smiths were visiting from Ireland. Childhood friendships are irreplaceable and to be treasured forever.

Joe and I have just returned from a wonderful two-week visit with our son Joe and his sweet five-year-old daughter Chloe in Uganda. We were impressed and delighted to tour his Priceless Farms property. Joe arranged some exciting wildlife safaris during our visit to Kenya and Uganda.

As I finish this chapter, we are packing to go to the Azore Islands with Juliana and Bella and friend Jema. We will stop in Boston and Cape Cod to finally meet our great-grandson Nolan Wyatt Via, who will be eight months old before we get to hug him. I love my life. I am happy. I am blessed.

Thank you for the privilege of your time in reading my life story.

Nolan Wyatt Via with his maternal great-grandparents Joe and Hope in November 2017 at the US Coast Guard air station on Cape Cod where his dad is an aviation survival technician.

Ashford Castle in Ireland provided luxury accommodations
for Joe and Hope, Ken and Marilyn Quinn, and Bob and
Cele Yager during a class reunion trip in April 2016.

CHAPTER 61

Epitaph

The following excerpts were taken from a letter written by my room-mate for life. It is my desire to have these exact words engraved on the back of our tombstone as it epitomizes our love and gives extra purpose to our lives.

It is my legacy, my epitaph.

My darling Hope,

Without you, I am nothing. With you, even if I have nothing, I have everything.

Your devoted husband,
Joe

Obviously, the secret to the lasting peace and happiness in our marriage is that God is the central focus of our lives. We also believe in and are grateful for our guardian angels that have faithfully watched over our family. Amen.

ABOUT THE AUTHOR

Hope Gander Goodwin currently lives in Springfield, Missouri, with her husband, Joe Goodwin Sr. Their offspring are disbursed across the continents from California to faraway East Africa. Seven grandchildren and one great-grandson are the pride, focus, and light of their lives. Despite visiting all seven continents, living over four decades in twenty countries, and having toured one hundred twenty-seven countries and territories, they still delight in continuing to travel extensively. Their family, friends, faith, and love sustain them. It is hoped that this tale of a life well lived will entertain, educate, and inspire readers.

CPSIA information can be obtained
at www.ICGtesting.com
Printed in the USA
BVHW03s1756150918
527595BV00001B/6/P

9 781643 502953